D0991518

R00997304561
The
Chicago Public Library
C
P L
JUV/Ref
PN 1972
.S46
1991
Call No.
Branch CARL B. RODEN

FANTASTIC THEATER

FANTASTIC THEATER

Puppets and Plays for Young Performers and Young Audiences

by Judy Sierra

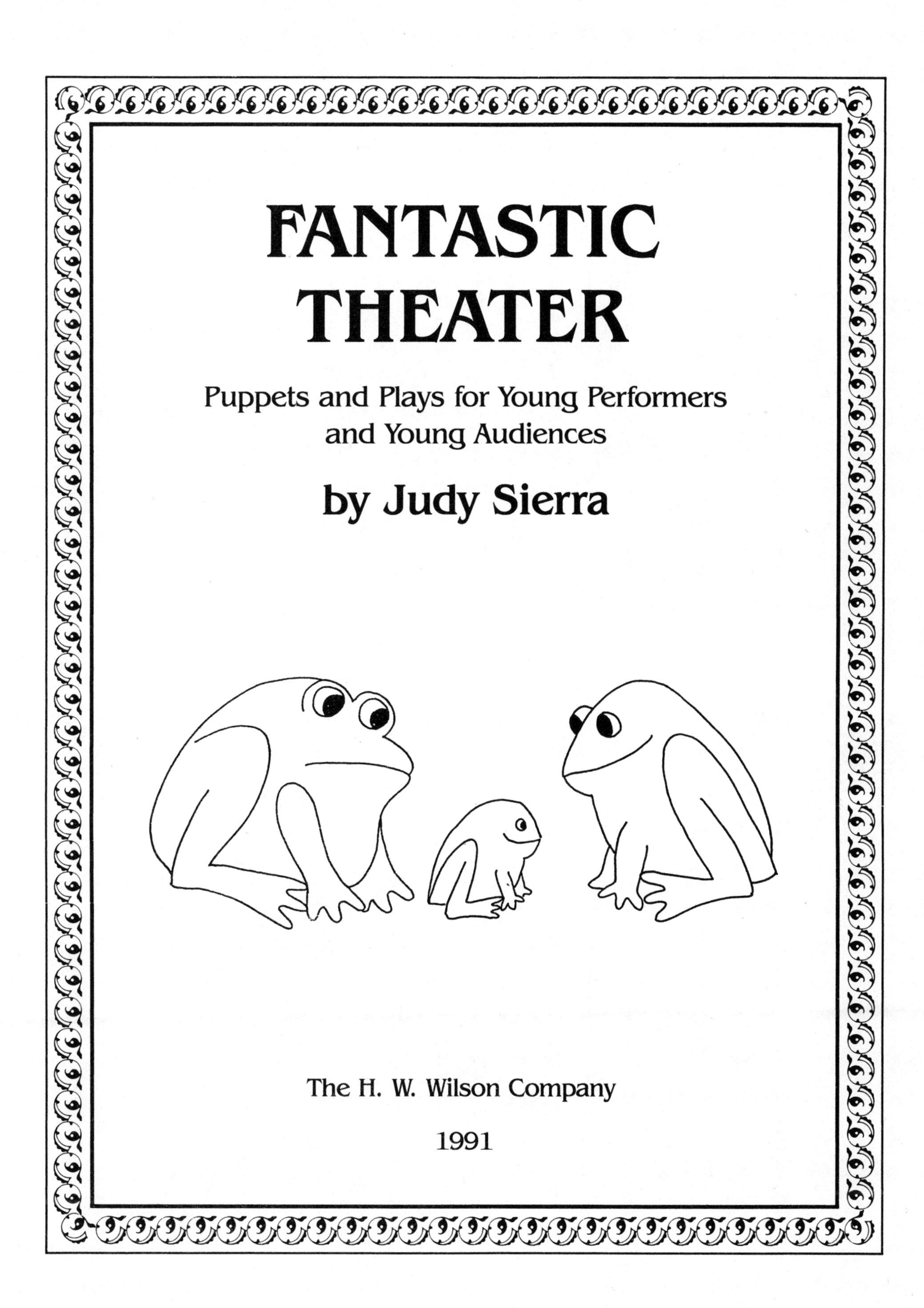

The H. W. Wilson Company

1991

For Jean and Joe,
who started me on my puppet career.

Library of Congress Cataloging-in-Publication Data

Sierra, Judy.
Fantastic theater : puppets and plays for young performers and young audiences / Judy Sierra.
p. cm.
Includes bibliographical references and index.
Summary: Thirty puppet plays adapted from nursery rhymes, folk songs, fables, poetry, folktales, and myths with instructional chapters on making and using rod and shadow puppets and puppet stages.
ISBN 0-8242-0809-9 : $35.00
1. Puppet theater—Juvenile literature. 2. Puppet making—Juvenile literature. 3. Puppet plays. 4. Shadow shows. [1. Puppet theater. 2. Puppet making. 3. Puppet plays.]
I. Title.
PN1972.S46 1991
791.5′.3—dc20

90-24438
CIP
AC

Printed in the United States of America
First Printing

Acknowledgments

I had the good fortune to learn from and work with the talented puppeteers of the San Francisco Bay Area Puppeteers' Guild, especially Jan VanSchuyver and Terry Ryder, and to study Balinese shadow puppetry with Larry Reed. I have also been blessed with a life partner who is as well a performing partner, a gifted artist and innovative puppeteer, Bob Kaminski.

This book would not have been possible without the experience I gained directing student productions in California and New Mexico as part of the National Endowment for the Arts' Artist-in-Residence Program. For the past year, I have had the dedicated assistance of the fifth-grade students at Rosemont Avenue School in Los Angeles, who are now master puppeteers, and whose work is captured in the accompanying photographs.

Table of Contents

Introduction

Puppetry is the ideal dramatic art form for children, both as actors and as audience. It is a theater of small scale and limited means, yet the effect of performance is magical as figures of fantasy and imagination come to life on the puppet stage.

Puppet performance is a tradition of long standing in public libraries. Creative children's librarians use puppets to dramatize books and introduce children to the unforgettable characters of children's literature and folklore. Library puppet clubs encourage children to share their reading experiences through art and drama.

In schools, puppetry is widely used to enrich the literature-based curriculum. Children involved in puppet plays effortlessly develop critical thinking and cooperative learning skills. Puppetry has proved to be a very effective tool in second-language acquisition, providing concrete and exciting contexts for language use. And, being safely concealed by the puppet stage gives students a safe opportunity to speak out, perhaps for the first time, in an unfamiliar language.

Because puppetry encompasses such a broad range of artistic expression—design, music, writing, and acting—it offers every child a chance to shine. Always attracting eager audiences, puppetry provides important recognition and appreciation of children's efforts. Children of all ages and abilities can produce delightful, enjoyable puppet plays.

This book contains thirty plays for puppets, based on the poetry, folk songs, fables, folktales, and myths of many world cultures. Folk material has been chosen because of its predictable, action-oriented plots, memorable characters, and its cultural diversity. This type of literature is enjoyed by children of all ages and by adults. Though the plays are written with child performers in mind, they are also highly recommended for adults to perform for child audiences. Some of the plays are designed to be presented as pantomimes to narration, singing, or recorded music, while others require learning the lines of a formal script. The plays are short, none much longer than fifteen minutes. Activities based on folklore, songs, children's literature, poetry, science, and children's own creative writing are included as follow-up projects to extend the knowledge and enthusiasm generated by the plays.

The book includes plays and other performance ideas for beginning and more advanced puppeteers and for all sizes of performing ensembles, from the solo performer to groups of twenty or more. The appendix contains lists which will further assist you in selecting the best projects for your group. There, the plays are classified by size of performing group and by geographic and cultural area. Supplemental performance projects which emphasize science, scriptwriting, poetry, and puppet design are also listed.

The plays in this book are designed for two styles of puppet, shadow and flat rod. Both have a long history of use in folk puppet theater. These types of puppets are faster for children to make than hand puppets, and much easier for them to use effectively. Shadow and rod puppets are able to represent the full body and natural posture of both humans and animals, with each character in its true proportion to the others. For this reason, they are better suited to the presentation of traditional literature. A shadow or rod puppet of the Greek hero Perseus, for example, can embody nobility and heroism in a way that a short, pudgy hand puppet could not.

Traceable puppet patterns are included in the book for all thirty plays. The size of these patterns is suitable for a small tabletop theater. If necessary, they can easily be enlarged on a photocopy machine. Using the patterns is optional, of course; children should always be encouraged to design their own puppets. All of the related performance projects described in this book involve creating original puppets.

Complete instructions are included for making puppets, puppet stages, props and scenery, and for using music and sound effects. The puppet director is guided through the process of rehearsal and performance. A section is included on the use of video as a rehearsal tool and to document performance.

Getting Started

A director brings both artistic vision and practical techniques to a theater production. This book is planned to help you develop both your ability to visualize puppet performances, and your technical expertise. Children's puppetry skills grow very rapidly; you will be able to delegate more and more responsibility to them in your second, third, and following productions. Experienced puppeteers aged ten and older will soon be able to use this book on their own.

Choosing a Performance Project

A good choice for a first performance is one that does not have any speaking parts—a pantomime to singing, narration, or recorded music, for example. Such pantomimes can be found in the first two sections of this book, "Puppetry and Poetry" and "Musical Puppet Plays." A list of other pantomime performances is included in the appendix.

Children will not be able to work from these scripts until they can read at a fourth-grade level. That does not mean, however, that children who have not achieved this competency cannot have speaking roles in puppet plays. Simply use the narration-improvisation technique described on page 35. Familiar picture book stories and folktales that can be easily adapted to this method are listed in the appendix.

Twenty-four scripts, adapted from world folklore, are included in the section, "Fables, Myths and Folktales." These scripts are arranged from easiest to most difficult. A recommended minimum and maximum number of puppeteers and support crew (narrator and musicians/sound effects personnel) is given at the beginning of each script. The minimum number assumes that some puppeteers will operate more than one puppet in the course of the show, but never more than one puppet at a time.

In selecting a play for your group, remember that there are many jobs in the puppet theater besides puppeteer that appeal to children:

Narrator: Most of the scripts in this book include a narrator. Narration helps the audience understand the setting and transitions of the play. In a small group, this role may be taken on by one of the puppeteers, or by the director. A narrator might also assume additional tasks, such as providing music and sound effects.

Musicians: Music and sound effects played on simple instruments add greatly to the effectiveness of puppet performances, and the role of musician is usually quite sought after. In addition, children who are accomplished musicians can play an overture before the performance or even compose music especially for it.

Artists: While most puppeteers want to make the puppets they will manipulate in the show, there are always additional jobs for talented artists: props and scenery, as well as posters, programs, and tickets to be designed and made.

Stage Manager: Puppeteers can always use assistance keeping puppets and props in order backstage. The stage manager can also keep a checklist of show equipment, and be in charge of arranging it before the performance and putting it away afterward. In formal performance, there are lights to operate and microphone levels to check.

Prompter: Prompting is important for a group that is new to learning a script. The prompter stands backstage, following along with a script, and whispers lines or cues to any puppeteers who have trouble remembering them.

Camera Crew: If you have access to video equipment, a camera crew can record rehearsals for performers to view and critique and can also provide a record of the finished production.

Director: Experienced puppeteers may be capable of taking on the roles of director and assistant director, assuming responsibility for the entire rehearsal process.

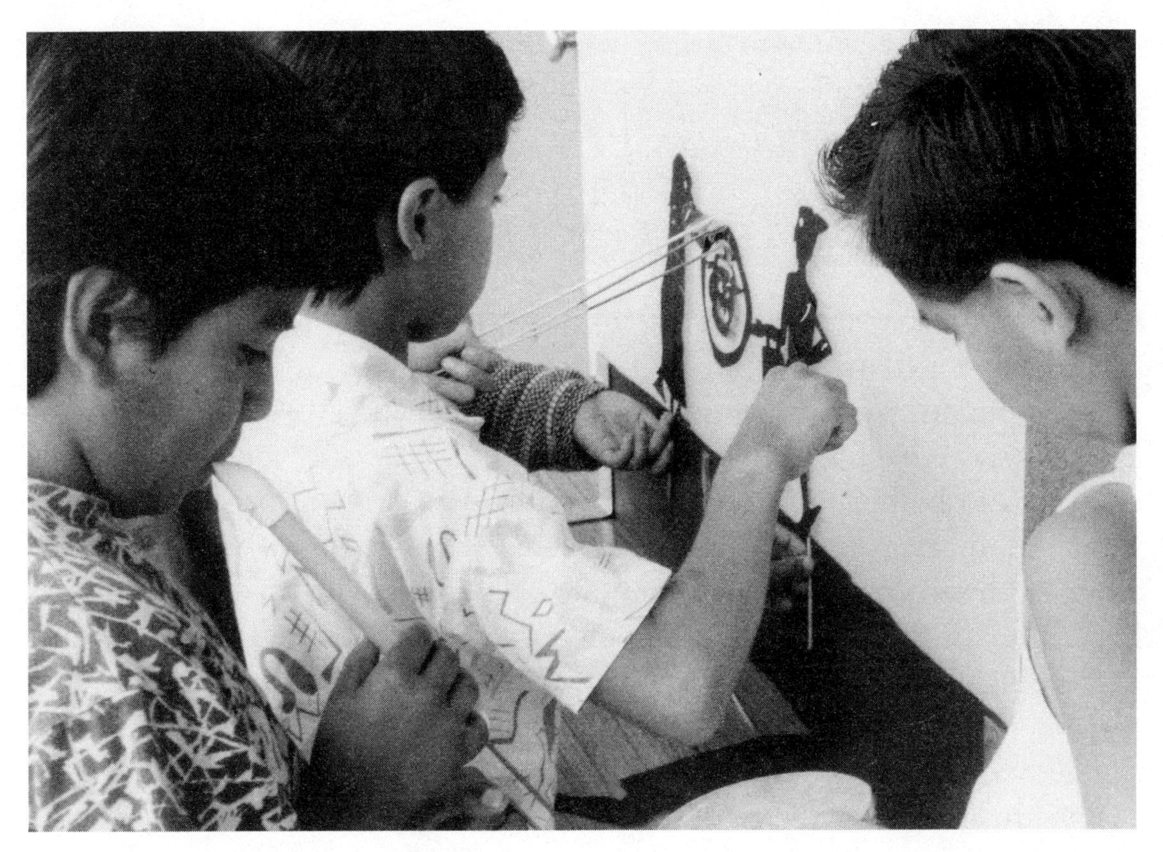

Musicians playing drum and slide whistle accompany a shadow puppet performance of the Greek myth, *Perseus and Medusa.*

First Step: Construction

Your first task will be to make a rod-puppet stage or shadow screen, if you don't already have one. Several stage designs are included for each type of puppetry, ranging from simple, inexpensive cardboard-box stages to slightly more elaborate ones which require some carpentry skills. If you are working with a small group, you may want to have them help you make the stage.

In certain situations, you might want to consider having the puppets already made for a group's first project. This is especially useful if the children are eight years old or younger, and are completely new to puppetry. Beginning with a performance quickly provides positive reinforcement. Success in a first attempt will build enthusiasm for following performances, in which children *will* make their own puppets. If you work in a library or recreation center, or as an art or drama specialist, you can use the same puppets again and again with many different groups. Having all your materials ready-made will allow you to coach a complete (nonscripted) puppet performance in an hour or less.

Shadow Puppetry

Shadow puppetry is a performing art which began about two thousand years ago in Asia (though exactly where remains a mystery). Shadow puppetry continues to be practiced today in its traditional forms in parts of Greece, India, Southeast Asia, Indonesia, and China. The audience gathers before a white cloth screen, illuminated from the back by an oil lamp or other bright light. Behind the screen, the puppeteers move flat jointed figures, acting out traditional stories. The effect is like that of film animation, since the placement of the light hides any human presence behind the screen from the audience's view.

Shadow puppetry attained a high degree of perfection in the royal courts of Java and Imperial China. The shadow puppeteer, or *dalang*, of Indonesia and the Malay Peninsula is still highly regarded for the ability to single-handedly play all roles in scenes from the Hindu religious epics, the *Mahabharata* and *Ramayana*. The artistry of shadow puppetry is not an imitation in miniature of human theater but has time-honored design and performance styles of its own. Its techniques can be adapted for use with modern stages, lighting, and readily-available construction materials.

Shadow Screens

Shadow-puppet performance requires a backlit translucent screen made of paper, cloth, or plastic. The partially-opaque nature of the screen, and the angle of the light, conspire to hide the puppeteers' hands and the puppet rods from view. For most performing situations, a screen thirty-six inches wide by twenty-six inches high is ideal. Shadow-puppet performance must take place in the dark. Thus, for daytime performance, a room's windows should be covered, and all lights except the shadow-screen light turned off. The three types of shadow-puppet screens described below are designed to sit on a tabletop.

Cardboard-Box Shadow Screen

A simple and inexpensive shadow stage can be made from a corrugated cardboard box. Choose a strong box with a well-glued bottom, as close as possible to the dimensions of twenty-six by thirty-six inches. Use a mat knife to trim the sides of the box to a depth of about ten inches. Then, cut a rectangular opening in the bottom of the box, leaving a margin of four inches on one long edge (this will be the bottom edge of the shadow screen) and one inch on the other edges.

The paper for the screen should be white, and about the weight of typing paper. The paper that comes in large rolls for school art projects is perfect. Cut a rectangle of paper three inches larger on all sides than the bottom of the box. Wrap it over the bottom of the box, folding the corners tightly. Pull the paper taut, and tape the edges securely to the box with duct tape. The paper screen is on the outside of the box; to make the box look more like a puppet theater, design a proscenium from colored paper, with an opening exactly the size of the rectangular opening of the box, and glue it on top of the paper screen. Secure the box to the tabletop with tape (or place a heavy book inside) to keep it from sliding during performance. Your screen is ready to light.

Cloth Shadow Screen

Cloth is the traditional material for the shadow screen. Select a white cotton or cotton-blend fabric about the weight of a bedsheet. Muslin is too transparent, and poplins are too heavy. The fabric is tightly stretched around a rectangular wooden frame, constructed from one-by-two-inch clear pine lumber. The easiest and fastest way to construct this frame, though, is to purchase wooden stretcher bars at an art supply store. These bars are used by oil painters to stretch their canvases and are specially cut at the corners so that they can be joined together without glue or nails. Stretcher bars are sold separately and in varying lengths, allowing you to choose the exact dimensions of your shadow screen.

Attach the cloth to the frame with a staple-gun. Trim the cloth so that it is about four inches larger on each side than the frame. Wrap the cloth up and over the frame, and staple it to the inner wide, flat side of the wood. Place one staple at the center of each side, stretching the cloth very tightly. Move out from these initial staples toward the corners of the frame, keeping the cloth tight and trimming and folding the cloth neatly at the corners for a mitered fit. If the cloth becomes soiled, you can wash it without taking it off the frame. Simply scrub it with soapy water and a soft nail brush, rinse, and then let dry.

For informal performances, this screen can be attached to simple support legs and set on a table top. When the room is dark, and the shadow stage is lit, the audience will focus on the screen, so a stage structure which masks the puppeteers' bodies is not necessary. Purchase four six-inch flat metal shelf brackets (not the decorative kind, but plain metal L's which are perfectly flat except for the one right-angle bend). These are held in place by two metal-spring gluing clamps, which resemble giant clothespins. Be sure to test these before you buy them, for they are often so tight that a person of average strength can't open them. Both brackets and clamps are available at hardware stores. Place two angle brackets at each end of the screen, like feet, and clamp them into place with the spring clamps. The brackets will need to be taped to the tabletop to keep the stage from sliding during performance.

This simple screen can be made into a more finished puppet stage by adding two hinged side pieces. The extra support this structure gives is

A puppeteer rehearses on a small cardboard box shadow screen, large enough for one or two performers.

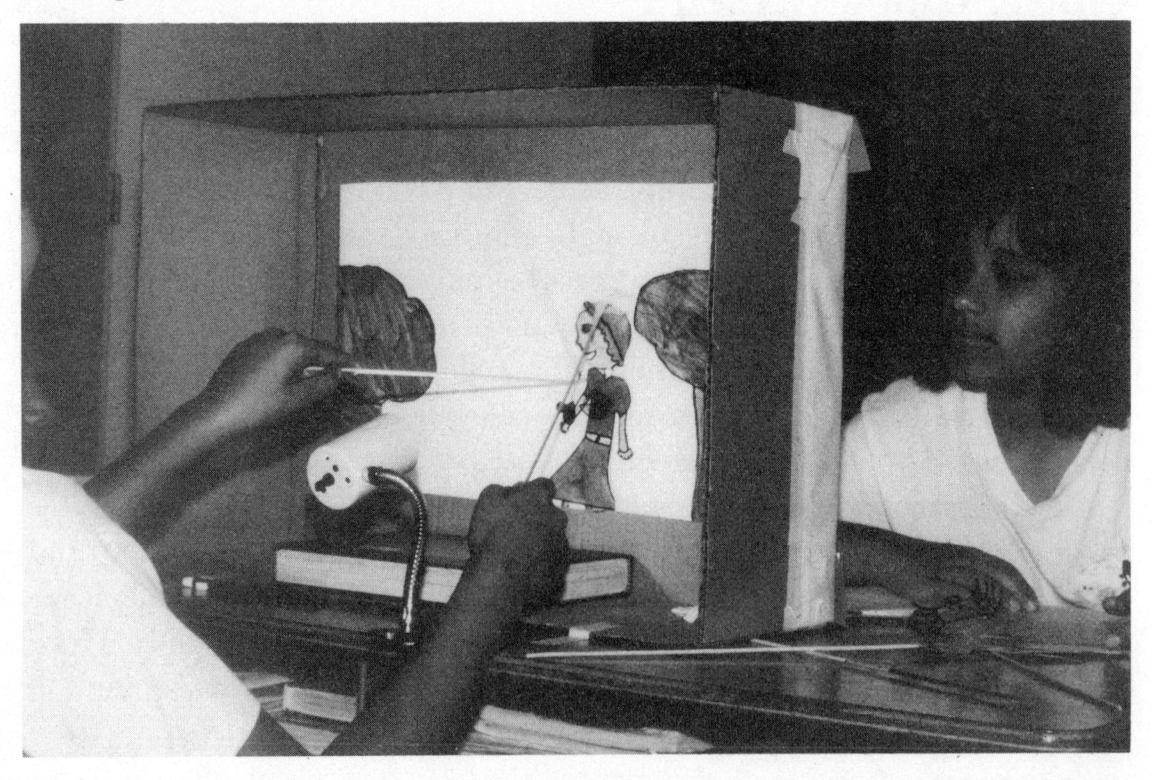

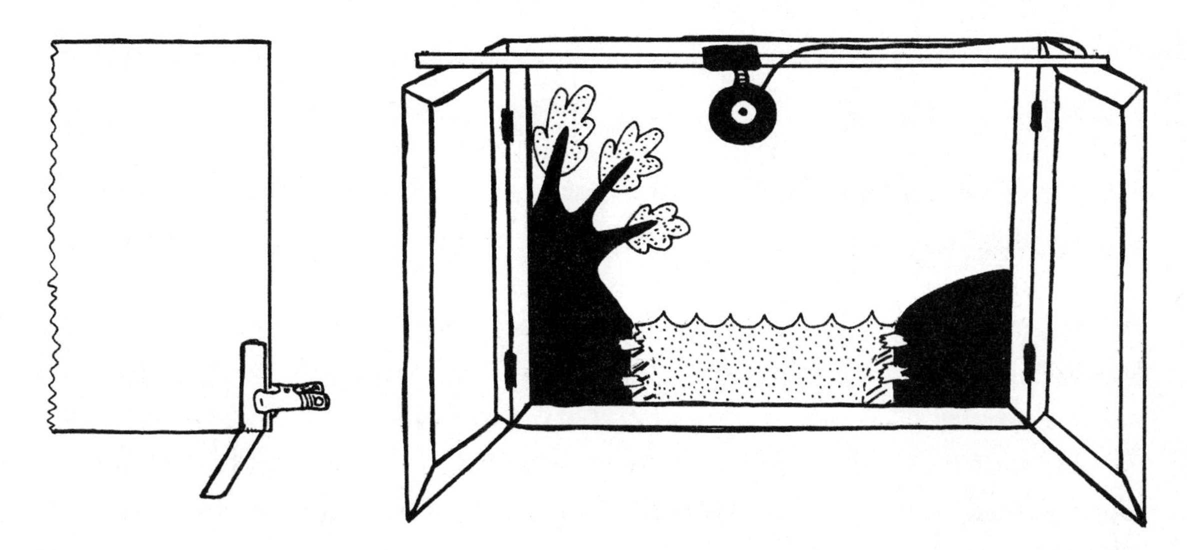

Left: Metal angle brackets and spring clamps can support a tabletop Plexiglas or a cloth shadow screen. Right: The addition of hinged side pieces adds stability to a large screen; this also allows the use of a light batten, which gives greater flexibility in the placement of the lamp.

recommended for screens larger than twenty-six by thirty-six inches. Make two more wood frames, each the same height as the screen, but half the width. Cover them with opaque fabric, then hinge them to the screen so that the stage will fold flat for storage. The side pieces will also allow you to add a light batten—a piece of one-by-two-inch clear pine set across the tops of the side pieces about six inches back from the screen. This will also place the light fixture in a better position for the larger screen.

Plexiglas Shadow Screen

Plexiglas makes a durable and easy-to-clean shadow screen. It is the best choice for a traveling shadow puppet screen. Choose a one-eighth inch thickness in semi-opaque white, usually called "milky white." Have the Plexiglas cut to the desired size and, for safety, ask that the corners be rounded. Make support legs for the Plexiglas using shelf brackets and spring clamps, as described above for the cloth stage.

This screen can also be made into a stage with side pieces. Attach one-by-two-inch clear pine along both short edges of the screen. The plastics distributor can drill holes in the Plexiglas for you, so that you can attach the wood with wood-screws. Two wood-frame side pieces can then be hinged onto these wooden supports, and the stage completed in the same manner as described above for the cloth shadow screen.

Lighting the Shadow Screen

The light for a shadow screen is positioned ***between*** the puppeteer and the screen, either at the bottom of the screen angling up or at the top of the screen angling down. The tabletop stages described above can be lit by a small, lightweight, clip-on light fixture attached directly to the top of a free-standing screen, or to the light batten of a stage with side pieces. On a Plexiglas screen or cardboard-box stage, you will probably need to insert a one-inch block of wood (or a small box of crayons) between the stage and the clamp, in order to give the lamp a firm enough grip. The light fixture should have a flexible neck (a "goose neck," and not merely a swivel) which will allow you to adjust its direction precisely so that hand and rod shadows are

A small light fixture is attached to the center top of this cloth shadow screen.

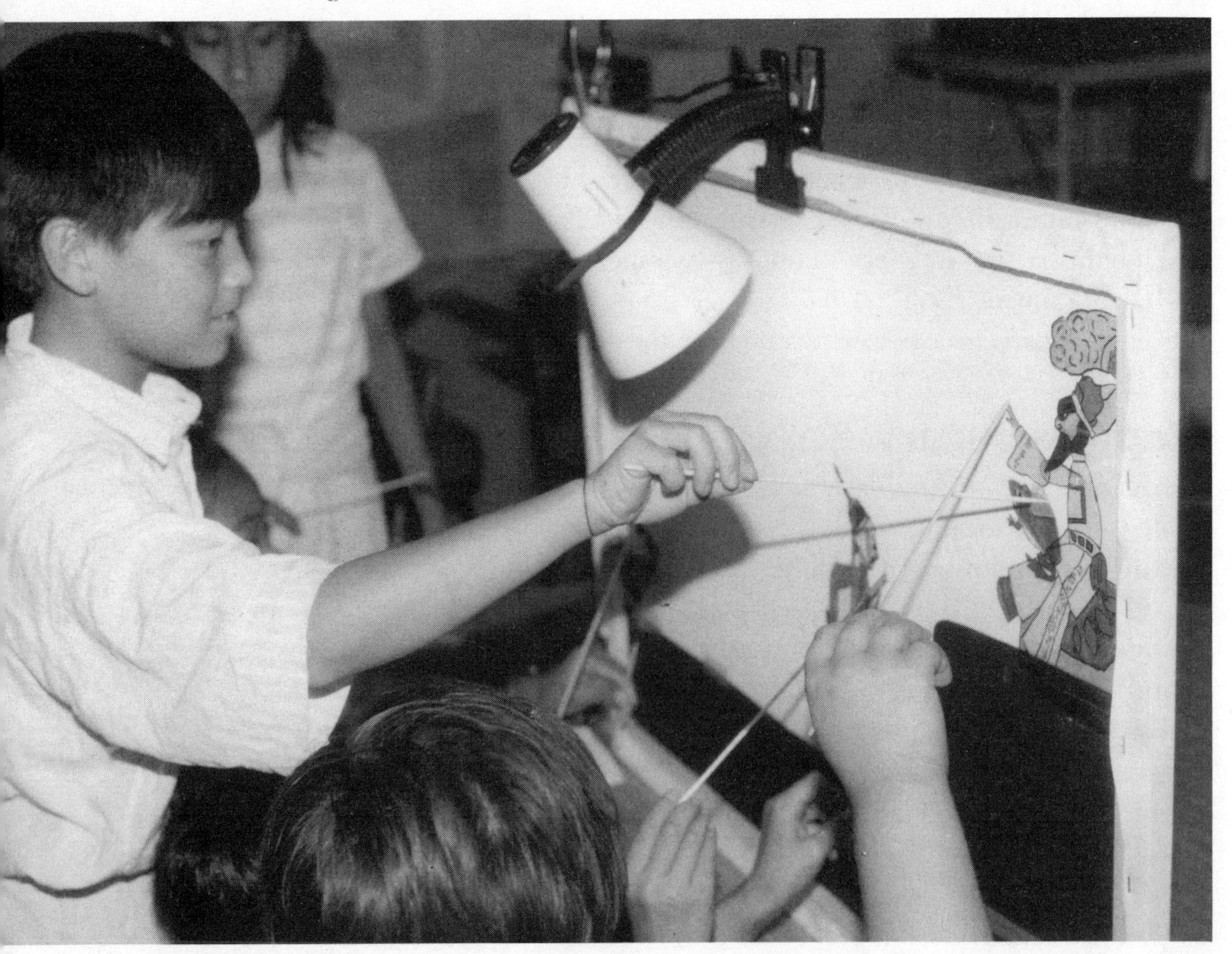

not projected onto the screen. Use masking tape to secure the lamp's electrical cord to the shadow screen, table, and floor, out of the way of the puppeteers.

A 60-watt soft-light bulb works best for screens up to twenty-six by thirty-six inches; use 75- or 100-watt bulbs for larger screens. The screen can only be lit by one light source at a time; with two light sources, double images will occur. Using a dimmer switch on your light will add to the theatricality of your show when used at the beginning and end of a performance. It is also possible to use a fluorescent-light source; dimmer switches do not function with fluorescent lights.

Plexiglas shadow screens can also be lit effectively by indirect sunlight. This is a real advantage if you are hesitant to have your group working near an electric light. To use indirect sunlight, on a clear day, place the shadow screen on a table in front of a window, with no direct sun rays entering. If your windows have blinds, you can tilt them up to convert direct sunlight to indirect. The room lights must be turned off and all windows covered except the one directly behind the shadow screen. The puppeteers sit or kneel behind the screen, between the table and the window. They will need to keep their bodies very low, so that as much light as possible hits the shadow screen.

Making Shadow Puppets

Shadow puppets are flat silhouette figures which are moved by means of rods held by the puppeteers. The figures cast either a black shadow or a brightly colored one, depending on the materials used to make them. They may consist of one piece, or of two or more pieces that are jointed together to give movement. Traditionally, shadow puppets are made from animal hides which have the thickness and stiffness of a drum head. The Javanese and Balinese puppets are exquisitely painted, but the colors do not show through the shadow screen. What does show, however, are the intricate patterns made by hundreds of small shapes incised into the leather. Traditional shadow puppets from China and India are made from hide scraped so thin that it becomes translucent. The puppets are both incised and tinted with dyes, and their bright colors can be seen by the audience.

Contemporary shadow puppets may be made of thick paper (construction paper, cover stock, lightweight posterboard), opaque plastic sheet (vinyl), or clear plastic (acetate). Paper and plastic puppets will last through many rehearsals and performances *if* they are not treated like toys—or weapons! Necessary repairs can be made easily with clear tape. Store the puppets as flat as possible in a safe, dry place when not in use.

Black Shadows

The simplest shadow puppets are cut from black or very dark paper or plastic, which makes a striking contrast to the white screen. Colored tissue paper can be added to cutouts in these puppets, producing a stained-glass effect. Use construction paper for beginning projects; for more important productions, purchase black cover stock at an art store, or use lightweight black posterboard that can be cut with scissors. Very durable puppets can be made from dark brown or black sheet vinyl, available in the form of report and book covers at office supply stores and photocopy shops.

Photocopy the puppet patterns you will use, enlarging them at the same time, if you wish. To trace the puppet patterns onto paper or plastic, first make the photocopies into transfers similar to carbon paper: color the back of each puppet pattern with a white or other light-colored crayon. You should be able to see the puppet's outlines through the paper; color along these lines, using firm, quick strokes. Place the pattern on top of the paper you will use for the puppet, crayoned side down, and go over the lines of the pattern firmly with a ball-point pen or pencil. Then cut out the puppet.

Lines or designs drawn onto black-shadow puppets will not be seen by the audience. To be visible, any surface decoration must be cut out, using scissors, hole punch, or sharp craft knife. Hole punches are available in many interesting shapes. For a stained-glass effect, cut out an area or areas of a black-shadow puppet, and cover with a slightly larger piece of colored tissue paper. Attach the tissue to the puppet with clear tape. The eyes of black-shadow puppets should always be cut out.

Shadow Puppets in Color

Brightly colored shadow puppets can be made from clear acetate which has been specially treated to accept ink. This acetate is widely available, thanks to the popularity of overhead projectors. A thickness of five mil is adequate for puppets the size of the patterns in this book, but seven- or ten-mil is necessary for larger puppets. This acetate can be purchased at school and office supply stores.

The colors and details on acetate shadow puppets can be seen clearly by the audience. The design of these two puppets (from the play, *Toad Visits the Emperor*) is adapted from the Chinese shadow theater.

Make a photocopy of the puppet patterns, enlarging them if you wish. When working from a paper pattern, lay a sheet of acetate directly on top of it. Tape both sheets to the tabletop so that they won't slip, and color with markers. It is possible to purchase acetate that can be used in a photocopy machine. This allows you to copy the patterns directly onto the material from which the puppet is made. Copier acetate comes in five- and seven-mil thickness, and is stocked by most copy shops and office supply stores. Color the acetate with permanent markers. Be sure to apply lighter colors first, darker colors last, and outline the puppet in black. Because the acetate is nearly invisible on the shadow screen, you need only cut around the general outline of the puppet. A deer's antlers, for example, will simply be cut as one rounded shape.

Caution: Acetate has a tendency to rip if there are any inward-pointing angled cuts, such as between legs. Make all cuts on acetate rounded.

Puppet Rods

The rods on shadow puppets allow the puppeteers to manipulate the puppets without their hands being seen by the audience. Rods are made from thin wooden sticks, such as bamboo barbecue skewers (available at supermarkets and variety stores). Choose the kind that are about one-eighth inch in diameter and at least ten inches long. You may want to remove their sharp points with pliers or wire clippers. Wood dowels can also be used.

There are two methods of attaching rods to shadow puppets, horizontally and vertically, and it is important to learn the advantages and limitations of each. A horizontal rod is attached perpendicular to the puppet. The puppeteer's hand, grasping the end of the rod, will thus be about ten inches away from the shadow screen. A puppet with a horizontal rod can travel anywhere on the shadow screen, *but* it can never turn to face the other direction. If a puppet character needs to both fly through the air *and* turn to face left and right, it will need to be doubled: Two identical horizontally-controlled puppets must be made, one facing left and one facing right; when the puppet must turn, one is quickly substituted for the other.

The horizontal rod should be attached to a point in the top half of the puppet. It is held in place with two pieces of clear tape, each of which bends at a right angle so that half of it adheres to the puppet, the other half to the rod. If you leave a very small gap between the puppet and the tip of the rod as you make this attachment, you will be able to fold the rod down, so that the puppet can be stored flat when not in use.

A vertical rod is attached flush with the puppet, extending below it like a lollipop stick, and providing the puppeteer with a handle. As the vertical rod also acts as the puppet's backbone, giving needed support to the paper or plastic, it should extend up into the puppet as far as possible. Puppets with vertical rods can easily turn to face left or right, but cannot rise up very far off the "ground," a four-inch-high strip of black paper that must be attached across the bottom of the screen when vertically-rodded puppets are used.

The actions a puppet will perform in a show determine how its rod will be attached, so specific instructions for rod attachments are given in the production notes for each play in this collection.

Shadow Puppets with Moving Parts

Shadow puppets can be made of two or more pieces which overlap and are joined together at a pivot point. These pieces are then moved by means of an additional rod. It's easy to get carried away with this concept and imagine a puppet with all the movement possibilities of an animated-film character.

In reality, each moving part (or series of parts) must have its own control rod, and each control rod must be held at all times. Thus, most puppets will have only one moving part, because the puppeteer will need to hold the main body rod and the moving part rod.

Some of the most common types of moving parts are shown below. The moving piece or pieces must be cut separately and have a sizeable overlap, usually circular in shape, which looks natural throughout a complete range of movement. Many of the puppet patterns in this book are designed with moving parts, for instance, *The Crocodile and the Hen, Toad Visits the Emperor,* and *Perseus and Medusa.* Use these as models when designing moving parts for other puppets. Join the moving parts together at the pivot point, which is marked with a dot on the patterns.

The traditional method of joining moving parts is with thread or string which is double- or triple-knotted on each side. Use an embroidery needle,

A moving part may be one piece, or a series of pieces, controlled by a rod attached to the top of the end piece. Inset shows the method of attaching a rod to a moving part, using thread taped to the end of the rod, and leaving a gap of 1/8 inch or less between the puppet and the rod.

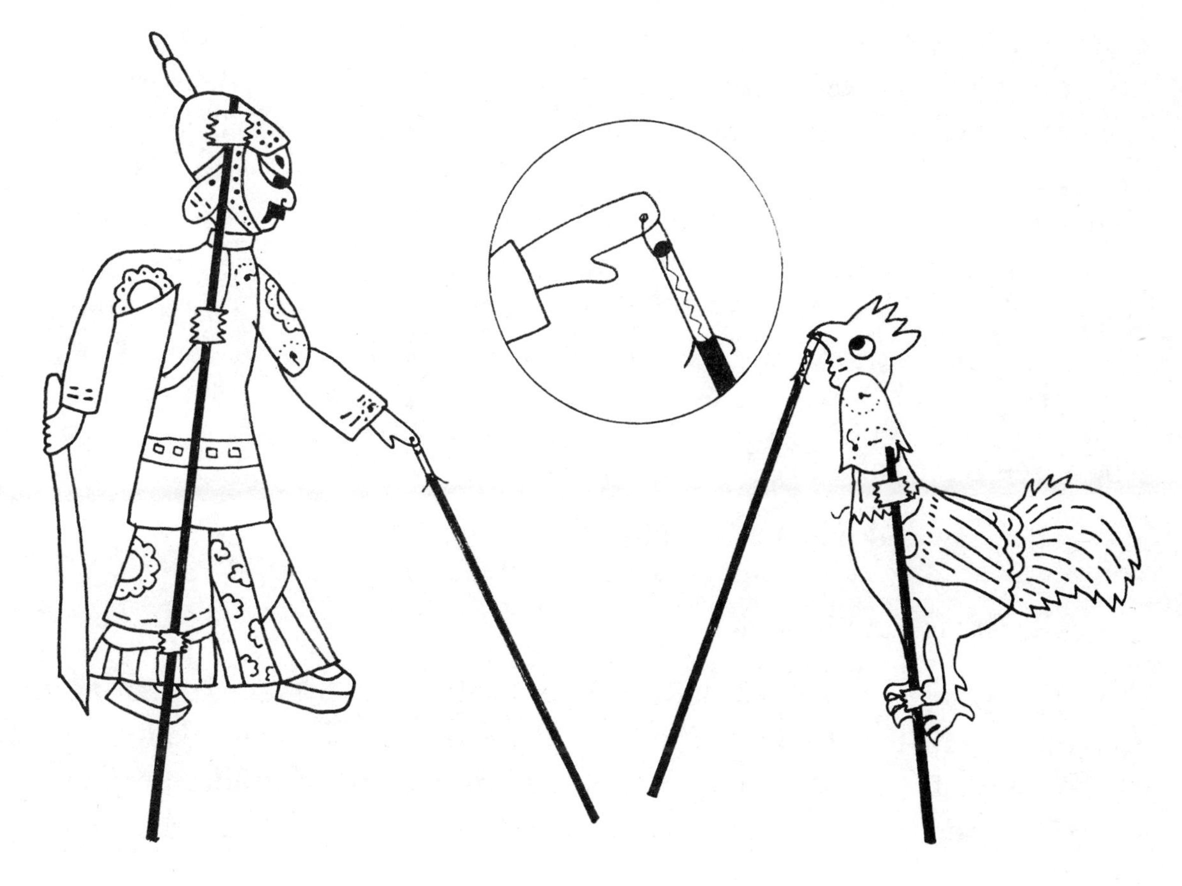

and either carpet thread or a double strand of waxed dental floss. Tie the second knot tightly by holding it against the puppet with your finger as you pull the thread. Seal each knot with a dot of white glue. Small brad fasteners can also be used to join parts. It is a good idea to reinforce the joint area first with clear tape.

Rods on moving parts of horizontally-controlled puppets should be attached in the same manner as the main rod. Rods on moving parts of vertically-controlled puppets are attached so that they can be lifted up and off the screen, whether the puppet is facing left or right. Use a one-eighth-inch dowel or skewer for this rod. Pass carpet thread or waxed dental floss—through a point near the extreme end of the moving part—and cut the thread so that two one-inch ends hang down. Tape these ends to the tip of the rod, leaving about one-eighth-inch of play between the tip of the rod and the moving part.

Designing Your Own Shadow Puppets

Puppet designs may be drawn directly onto paper, using a light pencil or crayon; use a crayon or wax pencil on vinyl. Designs for clear acetate puppets can be drawn on paper, then traced onto the acetate. Black-shadow puppets should almost always be drawn in profile; they will look more natural, in movement and interaction, if they face the side, rather than the front. If you do design a black-shadow puppet facing forward, you will need to cut out the facial features, or the area surrounding them, in order for the puppet's face to be visible. See the drawings for *All Stories Belong to Anansi* for an example of a forward-facing puppet with facial features designed to be cut out.

The three basic rules for shadow-puppet design are:

1. Draw the puppet in profile.
2. Simplify unimportant features.
3. Exaggerate important features.

Children eight years old and younger often have trouble beginning a puppet design. To get them started, I make a variety of basic head and body shapes of light cardboard for them to trace around. Young children will also need to be reminded that all arms, legs, and tails need to be fairly fat. Long,

These puppets were designed by fifth-grade students and cut from black cover stock, using scissors, hole punch, and craft knife. The puppet on the right was inspired by a demon figure in a display of Indonesian shadow puppets.

thin shadow-puppet parts tend to curl up and thus become invisible on the shadow screen.

Older children and adults will generally need to loosen up their drawing styles and overcome inhibition in shadow puppet design. The following exercise provides a highly enjoyable introduction to puppet design for puppeteers ages nine and older:

Four-Minute Shadow Puppets

Each person receives a sheet of black construction paper, a light-colored crayon, scissors, and a puppet rod—a bamboo skewer, or even a pencil for this beginning exercise. Provide several rolls of clear tape and hole punches for them to share. Write the three basic rules of shadow puppet design on a chalkboard, then inform the group that they will have only four minutes to draw a puppet, cut it out, and attach the puppet rod. The puppet should be drawn as one continuous outline, and be almost as large as the sheet of paper. Select a design theme you think will capture the group's imagination, such as monsters, space aliens, crazy cars, space ships, or unusual pets. Keep careful track of time: give the starting signal, then make announcements telling them when they have three, two, and one minute left to complete their puppets. This may sound impossible, but it really works, and it generates a great amount of energy and enthusiasm. When the puppets are finished, play some lively music and ask the puppeteers to go backstage one at a time and move their puppet on the shadow screen. They may wish to exchange puppets first, in order to be able to see their own design from the audience's perspective. Provide generous praise for the puppets, pointing out examples of simplicity and exaggeration that work well on the shadow screen.

Props and Scenery

Props are objects which the puppets (appear to) pick up, or otherwise manipulate. Shadow puppet props are attached to rods in the same manner as are puppets. Props which move through the air, or which are picked up or passed from hand to hand are usually attached to horizontal rods. If a puppet picks up a ball, someone backstage holds a control rod attached to the ball prop and follows the hand of the puppet on the screen. If the puppet throws the ball, the person manipulating the prop simulates its flight through the air. In shadow puppetry, it is best to be sparing in the use of props. Small ones are hard for the audience to see. Manipulating props is difficult for beginners and will slow down the performance. Small objects can merely be mimed, that is, spoken about while the puppets pretend to use them. This method is used in *Perseus and Medusa* when Athena shows Perseus a portrait of Medusa, and when Perseus steals the eye from the three gray sisters. There is no actual prop of either of these objects.

Shadow puppet scenery is usually confined to the edges of the screen. This type of puppet can never appear to be in front of any scenery, so too much scenery will severely limit the puppets' playing area. Of course, chairs, tables, beds, etc., will often be needed at center stage in order to set the scene, and to accommodate the action of the play. Make shadow puppet scenery from black paper or plastic; if colored acetate is used, it produces an

Puppeteers designed a scenery piece of a house to use in performing a play they wrote based on the nursery rhyme, *Little Miss Muffet.*

odd, see-through effect as puppets pass behind the scenery. Occasionally, this is desirable: in the case of water, for instance, blue tissue or acetate can be used, and so puppets will appear to be swimming.

There are several ways to attach scenery pieces to the shadow screen. If they are onstage only for a short period of time, they can be attached to vertical rods and held in place on the shadow screen by a puppeteer. A vertical rod can also be taped to the screen for a semi-permanent attachment. In the Indonesian shadow theater, set pieces as well as puppets are often held in place by pushing their rods in a pithy, split banana log which sits across the bottom of the screen. You can simulate this technique by taping pieces of Styrofoam, about one-inch thick, in strategic locations at the bottom edge of the shadow screen. Place masking tape right on top of the Styrofoam—it is easy for the sharp shadow rods to poke through the tape and into the foam. Trim the rods of the scenery pieces so that when they are stuck into the Styrofoam, they will be at the correct height on the stage. On a cloth screen, most scenery can be held in place by sandwiching it between the frame and the cloth. Instead of using a rod, simply extend the bottom of the scenery piece to account for the distance between the bottom of the screen and the top of the puppets' "ground." Add a paper tab to the back of the piece as a grip.

Patterns are provided in this book for those smaller scenery pieces whose precise size and design are important to the play. For other scenery, a small sketch is given which you will need to enlarge to fit your screen. No designs are included for generic scenery such as trees, mountains, and ocean waves.

The use of a four-inch-high ground is necessary to mask the puppeteers' hands when using vertically-controlled shadow puppets. This can be cut from black construction paper and taped to a Plexiglas screen with clear tape. Ground for a cloth stage should be made of stiff black paper, such as poster board, sandwiched between the wooden frame and the cloth. The ground is taken into account in the making of the cardboard-box stage.

Shadow-Puppet Manipulation

Puppeteers need to follow a few simple rules of shadow puppet manipulation:

1. Hold the rod at the tip or end, so that the audience cannot see your hand.
2. Keep the puppet pressed against the shadow screen at all times.
3. Keep your puppet's feet on the ground—unless it is flying!
4. Make the puppet move when it speaks; keep it still when it listens.

Manipulation Exercises

Use the following exercises to help puppeteers learn these basic rules, while becoming accustomed to manipulating their puppets.

Action

Puppeteers line up backstage in groups of four or five, and move their puppets across the shadow screen one at a time. As each puppet crosses, suggest any corrections which need to be made, such as, holding the rod at

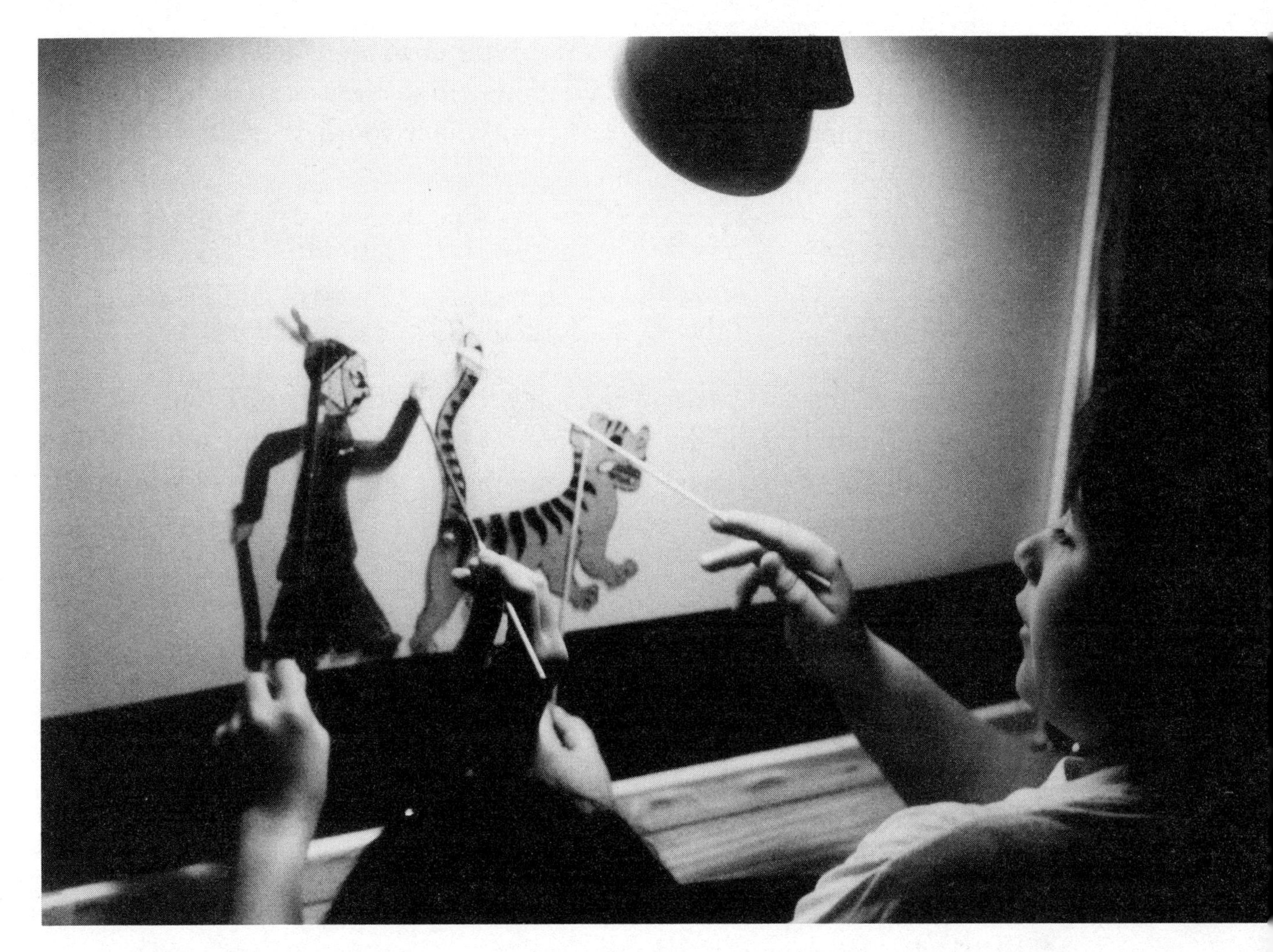

Good shadow-puppet manipulation results in the puppets seeming to move and act by themselves. These puppeteers are pressing their puppets firmly against the screen while keeping their hands out of sight of the audience. They are holding the puppets' vertical body rods below the black "ground" at the bottom of the screen, and gripping the horizontal rods that control the moving parts at the very end.

the end, making the puppet touch the screen, keeping the puppet on the ground.

Add two more levels of difficulty (and fun) to the exercise, making two sets of index cards. On the cards of the first set, write action verbs telling ways in which a puppet can cross the shadow screen, such as:

walk	float	run	ice-skate
skip	crawl	twirl	leap
swim	tiptoe	hop	walk backward
sneak	dance	fly	slide

Go through this pack, calling out a type of motion before each puppet crosses. When the puppeteers have done these exercises to their satisfaction, add another set of index cards, on which you have written adverbs, such as:

happily	bravely	sadly	timidly
quickly	menacingly	slowly	angrily
clumsily	sillily	gracefully	seriously

Go through the two packs of cards together so that you get random pairs of verbs and adverbs for the puppeteers to represent on the screen. They will soon discover that even a flat, one-piece puppet has a wide range of expressiveness through movement.

Reaction

As important as words and actions in a puppet play are reactions. Often, it is these small, subtle movements that bring the greatest delight to the audience. For this exercise, work with puppets representing human beings, preferably made with a moving arm. Affix one puppet at center stage, motionless, like a scenery piece. Have other puppets enter, one by one, and show in pantomime, by actions only, that the puppet onstage:

is its mother	is a monster
is a statue	is its friend
is hurt	is very funny

Then, cut a round, lumpy shape, about half the height of the puppets, and place it at center stage. Each puppet enters, and again in pantomime only, shows that the object:

is hot	is cold
is gold!	smells bad
is a rock	is made of candy
is dangerous	needs to be moved

Interaction

Puppeteers work in pairs. Two puppets enter from opposite sides of the screen, walk to center and stop. Then, the puppeteers improvise a short dialogue. The object of this exercise is to practice the move-as-you-talk rule.

The following are examples of opening lines that can be used to start the dialogues:

> "Can I borrow a quarter to make a phone call?"
> "My dog ran away. Can you help me find him?"
> "Which way to the haunted house?"
> "Aren't you (use the name of a TV or movie star)?"

Special Effects in Shadow Puppetry

Shadow puppets can perform magical acts not easily achieved in other types of theater, such as flying, disappearing, transforming into something completely different. A shadow puppet with a horizontal rod can move through the air, anywhere on the shadow screen. A puppet lifted an inch away from the screen grows large and fuzzy; a puppet lifted two or three inches away disappears completely. Quickly substitute another puppet in its place, and you have a magical transformation, as when the princess kisses the frog in *The Frog Prince.* Because shadow puppets can be made quickly, it is easy to use duplicate puppets of the same character in order to show changes of shape and of costume. After the wolf in *Red Riding Hood* eats the grandmother, for example, a second, fatter puppet of the wolf, dressed in one of Granny's nightgowns, appears onstage.

Advanced Shadow-Puppet Techniques

When making moving parts on a colored acetate puppet, leave the overlap area on one piece clear, so that the double layer of color doesn't make the joint obvious to the audience. Sometimes you will want to limit the range of movement of a moving piece. This is done by means of a thread stop, which must be specially engineered for each individual puppet.

A good way to advance your shadow-puppetry skills is to make and use replicas of Indonesian and Chinese shadow puppets. The design of the Indonesian puppets is exceptional in its creation of positive and negative designs on the shadow screen; the incised designs give the shadow a compelling, three-dimensional quality. The Chinese puppets that represent humans are made of eleven pieces; their delicate balance enables the puppeteer to simulate extremely lifelike movements with minimal effort.

Patterns drawn from authentic Chinese shadow puppets can be found in Edie Kraska's *Toys and Tales from Grandmother's Attic* (Houghton Mifflin, 1979). In order for the Chinese-style puppets of humans to sit, kneel, or walk, the ground on the shadow screen must be made of wood, at least one-fourth inch in thickness.

Maximum control of shadow puppets can be achieved by making them of the heaviest possible materials, such as ten-mil vinyl or acetate, and tilting the shadow screen forward at the top (toward the audience) about two inches for every foot of height. This will also allow you to attach the main body rod of the puppet in the same manner as the rod for a moving part, that is, by means of a thread loop attached to a rod, with a very small gap between rod and puppet. The traditional Chinese shadow puppet is attached to the rod at the front or back of the neck. This gives you a rod which is held horizontally but which also, with a flip of the wrist, allows the puppet to face in either direction.

Rod Puppetry

Rod puppets are performing figures that are manipulated by puppeteers from below the stage by means of sticks or rods. Rod puppets of human characters have a main body rod, and one or two arm rods. Perhaps the best known rod puppets are the Indonesian *wayang golek.* Traditional rod puppet theater has also existed in India, China, and Japan. The most sophisticated rod puppets, like the *wayang golek,* are carved, three-dimensional sculptures, while the simplest rod puppets—the Indonesian wooden *wayang klitik* and the Japanese paper theater, *kami shibai*—are flat. The European and American paper toy theater is also a type of rod-puppet theater.

The rod puppets in this book are designed to be flat and made from paper and cardboard. The puppets may be made the size of the patterns and operated in a small tabletop theater, or the patterns may be enlarged for use with larger stages.

Rod-Puppet Stages

Rod-puppet stages should be easy for the puppeteers to use, while permitting the audience to see the puppets clearly. If you have a hand-puppet theater, it will probably be suitable for rod-puppet performance.

Tabletop Rod-Puppet Stage

A tabletop stage can be made from a sturdy corrugated cardboard box, following the drawing below. This is an open-proscenium style stage, that is, it does not have front curtains that open and close, nor does it use background scenery. Instead, a black curtain behind the puppets allows the puppeteers to hold their puppets at face-level, looking through the fabric to see the puppets as they manipulate them. This black background focuses the

Left: A tabletop rod-puppet stage may be made from a corrugated cardboard box, plywood, or cloth-covered wood frames. The back curtain drapes over the puppeteers' heads. Right: Scenery pieces are held in place by wooden spring clothespins glued to the inside front of the stage.

audience's attention on the puppets, and also camouflages the black rods controlling the puppets and props.

Cut the box with a mat knife, following the drawing below, then either paint the outside or cover it with fabric, lapped and glued over the edges. Bend the sides of the stage out at a forty-five-degree angle, creating more room backstage for the puppeteers. Cut slots for two dowels that will hold the curtains—the curtain behind the puppets, or scrim, and back curtain, which will prevent the puppeteers from being seen by the audience. Both should be made from medium-weight black synthetic-knit fabric. Cut each piece the width of the corresponding dowel, plus six inches, and sew a slot at the top for the dowel and a hem at the bottom. The scrim should only extend one inch below the stage; the back curtain should be longer—it will enclose the puppeteers, and keep backlight from showing their shadows to the audience during the performance.

A more permanent stage can be made to these same dimensions, using frames of one-by-two-inch clear pine covered with opaque cloth and hinged together.

Large Rod-Puppet Stage

The size stage required for rod puppet performance is determined by the physical size of the puppeteers and by the number who will be backstage at any one time. For large groups, large puppets, and older children, a quick and easy playboard for an open-proscenium stage can be made from a one-by-six-inch clear pine board, cut to a length of six to eight feet. Attach three-quarter-inch Velcro to one long, narrow edge of the board, using white glue and heavy-duty staples (the kind you hammer in). Make a gathered front curtain, six feet in length, from lightweight but opaque fabric; sew the matching Velcro across the top edge of this curtain. The ends of the board can be set on a pair of tables, audiovisual-equipment carts, painting easels, book trucks, ladders, or the tops of bookcases. Use generous amounts of duct tape to attach the ends of the playboard to its supports.

Though the puppeteers can kneel or sit, standing is always preferable, especially for large performing groups and action-packed plays. If you like the flexibility of this very wide stage (I certainly do), ask someone with

The playboard of a large rod-puppet stage can be supported by two easels, or other supports of equal height which are taller than the tallest puppeteer. Scenery is cut from heavy paper or cardboard, and clipped to the playboard with metal spring clamps. Glue a right-angle support, cut from a small box with a securely glued bottom (see inset), to the back of each scenery piece.

carpentry tools and skills to design and build custom upright stands for your playboard.

Rod Puppets in the Round

Holding a puppet backstage and performing for an unseen audience can be too abstract an activity for many young puppeteers. For children ages five through eight, rod-puppet performances can be staged in a circle, like creative dramatics. This works best if you use fairly large, very colorful puppets. Both pantomimes to music (such as *Old MacDonald* and Pete Seeger's *The Foolish Frog*) and narrated picture-book stories (like Gerald McDermott's *Anansi the Spider* and Leo Lionni's *Swimmy*) adapt well to this method. The children hold their puppets at face level and manipulate them, while moving around the performing area as the sense of the story dictates. In this way, they participate in the puppet performance and see it at the same time.

Lighting the Rod-Puppet Play

For informal performance, it is not necessary to light the rod-puppet play; it is important, though, to minimize backlight (light from behind the stage) which might allow the audience to see the puppeteers' bodies through the curtains. Bright light on the front of the stage will usually counteract any backlight.

For formal performances, clip-on utility light fixtures and small, lightweight floodlight bulbs can be placed on stands to the side front of the stage. Spotlights are usually too harsh for puppets, unless they are sufficiently far away, such as the ceiling-mounted lights in theaters. If you don't have light stands, clip the lights to the backs of two chairs. Tape the lights' electrical cords to the floor with masking tape so that no one trips over them. For extra safety, also tape the legs of the stands or chairs to the floor with duct tape.

Making Rod Puppets

Flat rod puppets are almost always designed in profile, so that they can turn to face in either direction. They should be cut from a durable, good-quality paper. Heavy bristol, or light poster board are good choices for small- and medium-sized puppets. Corrugated cardboard and foam-core board are recommended for large puppets. Use the best possible scissors, or, for adults and older children, a combination of scissors and craft knife.

To transfer puppet patterns to the paper, first make photocopies, enlarging the patterns if you wish. Color the back of the photocopy with a dark crayon. The lines of the pattern should be visible on the reverse side, and you only need to color over those lines. Use a rapid back-and-forth stroke of the crayon. Then, lay the photocopy on top of the paper you will use for the puppet, crayoned-side down, like carbon paper. Secure the pattern to the paper with tape, so that it doesn't slip during the transfer process, and go over all lines with a pencil or ballpoint pen. Cut the puppet out. Most rod puppets need to be colored on both sides; transfer interior lines to the other side of the puppet after you cut it out. To transfer patterns for large rod puppets, duplicate the patterns onto clear acetate. Tape corrugated cardboard or foam-core board to a wall, project the puppet patterns onto it, using an overhead projector, and trace.

Smaller paper rod puppets can be colored with crayons or markers; paint larger cardboard and foam-core puppets with tempera or acrylic paint.

Three-dimensional rod puppets can be made from recycled paper and plastic products and/or paper sculpture. See Nancy Renfro's *Puppetry and the Art of Story Creation* (Nancy Renfro Studios, 1979), and Lis Paludan's *Playing with Puppets* (Plays, 1979) for examples and instructions.

Moving Parts

Moving parts are cut from the same material as the puppets. The parts must be designed with a generous overlap, usually rounded, that looks natural throughout the entire range of movement. Moving parts are joined to rod puppets with brad fasteners. A substitute for a brad fastener can be made from a one- to two-inch length of pipe cleaner, bent into a keyhole shape, the straight ends of which are then put through holes in the puppet and moving part and are opened flat, like a brad.

Note: If a rod puppet has a moving arm attached to one side, you will usually need to draw a second arm onto the side of the puppet opposite the moving part. Use the moving arm as a pattern.

Moving parts are attached to these rod puppets with brad fasteners, and are operated by means of thin black rods. The black cloth scrim behind the puppets helps camouflage these rods.

Puppet Rods

The main puppet rod not only provides a grip for the puppeteer, but also gives support to the puppet. It is the puppet's backbone and should extend as far up into the puppet's body as possible, leaving at least a three- to four-inch handle at the bottom for the puppeteer to hold. Rods for human puppets can often be disguised behind a leg. Camouflage the rod by coloring it to match the puppet's body, using paint or marker; color the area of the rod which extends below the body black.

There are several choices of materials for making rods. Bamboo barbecue skewers work well for small puppets. Clip off the sharp pointed ends with wire snips or pliers. Use three-eighths-inch wooden dowels as body rods on large puppets, one-eighth-inch for moving parts. The larger dowels work best when ripped in half lengthwise on a table saw, so that they have a flat side to glue against the puppet. Rods needn't be round; dowels are suggested merely because they are widely available. You may have another source of wood sticks that will work just as well. For large puppets, coat-hanger wire, or welding rod, bent with pliers into a flat circular handle at the bottom, works well both as a rod for moving parts, as a main rod for flying puppets such as birds, bats, and insects, and for props. Wedge the wire handle inside corrugated cardboard or foam-core board when the puppet, moving part, or prop is not in use.

To attach the end of a control rod to a moving part, use a needle and strong thread—carpet thread or dental floss. Pull the thread through the end of the moving part, about one-fourth-inch from the edge, leaving one inch of thread loose on either side. Tape the loose ends to the end of a control rod, leaving about one-eighth inch of play between the rod and the puppet. If the paper is too thick to be pierced with a needle, punch the hole with an awl. A wire rod for a moving part can be pushed through a hole in the end of the puppet part, then squeezed closed with pliers.

Props and Scenery

Props, objects the puppets (appear to) pick up, handle, and use, like rod puppets, are usually made from paper or cardboard. Attach them to the thinnest rods possible, painted black. Small props can simply be mimed, that is, spoken about as the puppets pretend to use them. For example, the grandmother in *Red Riding Hood* says she is going to put stones in the wolf's belly. She mimes doing this, but there are no actual props used for the stones. If you are using very large puppets, you may want to actually make such props.

Scenery pieces are objects such as trees, chairs, tables, and beds, which are necessary to the action of the play or help set the scene. Scenery is cut from heavy paper or cardboard. Large scenery pieces may need to be reinforced by wood sticks glued to the back. On a cardboard-box stage, scenery is held in place by a row of wooden spring-type clothespins glued to the inside of the stage, about two inches below the stage opening. Extend the bottoms of the scenery pieces by two inches before you cut them out, and glue a small paper handle onto the back of each piece.

Scenery pieces for a large rod-puppet stage should be cut from heavy paper and glued to a support which will hold them at a right angle to the playboard. Cut these supports from sturdy cardboard boxes, as illustrated on page 25, or use small box lids. Attach the scenery pieces to the stage with metal spring-type gluing clamps—these look like metal clothespins and can be purchased in hardware stores. Because this large stage has no wings or scrim to disguise exits and entrances, there must always be some kind of large scenery piece, taller than the tallest puppet, at each side of the stage. The puppets pop up quickly behind these and then walk onstage.

Rod-Puppet Manipulation

Like shadow puppets, rod puppets must not be handled roughly. For example, any forceful hitting or impact should be represented in performance by a sound effect followed by exaggerated recoil, rather than by actual contact.

The following are the basic rules for rod-puppet manipulation:

1. Try not to touch the stage with your puppet or your hand. Keep your puppet back two inches or more from the edge of the stage.

2. Always keep the flat side of the puppet to the audience. Turn it quickly and neatly.

3. Always know where the ground is in relation to your puppet's feet.

4. Move your puppet when it is talking. Keep your puppet still when it is listening.

5. Unless directed otherwise, always enter and exit from the far sides of the stage.

Puppeteers can practice these basic rules while using the manipulation exercises on pages 18–21.

Music and Sound Effects

Sound effects are marked with an asterisk (*) in the scripts. These represent the minimum of sound and musical accompaniment for each play. Music and sound effects have always been an integral part of puppetry, and they add immensely to the impact of any performance. Sound effects punctuate actions such as hitting, flying, and falling. Music makes the pauses between scenes flow naturally.

Sound effects can be produced on simple and inexpensive instruments, many of which are included in basic school rhythm instrument sets. The instruments below are recommended as a basic puppet orchestra:

a. A clavé, or wooden blocks, which produce a sharp rap.

b. Slide whistles are very effective as accompaniments to rising (slide up) or falling (slide down) actions. These very inexpensive instruments require

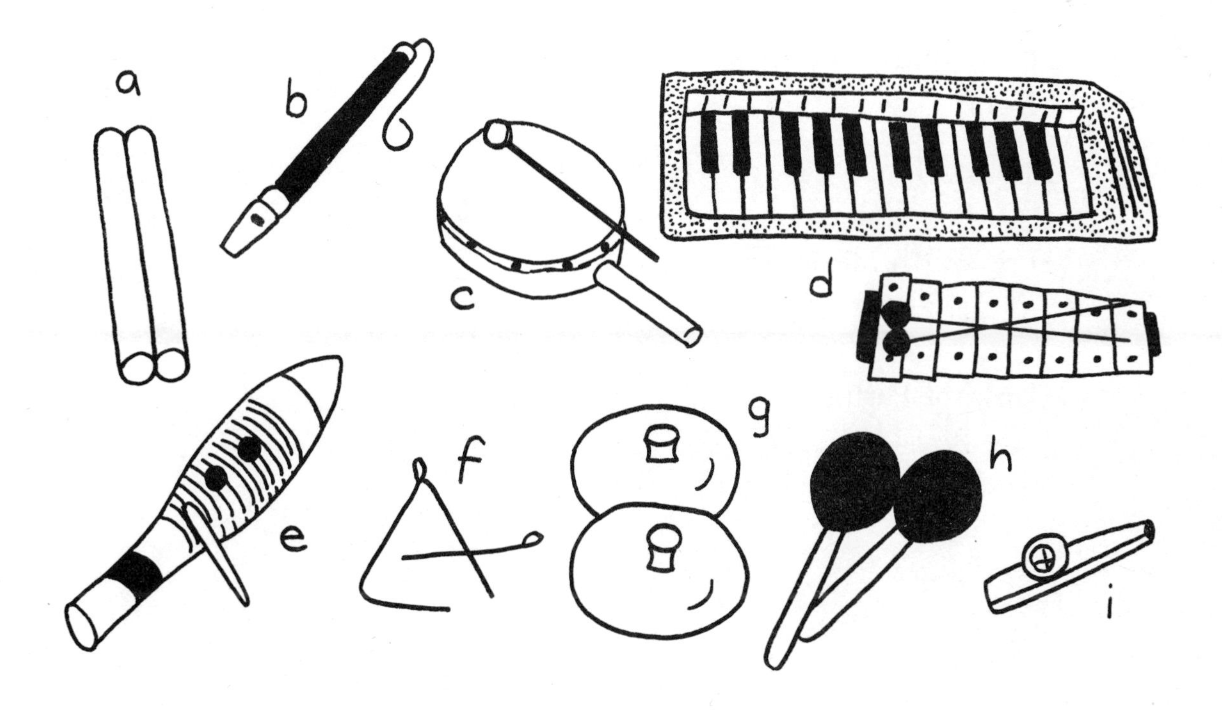

occasional simple maintenance: if the plunger sticks, put a few drops of vegetable oil through the air hole, rotate the whistle, and work the plunger until it is well lubricated.

c. A hand drum with a good, resonant tone.

d. A small electronic keyboard, which can simulate several instruments, is extremely useful. It can be used to play overtures and scene change music and also to produce sound effects. Alternatively, a xylophone can be used for simple melodies.

e. A Mexican *guiro,* or a raspy Halloween noisemaker can be used to make the cutting and digging sounds.

f. A triangle draws attention to occurrences which are surprising or magical.

g. Cymbals can be used to announce the entrances and exits of royalty, and also to simulate thunder and battle sounds.

h. A rattle or maraca mimics rain and digging noises.

i. A kazoo is particularly useful to small ensembles, allowing a puppeteer whose hands are occupied to play a tune as overture or scene change. (Siren whistles, samba whistles, and hunters' animal calls are other no-hands instruments, which can even be mounted on a harmonica stand for use by the busy puppeteer.)

Hundreds of kinds and sizes of inexpensive musical instruments can be ordered from:

Rhythm Band Inc.
P.O. Box 126
Fort Worth, Texas 76101

and

World of Peripole
P.O. Box 146
Browns Mills, New Jersey 08015

Recorded Music

A tape recorder is preferable to a record player for musical accompaniment. When recording a musical piece to use with a performance, repeat it several times on the tape, leaving a short silence between repetitions, so you won't have to rewind the tape during rehearsals. If you are recording two or more musical pieces to use in a performance—overture and scene-change music, for example—leave a five-second silence after each piece. Play the music on a tape player that has a pause button. This allows you to stop and restart the tape player noiselessly.

Amplification

Most children have a hard enough time being heard onstage without having to talk through a puppet stage. It is important (and absolutely necessary in large rooms) to amplify their voices. The most effective way is to place a floor microphone stand at maximum height to the side front of the puppet stage, and bend the flexible end of the microphone holder down, pointing toward the puppeteers. Use an omnidirectional microphone. The puppeteers should not talk into it; it will pick up their dialogue well enough if their voices are directed forward, toward the audience. Ideally, the narrator will have a separate microphone.

Rehearsal and Performance

Note: In stage directions given in this book, *left* and *right* refer to the sides of the stage from the puppeteers' point of view. *Offstage* means that the puppet is heard, but not seen.

A formal performance probably should not be the goal of beginning puppet projects. Yet some kind of performance ritual makes the whole playmaking process more exciting and rewarding. A group of children two or more years younger than the performers usually makes an appreciative audience. In a school, this can often be arranged on the spur of the moment, whenever the puppeteers feel that their play is ready to share. Making and viewing a videotape also provides a satisfying culmination for an early effort.

In working toward formal performance, I have found that the most important step is the initial session between group and leader, in which I explain the play or project to them. They have an opportunity to ask questions and propose alternatives, and we all agree to work toward a specific goal. Once a group commits to performance, they are willing to make whatever efforts are necessary to ensure success; children will take scripts home, stay after school to complete puppets and props, and make giant strides in the learning and interpretation of lines in a very short time.

As in all theater, the amount of time from first rehearsal to performance should not be too long, or a certain edge is lost. The ideal length of time will vary according to the maturity and experience of the group; younger children will need to have fewer, shorter, and more frequent rehearsals than older children. (See the sample rehearsal schedules on pages 40–41 for specific projects and time frames.)

Plays Without a Script

Plays which are performed as pantomimes to music or narration require that the puppeteers learn their cues (when to enter, what to do, when to exit) through repetition, not through reading and memorizing. As director, you will need to form a clear picture of puppet action and prepare a written outline of it. Before each rehearsal, have the group listen to the show's music or narration several times together. Talk the group through the first few rehearsals, until they learn their cues and the pattern of movement backstage. Keep rehearsals short, stopping before enthusiasm wanes. After each rehearsal, review what was accomplished, and discuss what work remains to be done.

Narration-Improvisation Technique

This is a method of presenting a story in puppetry without a script. I use it when I am working with a group for only one or two sessions, but it is also useful when working with children who are not ready to learn a script, but who can remember and interpret lines that they have heard. This technique is perfect for use with the picture books and folktales that are recommended as follow-up activities to the plays in this book. Mark the text you are working with, taking out any passages that will be made redundant by the puppets' actions. Highlight or underline dialogue. Begin by reading the text as the puppets act it out. After the children have heard the story several times, start allowing them to provide the dialogue. You may need to give them very pointed cues, such as, "and then the troll said. . . ." I often tell—rather than read—the stories. This allows me not only to cue dialogue, but also to change the words of the story in order to help direct the puppets' actions (for instance, "the little goat trembled with fear, and began to cry"). The language of many stories deserves reading, however; the language of an author like Dr. Seuss *necessitates* reading!

Working from a Script

It is sometimes assumed that since puppeteers are not seen by the audience, they can simply read their lines from a script. Puppet plays produced in this way fall far short of puppet theater's potential. For puppetry to be truly a performing art, the puppeteer needs to be aware of the puppet and its movements at all times. And, in learning a script, the puppet's lines are not so much memorized as "learned by heart," so that during performance, both words and actions proceed from the heart.

As a safety net for inexperienced performers, a prompter can hold a script backstage during rehearsals and performances. It is best never to allow puppeteers to take a script backstage. This forces the puppeteers to learn their lines early in the rehearsal process; those who have not done their homework will either quickly shape up or can be replaced by others who are willing to make the effort.

It's best not to even consider the alternative of prerecording the script. Such a recording ties the performance forever to an early, probably stilted, line reading. Let the puppetry work its magic, part of which is to give children the desire and the means to reach beyond themselves and achieve new levels of competence. Though having sat through many tedious, prerecorded puppet shows, I too tried this method once out of desperation. I was working with a group of extremely soft-spoken seventh-graders, with limited English language skills. After rehearsing once to a tape recording

Fifth grade students rehearse a shadow-puppet performance of the Greek myth, *Perseus and Medusa.* Their high level of involvement and concentration would not be possible if they were reading lines from a script.

they had made, the group unanimously rejected it. They knew they could do better and proved it in their subsequent performances. Presenting a show mimed to a professional tape, such as Pete Seeger's *Abiyoyo*, is a different matter. Many commercial recordings make fine puppet shows, as puppeteers strive to match the puppet visuals to the excellence of the audio production.

Learning Lines

Prepare a photocopy of the script for each member of the group, performers and crew. Puppeteers' and narrator's copies should show their lines marked with a yellow highlighting pen.

The actual memorization of lines takes place outside of the puppet sessions. Different methods work best for different people. Some children may already have experience learning scripts, and they can be asked to share their techniques with the group. Puppeteers not only must learn their lines, but also their cues—what is said or what happens just before they do or say something. After studying their parts on their own, they should ask a friend to test them by reading the script aloud (including stage directions) and pausing for them to deliver their lines. Set a deadline early in the rehearsal process for knowing all lines.

Line Rehearsals

Line rehearsals may be held while you are still making the puppets. The director reads the stage directions, and puppeteers recite their lines. Don't worry about minor mistakes at this point, or about the portrayal of character. An older group will enjoy speed line rehearsals, in which everyone says their lines as rapidly as possible while still being understood.

Walk-through

The first rehearsal backstage will be a walk-through, in which the director talks the group through the entire play, and each puppeteer goes through the motions of the performance. Puppeteers, and any associated crew such as stage manager and prompter are backstage. All puppets, props, and scenery are used. Musicians and narrator take their places. This is a time to agree upon the execution of entrances, exits, and scene changes. In puppetry, there are two patterns of stage traffic—that of the puppets and that of the puppeteers. The actions of the puppets must always make sense to the audience, thus the puppeteers do whatever is necessary backstage so that the play looks good. This may include some bodily contortions, passing puppets back and forth, and perhaps manipulating a puppet while someone else speaks for it.

Musicians need to have a good view of the puppets, because music and sound effects must be closely timed to the onstage action. For shadow-puppet performances, musicians may sit either in back or in front (and to the side) of the stage. Musicians for a rod-puppet performance will have to sit to the side front of the stage.

Continue having walk-throughs, with follow-up discussions until all basic traffic patterns have been agreed upon and all special actions, such as prop handling, scene changes, coordination of movement with music and sound effects, have been worked out.

Scene Rehearsals

Divide the script into scenes or other short units, which will be rehearsed from beginning to end without stopping. Set up the stage as it will be during performance. At this point, it is wise to begin stressing the importance of silence backstage. After each scene, talk through any major problems, such as puppets who disappear or sink out of sight, missed cues, etc., and repeat the scene again. Each rehearsal is a learning process. It is important that the mechanics of the play go smoothly, that the audience can see everything and understand what is happening. The director can help puppeteers find interesting and appropriate movements for the puppets. In matters of acting, be slow to criticize or to praise. As actors, children must be treated with great delicacy and allowed to discover their characters over the course of the rehearsal process.

Final Rehearsals

Keep rehearsals short, ending them when attention is lagging. Experienced puppeteers may be able to take over the rehearsal process at this point. In a classroom situation, they can be given time to rehearse by themselves. As soon as the group can make their way through the play from beginning to end without major mishaps, videotape it if possible, so that they can see it from the audience's point of view.

Fine-tuning the Performance

When directing children, it is always good to strive for a balance between suggesting that they do things in specific ways, and letting them make discoveries for themselves. Part of directing is teaching children what puppets are capable of, particularly in terms of action and timing. I try to concentrate on fine-tuning two or three of the action scenes of a play, ones I know the audience will appreciate for their humor or suspense, and let the rest of the show depend on the group's initiative. Similarly, in matters of acting, I choose to make only strategic corrections, and to make them as tactfully as possible. A puppeteer's misinterpretation of a character's motivation can throw off the other performers and confuse the audience. Sometimes a puppeteer needs private, one-on-one coaching; this kind of special attention often results in great improvement.

Note: There are plenty of nooks, crannies, and even wide-open spaces in these scripts for improvisation, both in action and in dialogue. Please use them!

Dress Rehearsal

Schedule one or more dress rehearsals if formal performance is your goal. Dress rehearsal should take place under conditions as close as possible to those of performance (the puppets, of course, are always dressed). The director sets a tone of seriousness. Have the group practice responding to the cue words *places,* to indicate that everyone should be standing where they will be standing at the beginning of the performance, completely silent; and *lights,* to indicate that room lights go out and stage lights go up. Dress rehearsal needn't be perfect, but it should be a matter of concern if there is any part of the play which has *never* gone well in any rehearsal. Don't forget to rehearse taking a group bow after the performance.

Formal Performance for an Audience

Make sure that your performing space will be set up so that the audience can see the puppets. Performing for a large audience may require that the puppet stage be on a raised stage. For shadow puppetry, see that the room can be darkened sufficiently at the time of day when performance will take place. Set up the puppet stage as it will be during performance. Check sight lines. Will audience members sitting at the far sides of the front rows have an adequate view, or will you have to make these areas off-limits?

For a professional effect, your group may want to make tickets, posters, and programs. Programs serve as keepsakes for the cast, crew, and audience, as well as crediting all who participated.

The performers may not know what to expect from an audience. A quiet audience will often cause nervousness on the part of the performers, who may then try to use slapstick and silly improvisations to provoke laughter. Assure them that silence is a sign the audience is enjoying the play. Silence from a child audience is the equivalent of a standing ovation. When the audience does laugh, puppets should freeze until the laughter begins to die down; otherwise, some of their lines will not be heard.

Saying a few words to the audience before the play begins can help assure a successful performance. Welcome them, and give some background about the play, the style of puppets, and the process of puppet making and rehearsal in which the group has been involved. Tell them how excited and happy the group is to perform for them. After the play, the audience will be curious to know which puppeteer played which part, so announce this after applause has died down and also recognize the members of the support crew by name. You may also want to hold a short session after the show, during which the puppeteers can respond to questions from members of the audience.

Sample Rehearsal Schedules

Play: *Old MacDonald Had a Farm*
Length of performance: Five minutes
Type of puppets: Black-paper shadows
Group: Twenty-eight second graders
Goal: Performance for parents' night
Length of puppetry sessions: Twenty to thirty minutes (session 1 may be longer)
Total number of sessions: Seven (every other day for 2½ weeks)

Session 1: Make shadow puppets: Old MacDonald, plus three each of nine animals.

Session 2: Sing the song together several times. Then, practice singing it, having the children hold their puppets up when they are named in the song.

Session 3: Set up shadow screen and light, and do the basic shadow-puppet action exercises on pages 18–21.

Session 4: Practice the backstage movement of puppeteers: where they will stand as they wait their turn, and where they will go after their turn is over. Sing through the song twice while going through all the movements.

Session 5: Decide together what actions will accompany each stanza of the song. Rehearse each stanza separately, several times.

Session 6: Repeat Session 5 rehearsal technique.

Session 7: Dress rehearsal.

Play: *Perseus and Medusa*
Length of Performance: Fifteen minutes
Type of puppets: Fifteen-inch-high corrugated-cardboard rod puppets
Group: Library puppet club: eight children, ages ten to thirteen
Goal: Performance at family story hour
Length of puppetry sessions: Forty-five to sixty minutes
Total number of sessions: Seven over seven weeks

Session 1: Read through the script two or three times. Trace and cut out puppets and props. Assignment: learn lines.

Session 2: Paint puppets and props. Line rehearsal without script.

Session 3: Attach moving parts and rods. Line rehearsal without script. Walk-throughs of performance with sound effects. Group discussion: revise scripts, add sound effects, etc.

Session 4: Line rehearsal without script. Rehearse scenes 1 and 2 several times, and discuss. Make posters.

Session 5: Line rehearsal without script. Rehearse scenes 3 and 4 several times and discuss. Design program for reproduction.

Session 6: Complete rehearsal; repeat as time allows. Videotape if possible.

Session 7: View videotape. Dress rehearsal.

Using Videotape

Videotape can be used with puppetry, both as a rehearsal tool and to produce a final product. As a rehearsal tool, it is of the most use to older children, and particularly to adult puppeteers, since it allows them to be their own directors. If the camera crew has seen several rehearsals, they will be able to follow the action closely, zooming in on characters who are standing still, and pulling back to capture action scenes.

Rod Puppets

Flat rod puppets acting in front of a black curtain make a striking video subject. Set up the camera frame so that the edges of the stage are not seen, and fade and stop the camera during scene changes, and you should be able to produce a high-quality puppet video. Lighting the stage effectively without harsh shadows is a problem with puppets. You can videotape outdoors in natural light if the noise level is low; otherwise, use a combination of fluorescent room lights and two or more small lamps or floodlights aimed at the playing area from four to eight feet away. Back the stage as close as possible to a wall, so that no light comes from behind it, or the puppeteers may be visible through the black backdrop.

Shadow Puppets

Most video cameras will reproduce the electric light shining through the shadow screen much brighter than it really is and the surrounding screen area much darker. Keep this in mind when viewing videotaped rehearsals; in terms of lighting, what you see on the video is not what the audience sees. When making a shadow puppet video as an artistic product to be viewed by others, indirect sunlight on a Plexiglas screen is the best medium to use.

Puppetry and Poetry

Nursery rhymes are so familiar, that they instantly engage both the puppeteers and the audience. Most of the Anglo-American Mother Goose rhymes are visual and dramatic. This makes them ideal for performance by children ages five through seven. These very young performers can either make their own puppets, or use puppets which have been made for them, and act out the rhymes as they are spoken by a narrator. Older puppeteers will want to expand and embellish the actions of the rhyme, improvise dialogue, and write original scripts based on nursery rhyme characters.

Hey Diddle Diddle

Even the fiddle and the Moon are puppets in this nonsense rhyme.

Puppeteers: Two to seven, plus narrator and musician.

Puppets:	Cat	Dog
	Fiddle	Dish
	Cow	Spoon
	Moon	

Hey diddle diddle, the cat and the fiddle.
The cow jumped over the moon.*
The little dog laughed to see such sport,
And the dish ran away with the spoon.*

Production Notes

Each line of this rhyme features different characters. Their actions will take much longer than the reciting of the words, so the narrator should pause after each line and wait for the puppets to complete their actions. Younger

Moon
Fiddle
Cat
Spoon
Dog
Dish
Cow

children can perform the actions as they are described in the rhyme, while older children can add touches of visual humor. Perhaps the cat has to chase and catch the fiddle before playing it, for example; the cow fails at her first few jumps, then the dog laughs at her, and she is motivated to succeed; the dish and spoon can do a little dance together before they run away. Dialogue between the characters may be improvised, such as the dish trying to convince the spoon to leave home.

Shadow Puppets
Use horizontal rods on all puppets.

Rod Puppets
The cow and the moon will need long enough rods to elevate them convincingly high in the stage-set sky.

***Sound Effects**
Use a slide whistle as the cow jumps over the moon and clavé to represent the footsteps of the dish and the spoon. Screechy fiddle noises can be made by mouth.

Little Miss Muffet

Puppeteers: One or two, plus narrator.

Puppets: Miss Muffet
Spider

Scenery piece: Tuffet

Little Miss Muffet
Sat on a tuffet,
Eating her curds and whey.
Along came a spider,
Who sat down beside her,
And frightened Miss Muffet away!

Tuffet
Miss Muffet
Spider
Mouse
Clock
1
2
3
4
5
6
7
8
9
10
11
12

Production Notes

The puppeteers can improvise voices and actions after each line of the rhyme. For example, Little Miss Muffet sings as she walks over to the tuffet and makes loud slurping noises while she eats. The spider says "Hello" to her—then "Boo!"

Shadow Puppets

Attach Miss Muffet to a vertical rod, the spider to a horizontal one. The spider can enter from above, as if it is descending on its dragline.

Rod Puppets

The spider enters hopping along the ground.

Hickory Dickory Dock

Puppeteers: One, plus narrator

Puppet: Mouse

Scenery piece: Clock

Hickory dickory dock,
The mouse ran up the clock.
The clock struck one,*
The mouse ran down,
Hickory dickory dock.

Production Notes

Pause in the narration after the sound effect of the clock striking one. The mouse jumps in surprise and squeaks before running down.

Shadow Puppets

The mouse is attached to a horizontal rod. Make the clock of black paper and cut out the clock face. Cover the area with colored tissue paper and draw the clock's hands and numbers onto the tissue with black marker.

Rod Puppets
Make the mouse's rod long enough to allow the mouse to run to the top of the clock. Young children can perform this play individually, without a stage. Each child holds the clock in one hand, the mouse in the other. An entire classroom of kindergartners or first graders can recite the rhyme together, and simultaneously act it out with their puppets.

***Sound Effects**
Use a triangle for the clock striking.

Follow-up Activities

More about Nursery Rhymes
Working individually or in small groups, write stories or scripts that expand upon the nursery rhymes. Younger children can dictate their stories into a tape recorder, while older children can write scripts to perform, designing and making additional puppets as needed. Possible subjects include:

The cat takes music lessons.
The cow trains to get in shape for moon jumping.
What became of the dish and the spoon after they ran away.
How Miss Muffet later got revenge by frightening the spider.
What happened when the elephant ran up the clock.

Mother Goose Playhouse
Several nursery rhymes can be presented together in one puppet production, with Mother Goose herself acting as mistress of ceremonies. This makes an especially good performance to present to preschoolers. Other nursery rhymes which adapt well to puppetry include:

Dickery, Dickery Dare
Jack Be Nimble
Mary Had a Little Lamb
Higglety Pigglety Pop
Humpty Dumpty

Illustrations in the following Mother Goose anthologies should provide inspiration for both puppet design and dramatic interpretation:

Brian Wildsmith's Mother Goose.
New York: Franklin Watts, 1964.

Mother Goose Treasury, illus. by Raymond Briggs. Boston: Little Brown, 1976.

Random House Book of Mother Goose, illus. by Arnold Lobel. New York: Random House, 1986.

Puppets and Poets

Keep a file of short poems for puppetry—haiku and mood pieces, humorous and nonsense verse. Plan a puppet session in which groups of two or three puppeteers will select a poem, make puppets, and act it out to narration. Encourage them to take the puppet design and action beyond the surface meaning of the poem, extending the words of the poet or even contradicting them.

Musical Puppet Plays

Parades and processions to instrumental music are perfect puppet projects for beginners. Slightly more difficult are puppet performances dramatizing such narrative songs as "There Was an Old Lady Who Swallowed a Fly." Creating puppet pantomimes to the music of Saint-Saëns' *Carnival of the Animals* is a challenging endeavor for older children and adults.

Old MacDonald

A puppet show of *Old MacDonald* can be performed to a recording, but having the group sing it live is more fun and lets you decide the number and kinds of animals that will be included.

Puppeteers: Two or three nimble puppeteers can handle the entire play, or it can be adapted so that a group of up to thirty children participate—a few at a time, of course!

Puppets: Old MacDonald
Animals

Old MacDonald had a farm,
E - I - E - I - O,
And on that farm he had a cow,
E - I - E - I - O.

With a moo moo here,
And a moo moo there,
Here a moo, there a moo,
Everywhere a moo moo.
Old MacDonald had a farm,
E - I - E - I - O!

Old MacDonald had a farm,
E - I - E - I - O,
And on that farm he had a pig,
E - I - E - I - O.

With an oink oink here,
And an oink oink there,
Here an oink, there an oink,
Everywhere an oink oink.
Old MacDonald had a farm,
E - I - E - I - O!

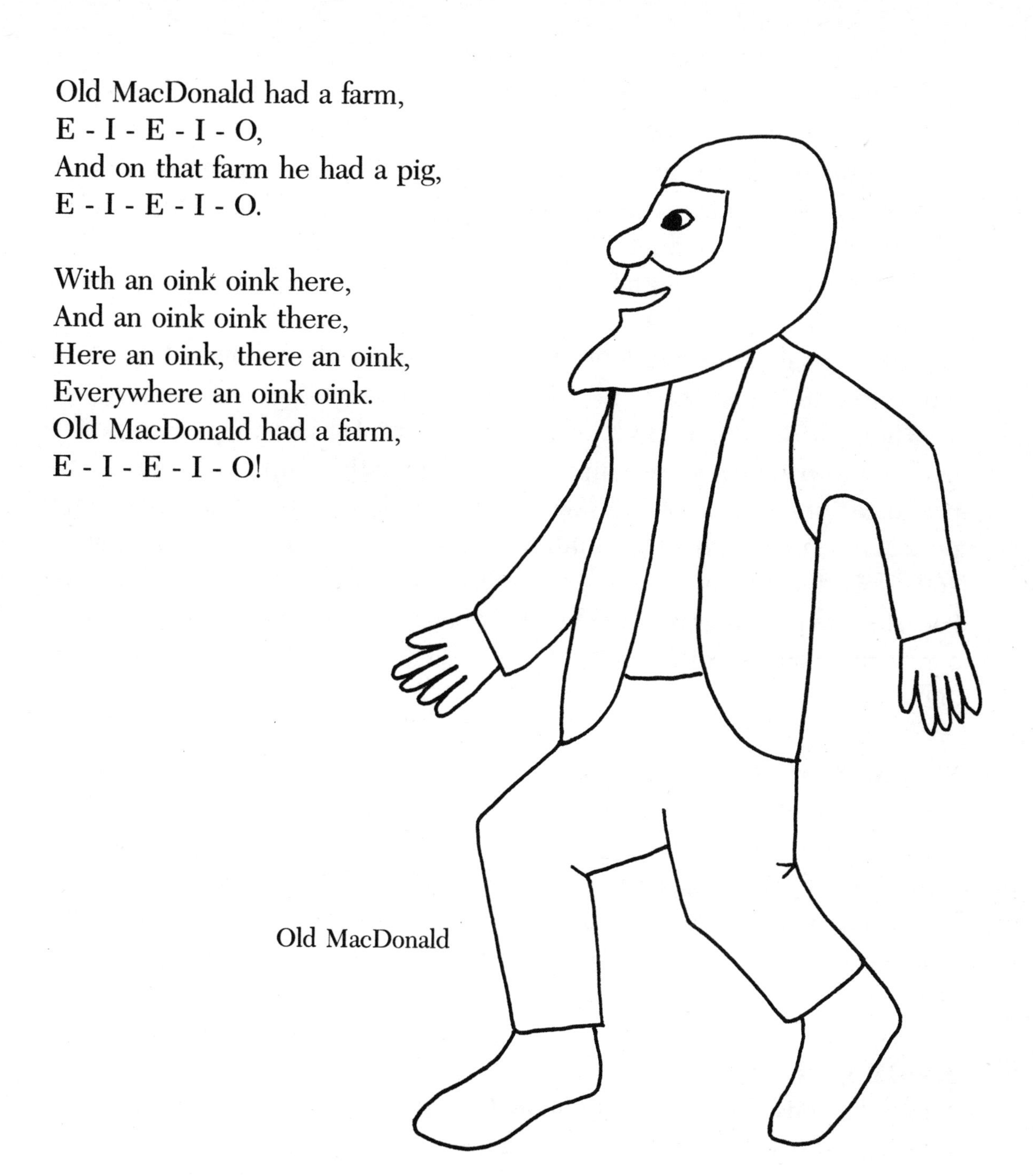
Old MacDonald

Production Notes

Patterns for farm animals to use with this song can be found with *There Was an Old Lady Who Swallowed a Fly* (page 58) and *The Runaway Pancake* (page 101). Plan the performance to suit the size of your group. One puppeteer needs to devote full time and attention to the puppet of Old MacDonald. Animals can appear one at a time ("a cow"), or in small groups ("some cows") in order to create roles for more puppeteers. Change the wording of the song accordingly.

To set the mood, make farmyard scenery for this play—fence, barn, trees, tractor, etc.—and place it at the sides of the stage, leaving a large central playing area for the puppets.

The puppeteers should take time to plan the way each animal will enter and exit. Will it walk, hop, or jump? Will it move slowly or quickly? Will Old MacDonald pet it? Ride it? Will it chase him? The show will be more interesting to the audience if each scene is different.

When a large group of children performs a play like this—in a performance for parents, for example—they should line up, in order of appearance, to one side of the stage. Form the line to the side front of the performing area so that the children can watch the play as they sing along and await their turn. One by one (or group by group), the children go backstage to play their parts. When they have finished, they may either form a new line on the other side of the stage, or quietly take seats in the audience.

Shadow Puppets

All the shadow puppets in this production should have horizontal control rods, to allow maximum freedom of movement on the shadow screen. Remember that the placement of a horizontal rod determines the side of the stage from which the puppet enters. If you want a puppet to enter from the left side of the stage, for example, attach the rod so that the puppet faces right.

Rod Puppets

Make the rods long enough to allow Old MacDonald to ride the horse or goat, and the animals to jump and dance.

Music

Old MacDonald is widely available on children's records. Musical notation can be found in:

Eye Winker, Tom Tinker, Chin Chopper, by Tom Glazer. New York: Doubleday, 1973. Page 56.

What Shall We Do and Allee Galloo!, by Marie Winn. New York: Harper, 1970. Page 30.

Follow-up Activities

Animal Charades

A game of animal charades can be used as a warm-up or a follow-up for this performance. The group sits in a circle, and each player secretly decides on a farm animal to imitate. Then, each in turn goes to the center of the circle, moving and making noises like that animal. After the time allotted for the charade is finished, the group tries to guess the name of the animal.

More Musical Animal Puppet Plays

The following songs can be performed with rod or shadow puppets.

"I Got Me a Cat" in *The Flannel Board Storytelling Book,* by Judy Sierra. Bronx: H. W. Wilson, 1987. Pages 92–94.
All puppets will need to remain onstage until the very end of this cumulative folk song.

The Farmer in the Dell, illus. by Mary M. Rae. New York: Penguin, 1988.
The puppets dance to the refrain, "Hi, ho, the derry-o."

Oh, A-Hunting We Will Go, illus. by Nancy Winslow Parker. New York: Atheneum, 1974.
The hunters may be made as one "group puppet," operated by one puppeteer. Children can add their own verses to this simple song.

Over in the Meadow

This English folk song can be performed as the puppeteers and audience sing. It offers an opportunity for the group to explore the concept of animals sharing a habitat.

Puppeteers: Two to nine.

Puppets: Toad
Baby toad
Fish
Two baby fishes
Bird
Three baby birds

Scenery: Meadow

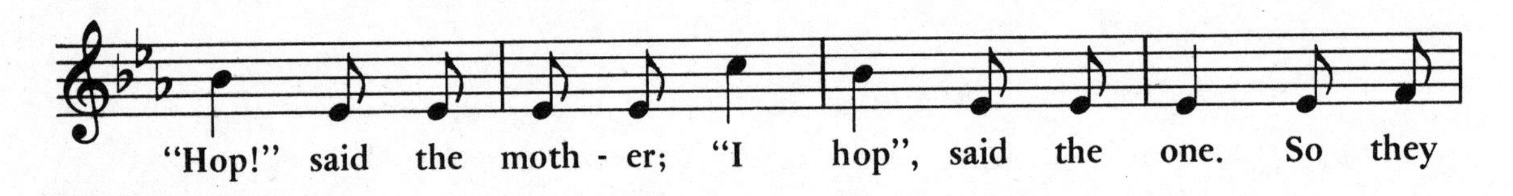

Over in the meadow, where the stream runs blue,
Lived an old mother fish and her little fishies two.
"Swim!" said the mother; "We swim," said the two.
So they swam and they leaped where the stream runs blue.

Over in the meadow, in a hole in a tree,
Lived an old mother bluebird and her little birdies three.
"Sing!" said the mother; "We sing," said the three.
So they sang, and were glad in the hole in the tree.

Little fish
(*make two*)
Mother bird
Little bird
(*make three*)
Mother fish
Baby toad
Mother toad
Meadow scenery
(*make to scale*)

Over in the meadow, in a hole in a tree,
Lived an old mother bluebird and her little birdies three.
"Sing!" said the mother; "We sing," said the three.
So they sang, and were glad in the hole in the tree.

Production Notes

Create a puppet set representing the meadow ecosystem, including a stream with a sandy bank, a tree with a hole for the baby birds to appear in, and a branch next to the hole for the mother bird's perch. The baby fishes and the baby birds may be made as a single "group puppet," operated by one puppeteer.

In performance, *Over in the Meadow* should be sung to a slow tempo, allowing the puppets plenty of time to move. Plan and rehearse the actions each animal will perform—hopping, leaping, swimming, flying. Use as much of the stage playing area as possible.

Shadow Puppets

Cut the scenery from black construction paper or poster board. The stream can be shown as a transparent blue area by incorporating colored tissue paper into the set, taped over a cut-out area in the construction paper. The audience will then be able to see the fish as they swim underwater, as well as when they leap into the air. Use horizontal rods on all puppets, making sure that mothers are facing their babies.

Rod Puppets

Use long rods on all the puppets: the toads need to hop, and the fish must leap. The rods of the birds must reach to the hole in the tree, so plan accordingly when you create the scenery.

Follow-up Activities

Way out in the Desert

Make up new songs and design new puppets for plays based on *Over in the Meadow.* It isn't hard! Some interesting places to explore are *Way out in the Desert, Down in the Ocean,* and *Deep in the Jungle.* You will need to decide on three types of animal families to include, and invent appropriate rhymes for one, two, and three (a rhyming dictionary is a big help), for example,

Way out in the desert, in the hot, hot sun,
Lived an old mother rattlesnake and her little rattler one.
"Rattle!" said the mother; "I rattle!" said the one.
So they rattled and they wriggled in the hot, hot sun.

Ecosystems in Shadow Puppetry

Shadow puppetry is an expressive art form that can be used to teach natural science in the elementary grades. The many ways in which animals share a habitat can be explored in shadow puppetry. Shadow puppets have the advantage of being able to move all over the puppet screen, unimpeded by gravity. Animals' secret hideaways can be revealed through cutouts in the shadow scenery and shadow puppets can vanish instantly from view—as a way to show one animal eating another, for example. Jointed shadow puppets allow puppeteers to simulate some of the subtleties of animal movement. Shadow puppets can change form as if by magic: simply lift one puppet off the screen and substitute another in exactly the same place. This method can be used to show a tadpole becoming a frog or a caterpillar forming a chrysalis.

Use the scenery of *Over in the Meadow* and make puppets of other animals who might live there. In shadow puppetry, show them in their homes, and show how they move.

There Was an Old Lady Who Swallowed a Fly

A wonderfully visual puppet show can be made from this favorite song of logic gone zanily amock. When it is performed in shadow puppetry, the audience can magically see the animals *inside* her stomach.

Puppeteers: Two to nine.

Puppets: Old lady, Fly (can be sound effect only), Spider, Bird, Cat, Dog, Goat, Cow, Horse

There was an old lady who swallowed a fly.
I don't know why she swallowed the fly.
I guess she'll die.

There was an old lady who swallowed a spider.
It wriggled and jiggled and tickled inside 'er.
She swallowed the spider to catch the fly,
But I don't know why she swallowed the fly.
I guess she'll die.

There was an old lady who swallowed a bird.
How absurd! She swallowed a bird.
She swallowed the bird to catch the spider
That wriggled and jiggled and tickled inside 'er.
She swallowed the spider to catch the fly,
But I don't know why she swallowed the fly.
I guess she'll die.

There was an old lady who swallowed a cat.
Fancy that! She swallowed a cat.
She swallowed the cat to catch the bird.
She swallowed the bird to catch the spider
That wriggled and jiggled and tickled inside 'er.
She swallowed the spider to catch the fly,
But I don't know why she swallowed the fly.
I guess she'll die.

Old Lady (*make to scale, cutting on dotted line for shadow puppet*)

There was an old lady who swallowed a dog.
She was a hog, to swallow a dog.
She swallowed the dog to catch the cat.
She swallowed the cat to catch the bird.
She swallowed the bird to catch the spider
That wriggled and jiggled and tickled inside 'er.
She swallowed the spider to catch the fly.
But I don't know why she swallowed the fly.
I guess she'll die.

There was an old lady who swallowed a goat.
Just opened her throat, and in walked a goat.
She swallowed the goat to catch the dog.
She swallowed the dog the catch the cat.
She swallowed the cat to catch the bird.
She swallowed the bird to catch the spider
That wriggled and jiggled and tickled inside 'er.
She swallowed the spider to catch the fly,
But I don't know why she swallowed the fly.
I guess she'll die.

There was an old lady who swallowed a cow.
I don't know how, but she swallowed a cow.
She swallowed the cow to catch the goat.
She swallowed the goat to catch the dog.
She swallowed the dog to catch the cat.
She swallowed the cat to catch the bird.
She swallowed the bird to catch the spider
That wriggled and jiggled and tickled inside 'er.
She swallowed the spider to catch the fly,
But I don't know why she swallowed the fly.
I guess she'll die.

There was an old lady who swallowed a horse.
She's dead, of course.

Cat
Cow

Production Notes

To make the old lady, enlarge the pattern pieces to fit the size of your stage: the puppet should be about two-thirds as tall as the stage opening. Her arm and head are moved by long rods. On tabletop rod-puppet stages and shadow screens, she is attached to the stage like scenery.

The old lady puppet eats each animal after lifting it up to her mouth with her hand. In order to accomplish this, the puppeteer manipulating the old lady and the puppeteer manipulating the animal work together to make the action as smooth as possible. As each animal moves into her mouth, the old lady closes her jaws. The animal puppet is then moved down and offstage behind her. Plan and rehearse some small, lifelike actions for the old lady to perform when not eating, such as wiping her mouth, patting her hair, and scratching her nose. After the words, "She's dead, of course," have the old lady say, "Oh, no, I'm not." She can then open her mouth wide, letting all the animals escape.

Shadow Puppets

The shadow figure of the old lady is cut from heavy black paper, such as railroad board (construction paper won't stand the wear and tear). Cut out her eye and cut the stomach opening on the dotted lines. Cover the stomach with colored tissue paper. Attach the head and arm pieces to the body with brad fasteners, placing the rounded head of each fastener toward the shadow screen and adjusting them so that all the parts move easily and freely. Attach horizontal rods to the back of the puppet's head and hand; a single puppeteer can operate both rods.

All the animal puppets are mounted on horizontal rods. As you attach the rods, make sure that the puppets will be facing the old lady when they are placed onto the shadow screen. After each puppet is swallowed during the performance, it will be seen again briefly inside the old lady's stomach (through the tissue paper). The spider puppet reappears, and crawls around her stomach, every time its name is mentioned in the chorus of the song.

Rod Puppets

Make the old lady puppet of heavy cardboard (corrugated cardboard works well). For a tabletop stage, enlarge the pattern pieces so that the puppet is about two-thirds as high as the top of the back curtain. Paint the four pieces

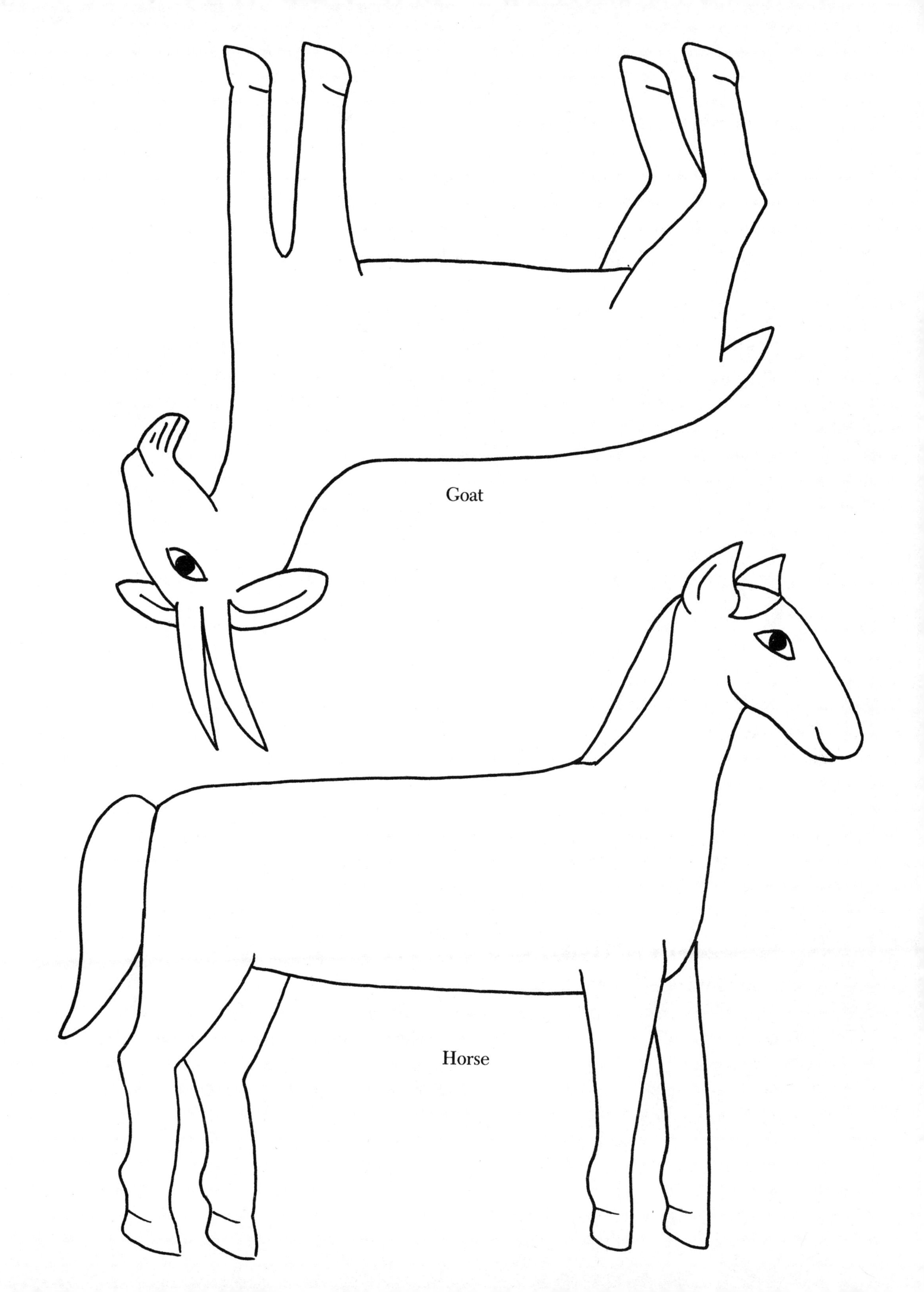
Goat
Horse

with tempera before joining them together with brad fasteners. Do not cut out the stomach. Attach the puppet to the inside front of the stage as if it were a scenery piece. The arm and head are operated by means of long dowels attached to the back of the puppet's hand and head with strong tape, such as duct tape, in the manner of horizontal shadow-puppet rods.

On a large rod-puppet stage, the old lady should be operated as a puppet by means of one body rod, a head rod, and an arm rod. She will need to be operated by two or three puppeteers.

The animal puppets are operated on vertical rods, colored black, which must be long enough to reach from the bottom of the stage opening to the old lady's mouth without revealing the puppeteers' hands.

Music

Words and music:

> *The Fireside Book of Children's Songs,* edited by Marie Winn and Allen Miller.
> New York: Simon & Schuster, 1966. Page 116.
>
> *The Fireside Book of Birds and Beasts,* edited by Jane Yolen.
> New York: Simon & Schuster, 1972. Page 216.

Records and cassettes:

> *Best of Burl's for Boys and Girls,* by Burl Ives.
> New York: MCA, n.d.
>
> *Birds, Beasts, Bugs and Little Fishes,* by Pete Seeger.
> New York: Folkways, 1955.

Follow-up Activities

Cumulative Folk Songs

There Was an Old Lady Who Swallowed a Fly uses a cumulative storytelling technique which challenges the memories of both storyteller/singer and audience. This is an enjoyable and painless way of developing memory and language skills, since listeners just can't help singing the ever-lengthening lists. Learn these two other cumulative folk songs:

The Rattlin' Bog

Words and music in *Hi! Ho! The Rattlin' Bog,* edited by John Langstaff.
New York: Harcourt, Brace, 1969. Page 11.

Record and cassette: *Polka Dot Pony,* by Fred Penner.
New York: Shoreline, 1981.

There's a Hole in the Bottom of the Sea

Words and music in *Eye Winker, Tom Tinker, Chin Chopper,* edited by Tom Glazer.
New York: Doubleday, 1973. Page 78.

Record and cassette: *A House for Me,* by Fred Penner.
New York: A&M, 1985.

Puppet Plays to Recorded Music

Recordings of both songs and instrumental music can be used as the sound tracks for puppet shows.

Carnival of the Animals, by Camille Saint-Saëns.

There are many recordings of this orchestra classic. Try to locate one that includes a narration of the zoo poems of Ogden Nash. The "Fossils" segment of this piece makes a splendid accompaniment to a dinosaur parade!

"Abiyoyo," on the cassette, *Stories and Songs for Little Children,* by Pete Seeger (High Windy Audio, n.d.). Also available as a picture book of the same title, text by Pete Seeger, illustrations by Michael Hays (New York: Macmillan, 1986).

Shadow puppets are particularly suitable for the dancing and disappearing featured in this story.

"The Foolish Frog," on the cassette, *Stories and Songs for Little Children,* by Pete Seeger (High Windy Audio, n.d). Also available as a picture book of the same title, text by Pete Seeger, illustrations by Miloslav Jagr (New York: Macmillan, 1973).

Either use an extra-wide rod-puppet stage to accommodate this very large cast of characters, or present it as a rod-puppet play in the round. It can be played on a large tabletop, where a cardboard box has been made into the corner grocery store. Make large, colorful puppets and, for formal performance, have the puppeteers dress in black.

Fables, Folktales and Myths

The Fox and the Grapes

This fable and the following one, both from Aesop, make excellent solo-performance pieces for beginning or advanced puppeteers. Though brief, they provide the puppeteer with good experience in building a scene and keeping an audience engaged. Improvisation in action and monologue should be encouraged.

Puppeteers: One, plus narrator.

Puppet: Fox

Scenery piece: Arbor with grapes

Setting: A country garden; arbor to right of center stage.

Narrator: A fox was out walking one afternoon, when he spied a bunch of grapes hanging from an arbor.

Fox: (*Enters left and looks up.*) Mmmm. Those grapes look delicious.

Narrator: The fox jumped up and tried to grab the grapes with his teeth. But he couldn't reach them.

Fox: (*Excited.*) Ha! I'll get you! (*Jumps.*) You won't escape me, you juicy, delicious grapes. (*Jumps.*) I'll get you.

Narrator: The fox kept trying to reach the grapes, but he just couldn't jump high enough.

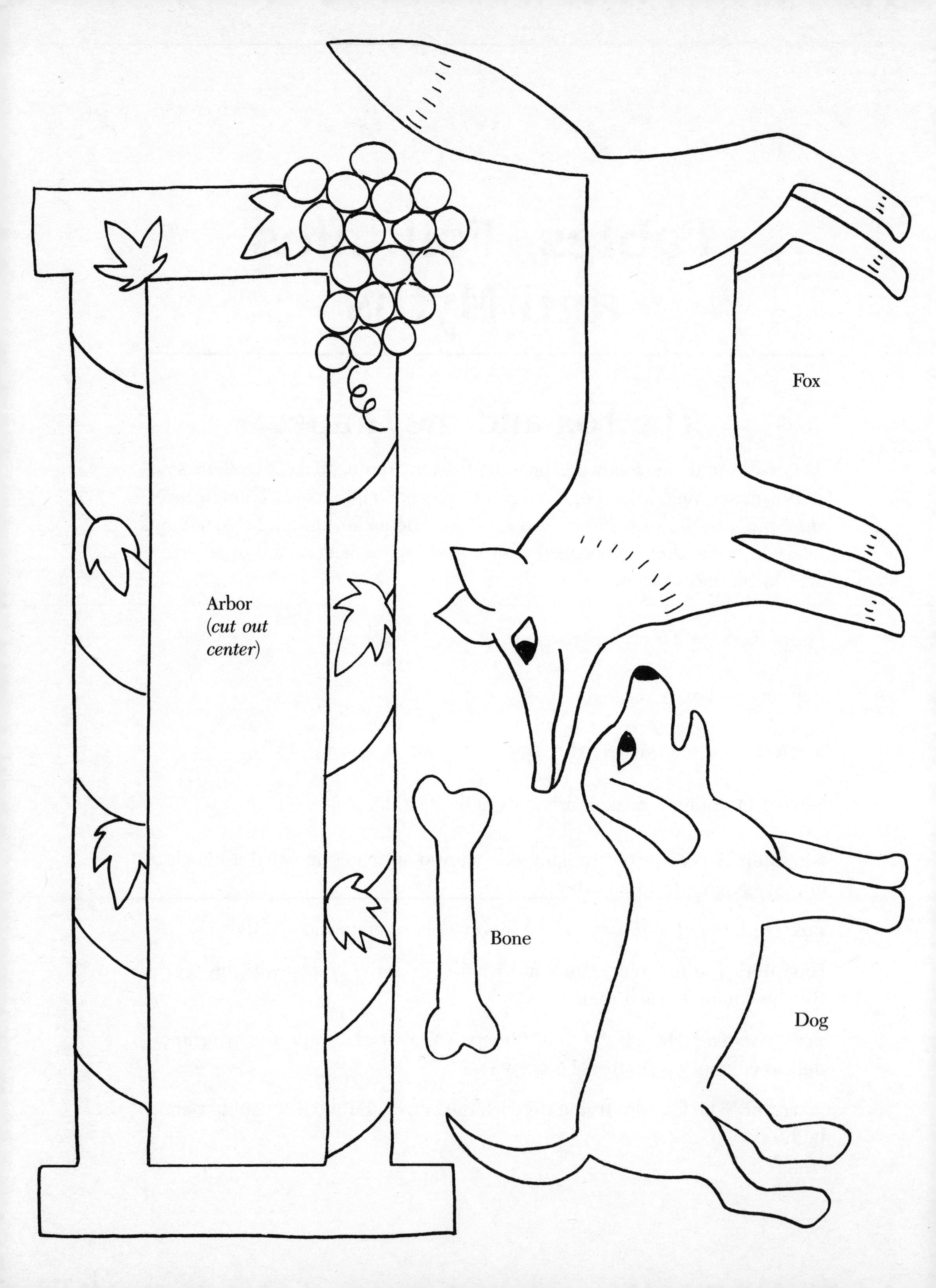
Fox
Arbor
(*cut out
center*)
Bone
Dog

(*Snarling angrily, Fox jumps three more times.*)

Narrator: Finally, the fox walked away.

Fox: (*Stops just before he exits.*) I didn't want those grapes anyway. They were *sour.* (*Exits.*)

The Dog and His Bone

Puppeteers: One, plus narrator and musician.

Puppet: Dog

Prop: Bone

Scenery piece: Stream

Setting: A forest path; stream at right of stage. Trees and other scenery are optional.

Narrator: One day, a dog found a large bone with lots of meat on it. He was carrying it home, so that he could eat it in a secret place.

Dog: (*Enters left, stops, and growls.*) Grrrr! No other dog will share this bone. It's mine. All mine. Mine. (*Continues walking toward stream.*)

Narrator: As the dog walked along, he passed by a stream. Looking down at the water, he was surprised by what he saw.

Dog: What? There's a dog down there. And he is carrying a bone. It looks like my bone . . . but it's . . . it's BIGGER. Grrrr! Look out, you cowardly cur. I'll take your bone and my bone, too.

Narrator: The dog opened his mouth to steal the other dog's bone.

(*Dog drops his own bone into the water.**)

Narrator: But his own bone fell into the water. The dog saw by the rippling surface of the stream that the other dog had merely been his own reflection. And instead of two bones, he had none.

(*Dog exits, whining.*)

Production Notes

Concentrate on contrast in puppet voice and movement (slow/fast, large/small) and on pauses and hesitations to convey the building anger of the dog, the fox's eagerness turning to disdain.

The puppeteer playing the part of the dog should speak through clenched teeth until the bone is dropped. Hold jaws motionless (bite across the middle of a pencil if necessary), and speak slowly, enunciating clearly.

Shadow Puppets

The fox puppet is attached to a horizontal rod: he will only face one direction during the performance, and the horizontal rod will allow him to jump high. A moving part—head or tail—gives the puppet added expressive possibilities.

The dog and his bone should also be placed on horizontal rods. To represent the stream on the shadow screen, cut away part of the right-hand side of the black paper ground which stretches across the bottom of the screen, and cover it with blue tissue paper. As an added challenge, try designing a puppet to play the part of the dog's reflection in the water.

Rod Puppets

Make the fox's rod long enough to allow him to jump up at the grapes.

Cut an oval of shiny blue paper or plastic, and drape it over the front of the stage to represent the stream.

*Sound Effects

Use a light drumbeat or an electronic keyboard *plunk* for the sound of the bone hitting the water.

Follow-up Activities

Plays on Proverbs

Fables are short tales which usually end with an explicit moral, often in the form of a proverb. Make up your own puppet fables to illustrate the following proverbs.

> The early bird catches the worm.
> Too many cooks spoil the broth.
> An apple a day keeps the doctor away.
> You can't teach an old dog new tricks.

The plays may be serious or spoofs. Groups of two to five children can work on each, making the necessary puppets, and writing either a script or an outline for improvisation. Keep the proverb a secret from the audience until the end of the play.

Other One-person Plays for Talented Puppeteers

A play or story will work as a one-person puppet show as long as there are no more than two puppets onstage at any one time (although ambitious puppeteers can devise ingenious ways of keeping even more in sight and in motion at once). The following familiar tales can be rewritten in script format and performed as solo pieces.

"The Gunny Wolf"
"The Three Billy Goats"
"Little Cockroach Martina"

In *The Flannel Board Storytelling Book,* by Judy Sierra.
Bronx: H. W. Wilson, 1987.
Includes patterns suitable for rod and shadow puppets.

The Hungry Monster

Adapted from an Anglo-American folktale, *The Greedy Old Fat Man*, this play follows the familiar folktale pattern of the hungry person or animal who, when asked what he has eaten, promptly eats the inquirer!

Puppeteers: Three to nine, plus narrator and musician.

Puppets: Monster
Same Monster, only fatter
Boy
Girl
Dog
Cat
Fox
Squirrel
Monster's Mother

Scenery piece: Tree

Setting: A country road. Tree at far right. No scene changes.

Narrator: Once upon a time there lived a monster who could never get enough to eat.

Monster: (*Enters right, slowly walks to center.*) Food! (*Sniffs.*) Food! (*Sniffs.*) Food! (*Sniffs.*)

(*Girl and Boy enter left, skipping and singing.*)

Boy: Hello, Mr. Monster.

Girl: How did you ever get so fat?

Monster: Well, children, let me tell you. For my breakfast this morning, I ate one hundred pancakes, and I drank one hundred glasses of milk . . . and now, I am going to eat YOU! (*Eats Girl and Boy.*)

Dog: (*Enters left, barking happily.*) Hello, Mr. Monster. How did you ever, ever get so fat?

Monster: Well, for my breakfast this morning, I ate one hundred pancakes, and I drank one hundred glasses of milk, and I ate a little boy and a little girl, and now I am going to eat YOU! (*Eats Dog.*)

Cat: (*Enters right, meowing sweetly.*) Hello, Mr. Monster. I wonder how you ever got to be so very, very fat.

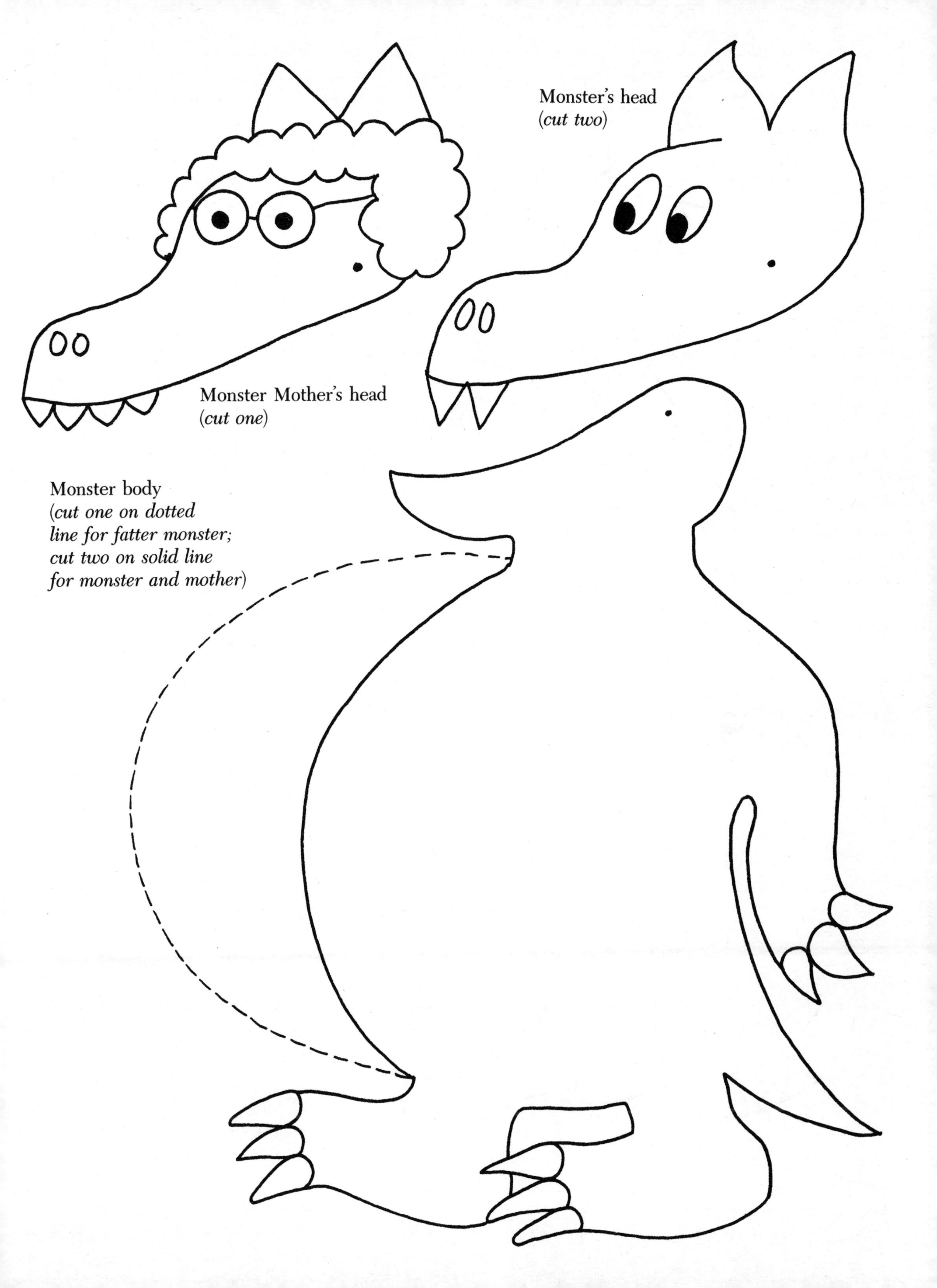
Monster Mother's head
(*cut one*)
Monster's head
(*cut two*)
Monster body
(*cut one on dotted
line for fatter monster;
cut two on solid line
for monster and mother*)

Dog
Cat
Squirrel
Tree
(*make to
scale*)

Monster: (*Turns.*) I'll tell you, Kitty Cat. For my breakfast this morning, I ate one hundred pancakes, and I drank one hundred glasses of milk, and I ate a little boy and a little girl and a dog, and now I am going to eat YOU! (*Eats Cat.*)

Fox: (*Enters left.*) Good morning, Mr. Monster. What makes you so fat?

Monster: For my breakfast this morning, I ate one hundred pancakes, and I drank one hundred glasses of milk, and I ate a little boy and a little girl and a dog and a cat, and now I am going to eat YOU! (*Chases Fox offstage left. When Monster re-enters, he is fatter—substitute second Monster puppet.*)

Squirrel: (*Appears in tree.*) Hello there, Mr. Monster. How did you ever get to be so fat?

Monster: It happened like this, you nosy squirrel. For my breakfast this morning, I ate one hundred pancakes, and I drank one hundred glasses of milk, and I ate a little boy and a little girl and a dog and a cat and a fox. And now I am going to eat YOU!

Squirrel: First you will have to climb up here and catch me!

Monster: Here I come! Here I come! Watch out! (*Slowly climbs tree, groaning and grunting. When he has gone as far as he can, he falls to the ground, landing on his back.**)

Squirrel: (*From tree.*) Look at that. The monster was so fat, his stomach just burst open.

Fox: *I'm out! (*Pops out of Monster's stomach and runs away.*)

Cat: *And I'm out! (*Pops out of Monster's stomach and runs away.*)

Dog: *And I'm out! (*Pops out of Monster's stomach and runs away.*)

Boy and Girl: *And we're out! (*Pop out of Monster's stomach and run away.*)

Squirrel: And I'm out—because I was never in! (*Jumps down from tree and bounces on Monster's stomach.* Exits left.*)

Narrator: And the hungry old monster called his mother, and she came and sewed up his stomach.

Fox
Boy
Girl

(Monster Mother comes, mimes sewing. Substitute the original Monster puppet at this point. Monster stands up and exits, following his Mother.)

Narrator: And he never bothered anyone ever again.

Production Notes

The monster can't realistically eat the other characters, of course. He should simply lunge forward at whatever he is eating; and, at the same time, that puppet is pulled down and out of the audience's sight. A lot of loud eating noises will make this seem real. When the puppets pop out of the monster's stomach, he is lying on his back, so they can simply appear from behind him.

When using a large cast of puppeteers, make sure that the backstage traffic flows smoothly and that puppeteers who are not immediately involved in the play move far back from the stage. Even more puppeteers can be involved if you change the script slightly and include two dogs, two cats, two foxes, etc.

Shadow Puppets

Use black shadows for this play; transparent acetate puppets would destroy the illusion of the monster eating the other puppets. Attach rods vertically to all puppets except the squirrel, who has a horizontal rod so that he can perch high in the tree and jump down onto the monster. If there is one puppeteer per puppet for the performance, try adding one moving part to each puppet. A moving arm works well for human characters, as do tails for dog, cat, and fox. The monster puppet is already designed with a mouth that opens amazingly wide when he swallows his victims.

Rod Puppets

The squirrel and the monster will both need long rods so that they can climb the tree.

*Sound Effects

Use a slide whistle down followed by a drum beat for the monster's fall from the tree and a slide whistle up as each puppet pops out of his stomach.

Follow-up Activities

Another World-Class Eater

Create a shadow puppet pantomime to a reading of Eric Carle's *The Very Hungry Caterpillar* (Collins-World, 1969), using colored acetate puppets, or black paper puppets with colored tissue overlays. Place a tree branch of black paper across the top of the screen, hung with green leaves of tissue or acetate, so that the audience will be able to see the caterpillar through the food it is eating. Make three caterpillars, progressively larger, a black paper chrysalis to cover the largest one, and, of course, a brilliant acetate or tissue-overlay butterfly. All the items the caterpillar eats should be manipulated on horizontal rods, like puppets.

Monster Parade

Design original monster puppets and present a monster parade to recorded music. Give each monster a unique voice. Have them tell their name, where they come from, what they eat, and other important information about themselves, as they cross the screen.

Mr. Bear Squash-You-All-Flat

Any house can hold just so many occupants and no more. How could Mr. Bear Squash-You-All-Flat ever fit into a clay pot? The nonsense of this tale from Russia is heightened by the silly names given to the animals, and the way in which they recite their names in unison to each newcomer.

Puppeteers: Six, plus narrator and musician.

Puppets:	Fly	Rabbit
	Mouse	Fox
	Frog	Bear

Scenery pieces: Pot
Jagged, broken pot

Setting: A snowy clearing in the forest. Winter woodland scenery, such as snow-laden trees, curious mounds of snow-covered logs and rocks, and snowdrifts, can be placed at the edges of the stage. No scene changes.

Narrator: One winter day, a man was driving his cart along a snow-covered road in Russia. As he passed through the forest, a large clay pot fell off the cart. It didn't make a sound as it landed in the soft snow, and it did not break.

(*The clay pot tumbles onto the stage and is placed far left, on its side, mouth facing right. All the animals enter from the right.*)

Fly: (*Enters with much flying and buzzing. Flies to mouth of jar.*) Hello! Hello! Is anyone at home? Bzzz. Whose little house is this? Hello! Hello! Bzzz. Nobody's home. Bzzz. I guess I'll just move in. (*Flies into clay pot.*)

Mouse: (*Enters and peeks timidly into pot several times.*) Whose little house is this?

Fly: This house belongs to me, Buzzer the Fly. Who are you?

Mouse: I am Nibble-Nibble Mouse. May I come live with you?

Fly: Yes.

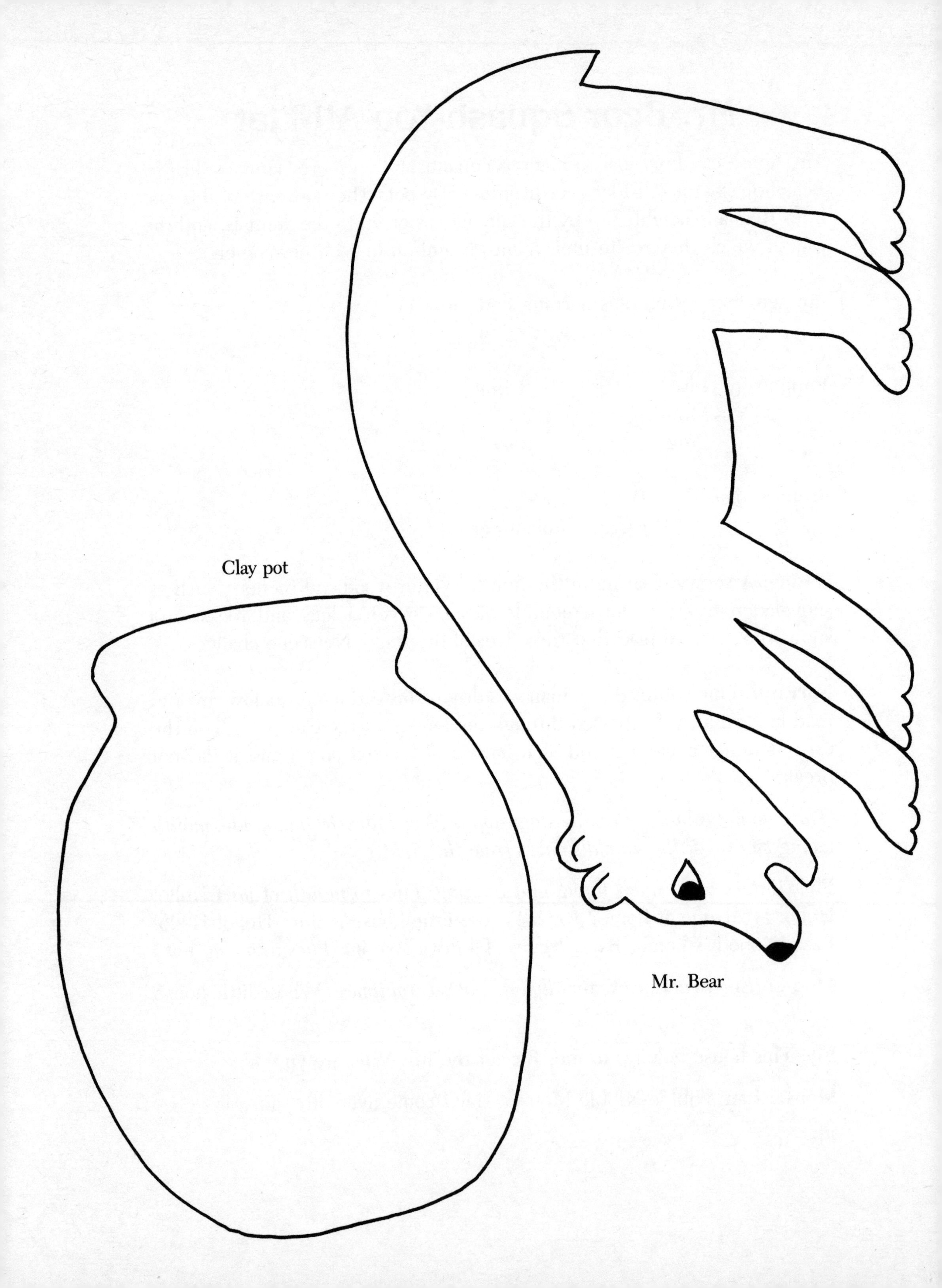
Clay pot
Mr. Bear

Mouse: Thank you. (*Scampers into clay pot.*)

Frog: (*Enters, hopping and croaking.*) Whose little house is this?

Fly and Mouse: It belongs to us, Buzzer the Fly and Nibble-Nibble Mouse. Who are you?

Frog: I am Croaker the Frog. May I come live with you?

Fly and Mouse: Yes.

Frog: Thank you. (*Hops into clay pot.*)

Rabbit: (*Enters, peeks into clay pot.*) Whose little house is this?

Fly, Mouse, and Frog: It belongs to us, Buzzer the Fly, Nibble-Nibble Mouse, and Croaker the Frog. Who are you?

Rabbit: I am Hoppity Rabbit. May I come live with you?

Fly, Mouse, and Frog: Yes.

Rabbit: Thank you. (*Hops into clay pot.*)

Fox: (*Enters and looks into clay pot.*) Whose little house is this?

Fly, Mouse, Frog, and Rabbit: It belongs to us, Buzzer the Fly, Nibble-Nibble Mouse, Croaker the Frog, and Hoppity Rabbit. Who are you?

Fox: I am Fluffy-Tail Fox. May I come live with you?

Fly, Mouse, Frog, and Rabbit: Yes.

Fox: Thank you. (*Goes inside clay pot.*)

Bear: (*Enters very slowly and looks into clay pot.*) Whose nice little house is this?

Fly, Mouse, Frog, Rabbit, and Fox: It belongs to us, Buzzer the Fly, Nibble-Nibble Mouse, Croaker the Frog, Hoppity Rabbit, and Fluffy-Tail Fox. Who are you?

Bear: (*Slowly, gruffly.*) I am Mister Bear Squash-You-All-Flat, and I am coming to live with you. (*Puts head into clay pot and gives a loud growl.*)

Fly, Mouse, Frog, Rabbit, and Fox: Oh, no! It's Mister Bear! He will squash us all flat!

(*Bear growls louder.*)

Fly, Mouse, Frog, Rabbit, and Fox: Please, stop!

(*Bear growls even louder.*)

Fly, Mouse, Frog, Rabbit, and Fox: NO!

Narrator: Then, the clay pot burst into a hundred pieces.* (*Clay pot disappears, and broken pot appears in its place.*) And Mister Bear just walked away.

(*Bear exits, growling.*)

Narrator: And Fluffy-Tail Fox ran away.

(*Fox hops out of pot and exits right.*)

Narrator: And Hoppity Rabbit hopped away.

(*Rabbit hops out of pot and exits left.*)

Narrator: And Croaker the Frog jumped away.

(*Frog hops out of pot and exits right.*)

Narrator: And Nibble-Nibble Mouse scampered away.

(*Mouse hops out of pot and exits left.*)

Narrator: And Buzzer the Fly flew away.

Fly: (*Flies out of pot, buzzes, flies some loops, then pauses.*) That's the end! (*Flies off.*)

Production Notes

Make a second prop of the broken pot, using the pot pattern as a model.

In this play, only one animal puppet appears onstage at any given time, though the voices from inside the pot give the impression of a crowd. Puppeteers whose puppets are not onstage, but whose voices are needed, should stand back from the stage.

Shadow Puppets

The pot prop is mounted on a vertical rod. It bounces on from the side of the screen and is fixed in place with strong tape or by pushing the end of the rod

Fox
Frog
Mouse
Rabbit
Fly

into a Styrofoam block. The fly must be on a horizontal rod; other animal puppets are attached to vertical rods.

Rod Puppets

The fly will need a long, thin, black rod. This puppet is very small; some shiny material, such as sequins or glitter, on his body will help the audience see him.

***Sound Effects**

There should be a loud cracking noise when Mr. Bear breaks the pot—find the best sound by test-hitting various (unbreakable) objects with a stick. As a special effect, puppeteers who are playing the animals in the clay pot can speak through cupped hands.

Follow-up Activities

Tales of Unusual Houses

Share these fictional accounts of unique houses and their inhabitants:

> *The Biggest House in the World,* by Leo Lionni.
> New York: Pantheon, 1968.
>
> Use the illustrations in the book as patterns for rod or shadow puppets; or, use two stages and combine rod puppet reality and a shadow puppet dream. Act it out as a pantomime to a reading of the book.
>
> "The Fearsome Beast," in *The Flannel Board Storytelling Book,* by Judy Sierra. Bronx: H. W. Wilson, 1987.
>
> This African folktale is accompanied by patterns suitable for shadow or rod puppets. Use the narration-improvisation technique to dramatize it.
>
> *Thidwick, the Big-Hearted Moose,* by Dr. Seuss.
> New York: Random House, 1948.
>
> Thidwick's head and antlers are the scenery of the play, upon which the puppet animals appear. Make a duplicate set of antlers to use during the final scene. A narrator reads the rhymed text as the puppeteers act it out.

Who Lives Here?

Shadow puppetry can be used to show hidden animal homes—in hollow trees and underground tunnels, for example. Create shadow puppet scenery to show the real homes of the animals in this folktale, using the puppets to show how the animals look inside their homes, where we might not be able to see them. Cut paper scenery of trees, ground, etc., and cut out the animals' tunnels and nests. Cover the cutouts with light-colored tissue paper. There are many excellent books about animal habitats to help you, including,

Animal Homes, by Sharon Elsewit. New York: Golden, 1984.

Animals and Where They Live, by John Feltwell. New York: Grosset, 1988.

The Big Book of Amazing Animal Behavior, by Annette Tison and Talus Taylor. New York: Grosset, 1987.

The Crocodile and the Hen

In this folktale from West Africa, a hen uses a tricky bit of reasoning to convince a hungry crocodile to leave her alone. Because the play relies more on dialogue than action, all three puppets are designed with moving parts; puppeteers can move the crocodile's mouth, the hen's head, and the lizard's tail as they speak.

Puppeteers: Three, plus narrator.

Puppets: Crocodile, Hen, Lizard (attached to rock)

Scenery pieces: Riverbank, River

Scene 1

The edge of a river. Riverbank at right. Hen enters right and walks slowly back and forth, making small clucking noises and pecking at the ground.

Narrator: In Africa, there once lived a hen who spent her days wandering along the riverbank, pecking for the little bugs and worms that lived in the mud. In the river lived a hungry young crocodile, who was always watching her.

Crocodile: (*Enters left, swimming. Puts front feet onto riverbank.*) You are eating the bugs and worms on ***my*** riverbank, so now ***I*** will eat ***you.***

Hen: Oh, brother of mine. Oh, brother of mine. Don't do it. You will regret it.

Crocodile: (*Turns so that he is facing away from Hen.*) She called me her brother. How ridiculous! I can't possibly be her brother. But suppose I was her brother. Then, it would not be right to eat her. (*Exits right.*)

(*Hen continues pecking and clucking.*)

Narrator: The crocodile went home. He thought and thought. Then he returned to the riverbank.

Crocodile: (*Enters right.*) Prepare to be my dinner!

Hen: Oh, brother of mine, do not eat me. You will regret it.

Crocodile: How can I possibly be your brother? You live on land, but I live in the water.

Hen: Still, you are my brother.

Crocodile: (*Turns, facing away from Hen.*) I'm confused. (*Exits right.*)

(*Hen continues pecking.*)

Narrator: The crocodile swam back home and thought some more. The next time he saw the hen by the riverbank, he crawled out onto the muddy shore.

Crocodile: (*Enters right.*) Now I shall really eat you. I know that I am not your brother, because you have feathers all over you, but I have scales all over me.

Hen: That is true. But you are my brother all the same. (*Exits left.*)

Crocodile: I shall have to go and ask Mbambi, the wise lizard, for her advice. (*Exits right.*)

Scene 2

Another place on the river. Mbambi sits on rock at right. Crocodile enters left.

Crocodile: Mbambi! Great Mbambi! I need your advice.

Mbambi: Yes, young crocodile.

Crocodile: I am befuddled. Each day, a lovely, fat hen comes and eats the bugs on my riverbank. Every day, I want to grab her and eat her. But she keeps calling me her brother. Certainly, I would never eat my sister. Yet how can a hen be the sister of a crocodile? She lives on land, but I live on water. She has feathers, but I have scales.

Mbambi: This is all true, yes, yes. However, the hen does lay eggs . . .

Crocodile: . . . and so do crocodiles! I never even thought of that. That hen could be my sister after all! (*Exits left.*)

Mbambi: It has always been so, it will always be so. Crocodiles do not eat hens.

Hen
Crocodile

Production Notes

The river is a strip of paper, cut in a pattern of waves, that stretches across the stage. It stays on during the entire play. The riverbank, about one-third as wide as the stage, rises several inches above the river, and is onstage only during the first scene.

Make the crocodile seem to swim by keeping his legs just below the bottom edge of the waves and rocking him up and down as he moves. Tilt his head up when he pulls himself up onto the riverbank to talk to the hen and open his mouth very wide each time he threatens to eat the hen. Use the moving parts of all three puppets to animate them when they are talking. Don't move the parts on every syllable, though. Use motion to punctuate important or stressed words.

Shadow Puppets

Make jungle leaves and flowers of colored tissue, and tape them across the top of the screen. Use vertical rods on all three puppets.

Rod Puppets

Make jungle scenery to decorate the sides of the stage. Mbambi and her rock need only be colored on the side facing the audience.

Follow-up Activities

More Egg Tales to Eggxamine . . . and Act Out

Chickens Aren't the Only Ones, by Ruth Heller. New York: Grosset, 1981.

Use the illustrations in this book as patterns or as inspiration for puppet designs, and have a parade of animals that hatch from eggs.

The Golden Egg Book, by Margaret Wise Brown. Illus. by Leonard Weisgard. New York: Golden Press, 1947.

Colored acetate shadows can be used to show the things the rabbit imagines are inside the egg.

Horton Hatches the Egg, by Dr. Seuss. New York: Random House, 1940.

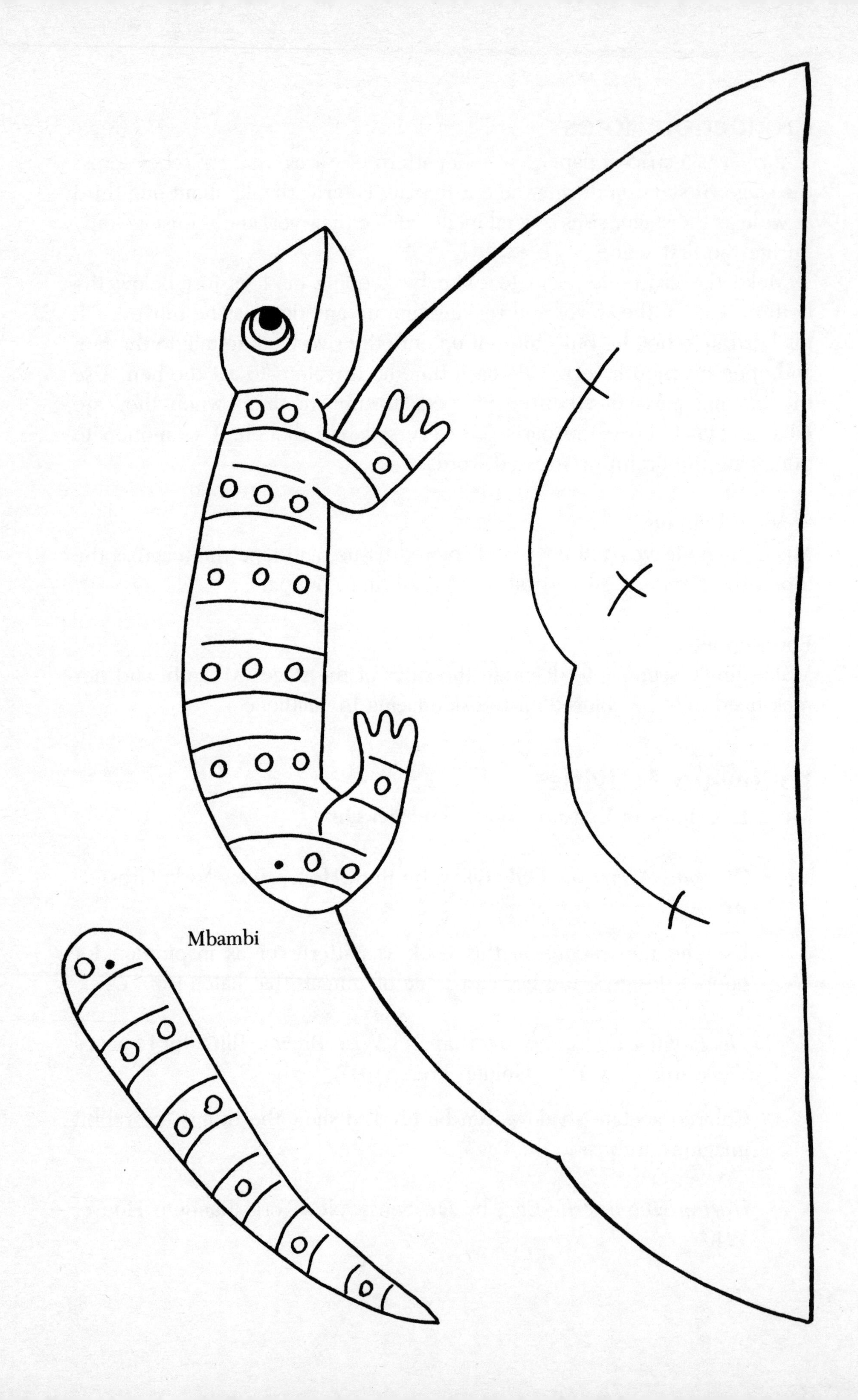
Mbambi

Simplify the puppets and scenery as much as possible. The three hunters can be one "group puppet," for example. Puppets pantomime the action to a reading of the rhymed text.

Who's in the Egg?

Each puppeteer chooses an animal that hatches from an egg, and makes realistic puppets of both the egg and of the young animal that will hatch from it. These can then be used to present one-person puppet shows, in an audience participation, question-and-answer format. The egg appears onstage, and members of the audience ask questions before guessing what animal is inside. The baby animal then comes out of the egg, tells its name, moves around the stage a bit, and exits. Puppeteers will need to do research about their egg, preparing answers to such questions as:

How large are you?

How long does it take you to hatch?

Where is your nest? What is it like?

How many other eggs are with you?

The Deer, the Fox, and the Tiger

This tale from China tells how two clever animals act together to trick an inexperienced tiger. The design of the puppets is taken from Chinese shadow theater.

Puppeteers: Two to three, plus narrator.

Puppets: Tiger Deer Fox

Scenery: Trees at the sides of the stage are optional.

Setting: A meadow.

(*Tiger enters right, walking slowly.*)

Narrator: A young tiger was walking across the meadow one morning. Suddenly he saw a strange new creature, one he had never seen before.

(*Deer enters left.*)

Tiger: (*Surprised.*) What sort of animal are you?

Deer: Don't you know? I am called "deer."

Tiger: Oh. And why are your ears so large?

Deer: So that I can hear a tiger coming from very far away.

Tiger: Oh. And why are your legs so long?

Deer: So that I can chase tigers and catch them.

Tiger: OH! And what are those great big pointed things on your head?

Deer: These are my tiger-forks. We deers use them to pick up tigers before we eat them.

Tiger: OHHHHH! (*Screams in fear, turns, and exits quickly right.*)

Deer: Foolish tiger! (*Turns and exits left.*)

Narrator: The tiger ran and ran.

(*Tiger runs across stage from right to left four times,* then enters right and stops, panting.*)

Fox: (*Enters left.*) Why are you running so fast, friend tiger?

Tiger: The ferocious deer! Help! Help! The ferocious deer is coming after me!

Fox: The ferocious deer?

Tiger: Yes, he wants to catch me with his tiger-forks and eat me for dinner.

Fox: Oh, no. You have it backward, my friend. Tigers are supposed to eat deer, not the other way around.

Tiger: Are you sure?

Fox: I am very sure. Let's go together to the place where you saw the deer. The two of us can share a feast of deer meat.

(*Tiger turns and walks right.*)

Fox: Stop! Wait!

(*Tiger stops.*)

Fox: You are walking too fast. I will never be able to keep up with you. Why don't you carry me on your back?

Tiger: Yes, certainly.

(*Fox jumps up on Tiger's back. They cross the stage left to right four times,* then enter left and stop. Deer enters right.*)

Fox: (*Jumps forward, landing on the ground in front of Tiger.*) Here you are, master. I brought you a tiger for dinner, just as I do every day.

Tiger: (*Screams.*) Aaaaaaah! (*Turns, runs off left.*)

Narrator: The tiger never returned to that part of the country again. And so, the fox, the deer, and their families were able to live in peace and safety.

Production Notes

A traditional way to suggest that puppet characters are traveling a long distance is to have them cross the stage several times in the same direction, as the tiger does in this production. This technique is most effective, of course, if there are no set pieces on stage, or only generic scenery, such as

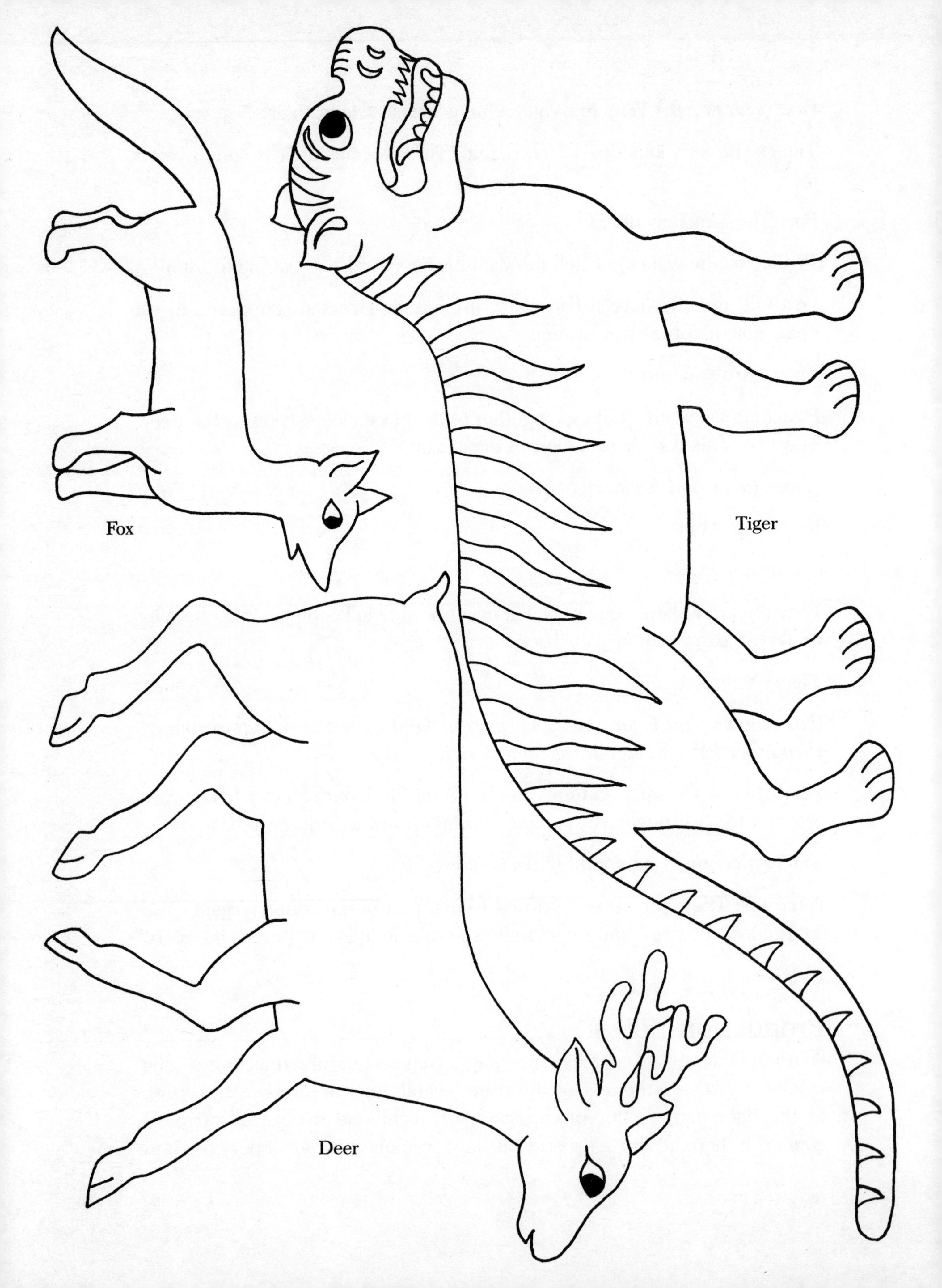
Fox
Tiger
Deer

the optional trees or grass to suggest the meadow setting of this play, at the far edges of the stage. Simple rhythmic percussive accompaniment is essential to an effective traveling scene.

Shadow Puppets
The deer and the tiger should be attached to vertical rods. The fox, because he needs to ride on the tiger's back, must be mounted on a horizontal rod.

Rod Puppets
Make the fox's rod long enough to permit him to ride on the tiger's back.

***Sound Effects**
Play a rhythm on drum, xylophone, and/or cymbal as the animals travel across the stage.

Follow-up Activities

Foolish Tiger Stories
The tiger is a large, frightening and extremely dangerous animal. It is perhaps to relieve their fear of this "man-eater" that people tell stories in which the tiger is made to look foolish. Compare *The Deer, the Fox and the Tiger* to the following folktales about tigers.

> *It All Began With a Drip, Drip, Drip,* by Joan Lexau. New York: McCall, 1970. (India)
>
> "The Tiger's War Against Borneo" (pages 22–27) and "Two out of One" (pages 119–123), in *Kantchil's Lime Pit,* by Harold Courlander. New York: Harcourt, 1950. (Indonesia)
>
> "The Tiger and the Rabbit," in *The Story Bag,* by Kim So-Un. Rutland, Vt.: Tuttle, 1955. Pages 58–64. (Korea)

A Two-faced Tiger
Cut tiger masks of heavy white paper. Cut out eyeholes, then draw and color a face on each side—one fierce and menacing, the other foolish and frightened. The masks may then be held up to the face and used in telling foolish tiger stories.

The Rabbit of Inaba

A small rabbit longs to leave her island home and visit the mainland—but how can she ever hope to get across the water? A chance encounter with a hungry crocodile, and some fast thinking, provide her with a convenient bridge. This Japanese folktale is a delightful account of tricking a dangerous enemy through flattery.

Puppeteers: Three to five, plus narrator and musician.

Puppets: Rabbit
Crocodile
Other Crocodiles—enough to reach from island to the mainland.

Scenery pieces: Oki Island
Mainland
Ocean waves

Setting: Oki Island, off the coast of Japan; island scenery piece is at far left, mainland at far right. There are no scene changes.

Narrator: Long, long ago, when all the animals could talk, there lived a small white rabbit. Her home was on the island of Oki, in Japan, just across the sea from the mainland of Inaba.

Rabbit: (*Enters left.*) Oki Island is so very lonely. How I would love to visit Inaba. (*Jumps in place twice.*) I think I can see other rabbits playing over there right now.

(*Crocodile enters right; the audience sees just the tip of his tail, then his head, then his tail again, as he swims back and forth.*)

Rabbit: I believe that I may soon get my wish. Even though that crocodile would just as soon eat me as carry me to Inaba, I know I can trick him into taking me there. (*Calls loudly to crocodile.*) Crocodile-dono! Crocodile-dono! Isn't it a lovely day?

Crocodile: Who said that? Who is calling my name?

Rabbit: I am! It's me! Over here, on the island!

(*Crocodile comes very close to the island.*)

Crocodile: Hello, rabbit.

Rabbit: Crocodile-dono, you live in the ocean, and I live on this island. Tell me, do you think there are more crocodiles in the sea than there are rabbits on the land?

Crocodile: There are more crocodiles than rabbits, of course, for the sea is far greater than the land.

Rabbit: Crocodile-dono, in my life I have seen many, many more rabbits than crocodiles. But then, you crocodiles are always hiding in the water.

Crocodile: (*Angrily.*) You foolish rabbit! If I were to call together all my crocodile relatives, your kind would be nothing compared to us.

Rabbit: I wonder . . . could there possibly be enough crocodiles to reach, head-to-tail and head-to-tail, from Oki Island all the way to the mainland of Inaba?

Crocodile: Of course there are! I will summon my family, and then you will see for yourself. (*Turns and exits right. Returns, followed by other Crocodiles.*) Just look, rabbit! It will be simple for us to make a line stretching from here to Inaba. There are enough crocodiles here to reach as far as China . . . or India. Did you ever see so many crocodiles?

(*The Crocodiles line up head-to-tail from the island to the mainland.*)

Rabbit: Oh, it's incredible! It's wonderful! I simply didn't believe this was possible! Oh please, please, you splendid creatures, let me ***count*** you. Don't anyone move. (*Hops from one crocodile to the next, counting as she hops.*) *One . . . *two . . . *three . . . *four . . . (*etc.*) Thank you so much, you generous crocodiles, for being my bridge to Inaba!

(*Crocodiles growl and hiss at the Rabbit.*)

Narrator: And so, the clever rabbit used her wits, and a few crocodiles, to make her way across the water to Inaba. Then, because she was wise as well as clever, the rabbit hopped away as fast as she could.

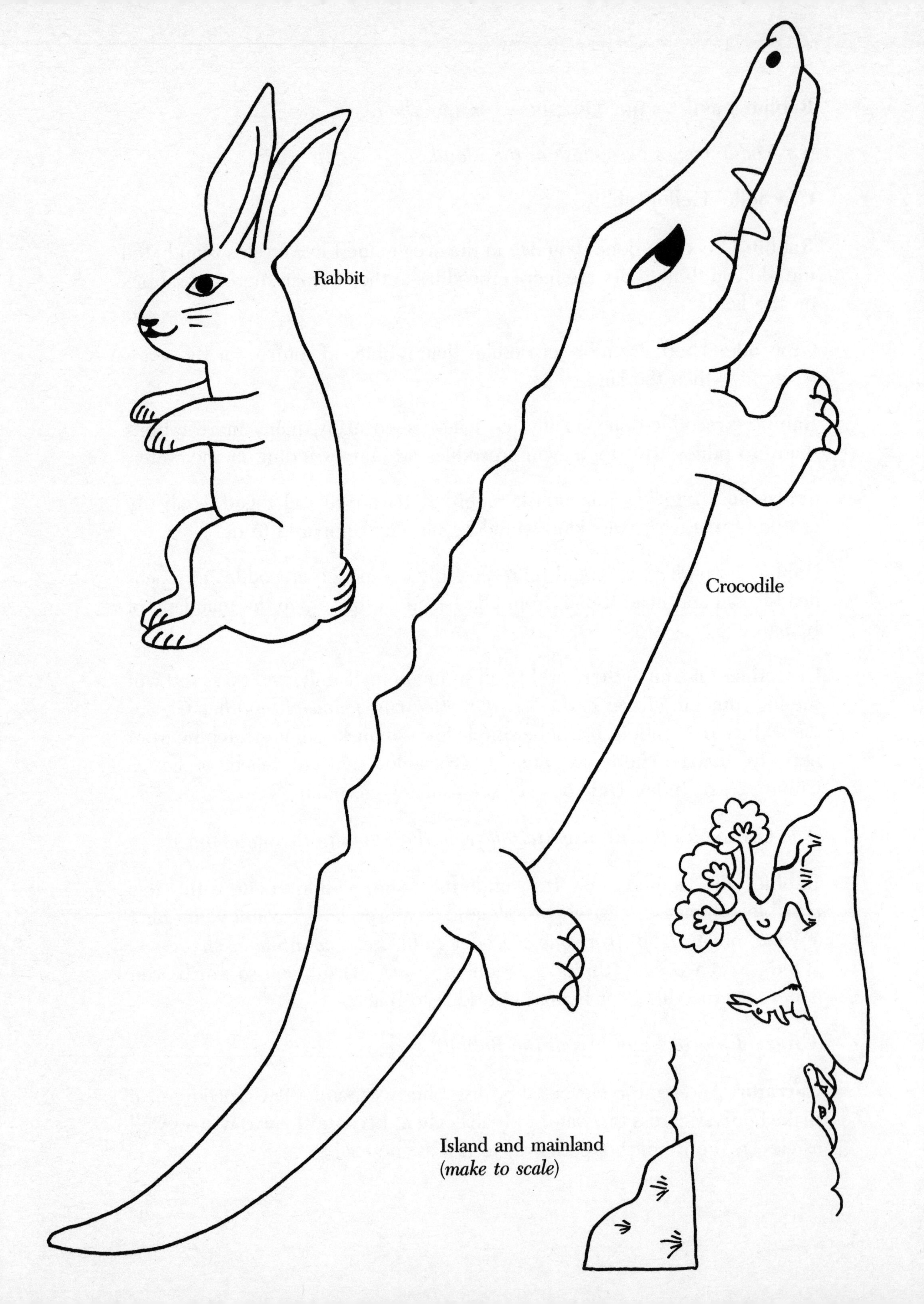

Rabbit
Crocodile
Island and mainland
(make to scale)

Production Notes

The wider the puppet stage, the better, for this play. If your stage is not very wide, you can heighten the feeling of distance between Oki Island and the mainland by making the puppets small. If your group is small, combine two or three crocodiles into one "group puppet." Then, one or two puppeteers can form the entire bridge of crocodiles.

Copy all crocodile puppets from the same pattern. Color them different shades of green and brown. Make a strip of blue paper waves, and place it between the scenery pieces of Oki Island and the mainland.

Add a humorous improvised scene: give each crocodile a name, and show them having a difficult time lining up (children have plenty of first-hand experience at this). The head crocodile becomes angry and exasperated with them, then cries, and finally begs them to line up properly.

"Dono" is a term of respect. The rabbit uses it as part of her strategy to flatter the crocodile.

*Sound Effects

Hit a drum or triangle, or create a bouncy tone on an electronic keyboard to punctuate the rabbit's jumps. Make the noise as she lands on each crocodile's back, just before she counts that crocodile.

Follow-up Activities

Tricky Rides and Tricky Riders

The rabbit of Inaba tricked the crocodiles into being her bridge to the mainland. In other folktales, animals have tricked or been tricked in rides on land, sea, and air. Read and compare these picture-book folktales.

Brer Rabbit Grossly Deceives Brer Fox. In *Jump! The Adventures of Brer Rabbit,* by Joel Chandler Harris. Adapted by Van Dyke Parks. New York: Harcourt Brace, 1986. Pages 27–32. (African-American)

The Cool Ride in the Sky, by Diane Wolkstein. Illus. by Paul Galdone. New York: Knopf, 1973. (African-American)

The Monkey and the Crocodile, by Paul Galdone. New York: Clarion, 1979. (India)

A Crossing-the-Water Riddle

Once a man was taking a wolf, a goat, and a sack of cabbages from one town to another. He came to a river, and there on the shore was a small boat—so small that it could only hold the man and *one* of the things he was taking with him. Now, he had a problem. He had to get all three things across the river. But that meant he would have to leave two of the things alone. If he left the wolf and the goat alone, the wolf would eat the goat. That would never do! And, if he left the goat and the cabbages alone, the goat would eat the cabbages. How could he get all three things across the river? See if you can solve this riddle by acting it out with puppets. Use the scenery from *The Rabbit of Inaba*, and make puppets and props of the man, the goat, the wolf, the boat, and the sack of cabbages.

The Runaway Pancake

The tale of the cake who runs away is known in many parts of the world, and by many names—Gingerbread Man, Johnny Cake, and Journey Cake, to name a few. This story about a pancake that flips itself in the frying pan and then rolls merrily out the door, is from Sweden.

Puppeteers: Three to seven, plus musician.

Puppets:
- Pancake
- Goody Poody
- Manny Panny
- Henny Penny
- Ducky Lucky
- Gander Pander
- Piggy Wiggy

Scenery pieces:
- Stove
- River
- Two trees

Scene 1

Interior of a house. Stove is center stage.

Goody Poody: (*Enters right and walks to stove, holding the pan over it as if she were cooking.*)

Mix a pancake
Stir a pancake
Pop it in the pan;
Fry the pancake
Toss the pancake
Catch it if you can.

Manny Panny: (*Enters left.*) When will our pancake be ready, Goody Poody? I'm hungry.

Goody Poody: Wait a bit longer, Manny Panny, until the pancake turns itself.

Manny Panny: I have lived a long time, but I have never seen a pancake turn itself.

Pancake: *Whee! (*Jumps up out of pan and down again.*)

Manny Panny: Well, I never saw the like. That pancake turned itself!

Pancake: Whee!* (*Jumps up out of pan again, bounces on Manny Panny's head, and exits left.*)

Goody Poody: Stop that pancake! Stop that pancake! Catch it, Manny Panny!

Manny Panny: (*Turns.*) Come back here, you bad little pancake! You're supposed to be my breakfast. (*Exits left, followed by Goody Poody.*)

Scene 2

Outdoors. Trees at each side of stage.

(*The Pancake crosses stage, right to left, three times, bouncing and giggling, followed each time by Manny Panny and Goody Poody, who yell things like "Stop!" "Come back!" etc. Finally, the Pancake enters alone. Henny Penny enters from the opposite side, and both stop.*)

Henny Penny: Good day, pancake.

Pancake: The same to you, Henny Penny.

Henny Penny: Pancake dear, don't roll so fast. Wait a bit and let me eat you up.

Pancake: I have rolled away from Goody Poody, and Manny Panny, and I can roll away from you, too.

(*Pancake crosses stage three times, right to left, chased by Henny Penny, who calls out "Stop!" "Wait!" "Come back!" etc. Finally, Pancake enters right, alone. Ducky Lucky enters from left, and both stop.*)

Ducky Lucky: Good day, pancake.

Pancake: The same to you, Ducky Lucky.

Ducky Lucky: Pancake dear, don't roll so fast. Wait a bit and let me eat you up.

Pancake: I have rolled away from Goody Poody, and Manny Panny, and Henny Penny, and I can roll away from you, too.

(*Ducky Lucky chases Pancake across stage, left to right, several times, calling out "Stop!" "Wait!" "Come back!" etc. Then Pancake enters left alone. Gander Pander enters from right, and both stop.*)

Gander Pander: Good day, pancake.

Pancake: The same to you, Gander Pander.

Gander Pander: Pancake dear, don't roll so fast. Wait a bit and let me eat you up.

Pancake: I have rolled away from Goody Poody and Manny Panny and Henny Penny and Ducky Lucky, and I can roll away from you, too.

(*Gander Pander chases Pancake across stage, right to left, several times, calling out "Stop!" "Wait!" "Come back!" etc.*)

Scene 3

The river. River set piece far left.

Piggy Wiggy: (*Enters right and turns around, leaving just enough room for the Pancake to enter to his right.*) Good day, Pancake.

Pancake: The same to you, Piggy Wiggy.

Piggy Wiggy: Why are you rolling so fast, you sweet little pancake?

Pancake: I have rolled away from Goody Poody and Manny Panny and Henny Penny and Ducky Lucky and Gander Pander, and I can . . .

Piggy Wiggy: (*Interrupts.*) But, pancake dear, how can you cross this river? You don't want to get wet, do you?

Pancake: Uh oh! I didn't think about that. The water would melt me into little wet crumbs.

Piggy Wiggy: I can swim, you know. Please allow me to help you across. Otherwise Goody Poody and Manny Panny and Henny Penny and Ducky Lucky and Gander Pander may catch you.

Pancake: Yes, please, dear Piggy Wiggy. Help me cross the river.

Piggy Wiggy: Have a seat on my snout, and I'll carry you to the other side.

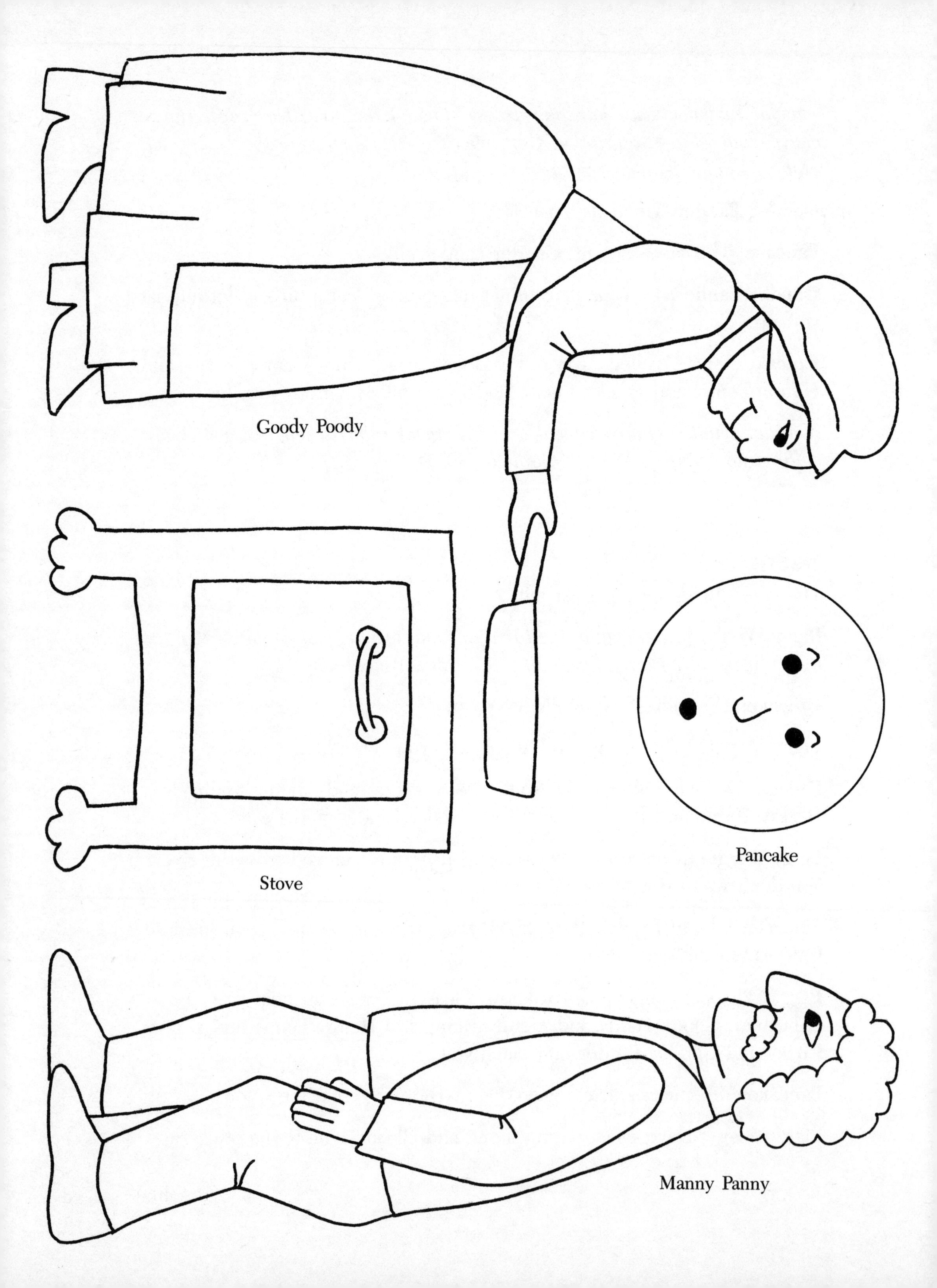
Goody Poody
Stove
Pancake
Manny Panny

(*Piggy Wiggy turns to face river, and the Pancake jumps onto his snout. Piggy Wiggy jumps into river, then tips up his snout, tossing the Pancake up into the air.**)

Pancake: Help! (*Lands on Piggy Wiggy's snout.*)

(*Piggy Wiggy tosses the Pancake up into the air again.**)

Pancake: Help! Stop! (*Lands on Piggy Wiggy's snout.*)

(*Piggy Wiggy tosses the Pancake up into the air again.**)

Pancake: Oh no!

Piggy Wiggy: Ouf! Ouf! Ouf! (*Eats the Pancake.*) Well, that's the end of one delicious pancake. (*Swims offstage.*)

Production Notes

Goody Poody's poem is by Christina Rosetti and is in *Sing Song: A Nursery Rhyme Book* (Dover, 1969).

The stove scenery piece should be attached to a rod and held by one of the puppeteers in the first scene, for a fast scene change. The river is a narrow band of paper, cut into a wave pattern, which extends halfway across the stage. Make two simple trees to place at either side of the stage during scenes two and three.

There are four separate chase scenes in this play; plan and rehearse them, so that each is different. For example, Manny Panny and Goody Poody may be far behind the pancake. This can be shown during the chase by having the pancake cross the stage alone, then leaving the stage empty for a few seconds before Manny Panny and Goody Poody cross in the same direction, yelling and shouting. Repeat this sequence twice, leaving the stage empty for a longer interval each time. One animal could be very quick at the chase, almost on top of the pancake, only to suddenly fall down in exhaustion. Another animal could be so slow that the pancake stops and calls "nanny, nanny"—giving the animal time to catch up and almost capture him!

To show Piggy Wiggy eating the pancake, move the pig puppet up and down, and make loud eating noises as the pancake puppet is quickly taken down and offstage.

Ducky Lucky
Gander Pander
Piggy Wiggy
Henny Penny

Shadow Puppets
The front-facing pancake is attached to a horizontal rod; thus, he can hop, jump, and roll in either direction. If you are making him from black paper, use a hole punch and small, sharp scissors to cut out his facial features. All the other puppets are attached to vertical rods, so that they can turn around and face in either direction.

Rod Puppets
Attach the pancake to a rod long enough to allow him to jump up high into the air.

***Sound Effects**
Use a slide whistle, up and down, when the pancake jumps into the air in the first and final scenes. Some chase music of the sort used with silent movies can be played on a keyboard to heighten the excitement . . . or use quick drumbeats.

Follow-up Activities

Dinner Theater
If this puppet show makes you hungry, follow it up by cooking your own runaway pancakes. Make a face on each one with raisins. Use the pancakes to re-enact the final scene of the play with each child playing Piggy Wiggy.

Edible Runaways
Compare the following picture book folktales to *The Runaway Pancake.*

The Bun, by Marcia Brown.
New York: Harcourt, Brace, 1972. (Russia)

The Gingerbread Boy, by Paul Galdone.
New York: Clarion, 1975. (United States)

Johnny-Cake, by Joseph Jacobs. Illus. by William Stobbs.
New York: Viking, 1972. (England)

Journey Cake, Ho! retold by Ruth Sawyer.
New York: Viking, 1973. (United States)

The North Wind and the Sun

In this fable from Aesop, the north wind and the sun compete in a contest of strength, and show that power is more than just physical force.

Puppeteers: Three, plus narrator and musician.

Puppets: Sun Wind Man

Prop: Cloak

Scenery pieces: Two mountains

Setting: A valley; mountains at left and right. There are no scene changes.

Narrator: One day, the sun and the north wind got into an argument about which one was the stronger.

Wind: (*Offstage.*) Me.

Sun: (*Offstage.*) No, me.

Wind: (*Offstage.*) I am.

Sun: (*Offstage.*) No, I am.

Wind: (*Enters left; goes to the top of the mountain at right.*) I am stronger.

Sun: (*Enters left; stays at the top of mountain at left.*) I am definitely stronger.

Wind: I am stronger than you are.

Sun: Impossible. I am stronger.

(*Man enters right, walking very slowly. As the sun and wind argue, he proceeds to center stage and stops.*)

Wind: You are not nearly as strong as I am.

Sun: Prove it, then.

Wind: I'll be glad to.

Sun: Do you see that man down there?

Wind: Yes.

Sun: Can you make him take off his cloak?

Wind: I'll blow it right off his back. (*Blows.**)

Narrator: The man wrapped his cloak more tightly around himself as the cold wind blew.

Wind: (*Blows twice more. Pants, out of breath, resting against mountain.*) Let's see ***you*** . . . make him . . . take off his cloak.

(*Sun moves to left of North Wind and twirls.**)

Narrator: As the sun shone, the man felt hotter . . .

Man: (*Groans.*) Oh!

Narrator: And hotter . . .

Man: (*Groans harder.*) Mmmmm.

Narrator: And hotter, until at last . . .

(*Man takes off his cloak, turns, and exits left.*)

Wind: He took off his cloak!

Sun: Of course he did. A little bit of warmth can accomplish things that cold, blustery blasts cannot.

Production Notes

The man and his cloak are on two separate rods. The cloak is held in front of the man (to the audience side) until he mimes taking it off, at which time, the cloak is held diagonally across his body as if he were carrying it.

The rule, "move the puppet when it is talking," is not appropriate for the sun and the wind, as they would look silly jiggling up and down in the sky. Instead, each puppet can make a slight move toward the other as it begins to speak. The listening puppet simultaneously moves back the same amount in the other direction.

Make mountain scenery pieces for each side of the stage; if stage space is limited, place just half a mountain, split vertically down the middle, at each side.

Sun
North Wind

Cloak
Man

Shadow Puppets

The sun and the wind are attached to horizontal rods. If they are made from black paper, the lines of their facial features should be cut out. Try making other decorative cutouts also. To represent the sun shining on the man, bring the sun off the screen an inch or so, then back into place, several times. Sound effects enhance this device. Both the man and his cloak are attached to vertical rods, so that the puppet can turn around to exit.

Rod Puppets

The sun and wind puppets will need rods long enough to lift them high in the sky. Color the two sides of the sun different colors, such as yellow and orange or orange and red. Add glitter or sequins to the sun and ribbons or Mylar streamers to the wind.

Keep the first (front) side of the sun toward the audience at the beginning of the show. Then when the sun "shines," twirl the puppet's rod for a special effect. The puppeteer will need to rehearse this movement many times, so that the sun puppet stays in place as it spins. Conclude the motion so that the puppet returns to its original color when the action is completed.

***Sound Effects**

Add sound effects for the wind blowing and the sun shining. Wind noises may be made by several puppeteers together—deep, airy whistles produced by rounding the lips and making the mouth cavity very large. Or blow gently across a microphone—but rehearse first so that you don't hurt the audience members' ears! Sunshine noise can be made by playing chords on an electric keyboard or by running a striker up the keys of a xylophone.

Follow-up Activities

Act Out a Group Poem

In this activity, children design and make their own shadow puppets, write a group poem, and put on a shadow show in which everyone plays a part. Give each child a piece of black construction paper (half an 8″ × 10″ piece will be enough), a light-colored crayon, scissors, a drinking straw, and two two-inch pieces of masking tape. Ask everyone to think back to a very windy day. What kinds of things did the wind pick up and blow? What other things *could* the wind whisk away? Pat Hutchins' picture book *The Wind Blew*

(Macmillan, 1974) can help provide ideas. Everyone decides upon and draws something that the wind might carry off on a windy day. Then, cut each object out and attach it horizontally to the straw with two pieces of masking tape.

With the leader acting as scribe, each puppeteer dictates the line of the poem that his puppet will act out. Alternate the children's lines with ". . . and the wind blew," for example:

> A leaf scraped across the street
> . . . and the wind blew,
> It picked up a man's umbrella, and the man, too,
> . . . and the wind blew . . .
> The trashcan rolled across the street,
> . . . and the wind blew.

To perform the poem, puppeteers line up to one side of the shadow screen, standing in the order in which their puppets are mentioned in the poem. One by one, as the poem is read, they move behind the stage, manipulate their puppet, and exit. Each windblown object will need to stay perfectly still for a few seconds during its journey across the shadow screen, so that the audience can focus on it. Add some soft background music.

Tales of Sun, Wind, and Sky

These stories about sun, wind, and sky can be performed as puppet plays:

How the Sun Was Brought Back to the Sky, by Mirra Ginsburg. Illus. by José Aruego and Ariane Dewey. New York: Macmillan, 1975.

Use the colorful illustrations as patterns for rod puppets, and perform in the round, using the narration-improvisation technique.

"The Rat's Daughter," in *The Flannel Board Storytelling Book* by Judy Sierra. Bronx: H. W. Wilson, 1987. Pages 128–133.

Includes traceable patterns suitable for rod or shadow puppets. Perform as a rod- or shadow-puppet play, using the narration-improvisation technique.

It Looked Like Spilt Milk, by Charles G. Shaw.
New York: Harper, 1988.

Use rod puppets made of white paper with blue outlines; for shadow puppets, use either acetate or heavy white paper, heavily outlined in dark blue. Perform as a pantomime to narration, pausing to give the audience a chance to guess each shape. Add more shapes to accommodate a large group.

Red Riding Hood

Most children know this tale well, and this makes their delight in performing it with puppets all the greater. There are many different retellings of "Red Riding Hood" in the oral tradition, and in books, plays, films, and cartoons. In the earliest European version published, that of Charles Perrault (1697), the wolf devours Red Riding Hood, and there the story ends. Most modern versions for children follow the Brothers Grimm (1812), who allowed the poor girl a second chance by letting her out of the wolf's belly. Performers may wish to use the puppets and sets for this play to improvise alternative endings of the tale.

Puppeteers: Four to five, plus musician.

Puppets: Red Riding Hood, Mother, Woodcutter, Wolf, Grandma, Wolf Dressed as Grandma

Prop: Tree (which will be chopped down)
Basket

Scenery pieces: Tree
Bed

Scene 1

Outside Red Riding Hood's house. Scenery of house at left optional.

(*Red Riding Hood and her Mother enter left. Mother is carrying basket.*)

Mother: These cookies are guaranteed to make your grandmother feel better, Red Riding Hood. (*Gives basket to her.*) Now, be sure you go straight to Grandma's house. Stay on the path, and keep an eye out for the Big Bad Wolf! (*Kisses Red Riding Hood.*)

Red Riding Hood: Don't worry, Mother, I will. Good bye! (*Turns, exits right, skipping and singing.*)

Mother: Good bye! (*Turns and exits into house.*)

Scene 2

The woods. Tree scenery piece at left. Tree prop at right is held by a puppeteer.

(*Woodcutter enters and chops tree at right four times.* It falls,* and he exits right.*)

Wolf: (*Appears from behind at left.*) Here comes a delicious . . . oops, I mean here comes a delightful little girl. If that woodcutter wasn't in the neighborhood, I'd eat her up right now. I'll hide behind this tree until she comes closer.

(*Red Riding Hood enters right, skipping and singing.*)

Wolf: (*Appears from behind tree.*) Hello, little girl.

Red Riding Hood: Hello! Who are you?

Wolf: Don't you recognize me?

Red Riding Hood: No.

Wolf: I'm a big, friendly puppy dog. Who are you?

Red Riding Hood: Everyone calls me Red Riding Hood.

Wolf: I'm pleased to eat you . . . Oops! I mean, I'm pleased to meet you, Red Riding Hood. Where are you going with that basket of cookies?

Red Riding Hood: To my grandma's house. She's been sick, and these cookies will make her feel better.

Wolf: What a kind little girl you are! And because you're so nice, I'll show you a shortcut to your granny's house. Go back that way, turn right and left around the rock under the tree beside the river.

Red Riding Hood: Thank you, big, friendly puppy dog. (*Turns and exits right, skipping and singing.*)

Wolf: While Red Riding Hood goes to Grandma's House the *long* way, I'll take the shortcut, and get there ahead of her. (*Exits left.*)

Scene 3

Inside Grandma's house. Bed at center. Grandma is in bed. There is a knock at the door.*

Grandma: Who's there?

Wolf: (*Offstage, in a high squeaky voice.*) It's your cute little granddaughter, Red Riding Hood.

Grandma: Come in, dear.

Wolf: (*Enters left. Speaks in regular voice.*) Hello, Granny!

Grandma: Oh, no! It's the Big Bad Wolf!

Wolf: The Big Bad *Hungry* Wolf! (*Eats Grandma.*) Now for a little disguise. (*Exits right. Reenters dressed in Grandma's clothes.*)

(*Knock at door.**)

Wolf: (*In regular voice.*) Who is it? (*Changes to high voice.*) Oops, I mean, who is it?

Red Riding Hood: (*Offstage.*) It's me. Red Riding Hood.

Wolf: (*Keeps high voice.*) Come in, dear.

Red Riding Hood: (*Enters left.*) Grandma, I brought you a basket of cookies.

Wolf: Thank you, dear.

Red Riding Hood: (*Walks to foot of bed.*) Oh, Grandma, what big ears you have!

Wolf: The better to hear you with, my dear.

Red Riding Hood: And Grandma, what big eyes you have.

Wolf: The better to see you with, my dear.

Red Riding Hood: Oh, Grandma, what big teeth you have!

Wolf: The better to eat you with, my dear! (*Jumps up and eats Red Riding Hood. Lies back down on bed and groans until the Woodcutter begins speaking.*)

Woodcutter: (*Enters left.*) There you are, you old criminal! I'll help you get rid of your stomachache. (*Cuts Wolf's stomach.**)

Red Riding Hood: (*Pops out of Wolf's stomach* and walks to right of bed.*) Oh, thank you!

Grandma: (*Pops out of Wolf's stomach* and walks to right of bed.*) Thank you for rescuing us from that awful wolf.

Red Riding Hood: He told me he was a big, friendly puppy dog! What should we do with him now?

Grandma: Since he's so hungry, I'll put these rocks in his stomach and sew him up! (*Mimes actions.*)

Woodcutter: And I'll tie him up and take him to the zoo. They should have a nice, safe cage for him. (*Mimes tying the Wolf.*)

Wolf: Grrrrr! Rrrrrr!

(*Woodcutter and Wolf exit left.*)

Red Riding Hood: I brought some cookies for you, Grandma.

Grandma: Thank you dear. Let's go into the kitchen and eat them together and have a little talk about wolves.

(*They exit right.*)

Production Notes

Each puppet in this play is designed with a moving arm. Make a second wolf puppet, fatter than the first, dressed in a nightgown and nightcap. When the wolf eats Grandma and Red Riding Hood, he simply jumps at them and makes a lot of noise and movement as they are quickly brought down and offstage.

Make two simple trees, lollipop-style, each a bit taller than the woodcutter puppet. One of the trees in scene two is attached to a rod and operated like a puppet, so that it can fall when the woodcutter chops it down.

*Sound Effects

Use a clavé for the woodcutter's chops at the tree and at the wolf's stomach, and for knocks at door. A slide whistle down represents the falling tree, slide

Mother
Red Riding Hood

Basket
Big Bad Wolf
Wolf in bed
(*backstage view*)

Grandmother
Woodcutter

whistles up accompany Red Riding Hood and Grandma popping out of the wolf's stomach.

Follow-up Activities

Pictures Tell the Story

This is an exercise that can be used to prepare a group to design their own puppets for *Red Riding Hood.*

The illustrators of picture books tell the story in art, alongside the words. And naturally, different illustrators will not draw the same folktale in the same way. Look at the following books, compare the ways in which the characters are portrayed by the artists. Are some versions more frightening than others? More humorous? How do the illustrations tell us where and when the story took place? How is this different in each book? Look for details the illustrators show us which are not contained in the words of the story.

Little Red Riding Hood, retold and illus. by Trina Schart Hyman.
New York: Holiday, 1983.

Little Red Riding Hood, illus. by Paul Galdone.
New York: McGraw-Hill, 1974.

Red Riding Hood, retold and illus. by James Marshall.
New York: Dial, 1987.

Red Riding Hood, by Beatrice Schenk de Regniers.
Illus. by Edward Gorey.
New York: Atheneum, 1972.

Wanted: One Wolf

Imagine that the wolf escaped from the woodcutter after the end of the play. The local authorities have asked you to help them recapture the beast by making a wanted poster. Include a drawing of the wolf, along with pertinent information such as aliases, habits, distinguishing marks, place last seen, and the amount of reward being offered. Use the posters to advertise your puppet show.

Wait Till Emmet Comes

This play, about a house haunted by supernatural cats, is adapted from an African-American folktale. Its eerie mood plays well in shadow puppets. For a rod-puppet production, turn the room lights off, and light the stage with lamps at either side. Or, use fluorescent paper or paints to make the puppets, and light the stage with black light.

Puppeteers: Four, plus narrator and musician.

Puppets: Preacher Man Three Cats

Scenery pieces: Chair Fireplace

Scene 1

A country road. Scenery is optional.

Narrator: A traveling preacher man was walking down the road one evening. The sun was just about to set. He was looking for a place to spend the night.

Preacher: (*Enters right, walks to center, and stops.*) Well, at last! There's a house over yonder and smoke comin' out the chimney. (*Exits left.*)

Narrator: The preacher man hurried toward the house. The front door was wide open, so he just walked inside.

Scene 2

Interior of house. Fireplace at far right; chair to left of fireplace, facing left.

Preacher: (*Enters left.*) Hello? Hello? Is anyone at home here? Guess I might as well just sit a spell by the fire. (*Sits.*) I'll wait until the folks that live here get back. This fire's mighty hot. That means they haven't been gone long.

Narrator: The preacher man sat and sat. Then, in came the biggest cat he had ever seen.

(*Cat 1 enters left and stands in front of Preacher Man. Cat's tail marches up* *its back until it reaches the Cat's head, waves at Preacher Man, then marches back to its original place.* The Cat hisses and growls.)*

Preacher: Oh, my goodness!

Cat 1: Should I? Should I? Oh, I'd really like to. But I'd better wait. I'll wait till Emmet comes.

Preacher: Who is Emmet?

Narrator: But the cat didn't answer him. It just sat and stared, its eyes glowing in the firelight. Then another cat came in, even bigger than the first.

Cat 2: (*Enters left: its front section takes three small steps, then its back section takes three small steps to join it.* Cat 2 stands next to Cat 1, growls, and hisses.*) Oh, look what came in. Do you think we should?

Cat 1: No, not now. Let's wait.

Cats 1 and 2: (*Mysteriously.*) Wait till Emmet comes.

Preacher: Who . . . uh, pardon me . . . who is Emmet?

Narrator: But the cats didn't answer him. They just sat by the fire. Their four eyes glowed like hot coals. They just sat, and stared, and stared at that preacher man. Then in came another cat, even bigger than those two.

Cat 3: (*Enters left. Growls and hisses. Stands to the left of Cat 2. Cat 3's head rises into the air, travels over Cats 1 and 2, and looks the Preacher Man in the eye.*) Look what I see! (*Head returns to Cat 3's body.*)

Cat 2: He's perfect, isn't he?

Cat 1: Shall we?

Preacher: No, don't!

Cats 1, 2, and 3: (*Mysteriously.*) Wait. Wait. Wait. Wait till Emmet comes.

Preacher: (*Gets up from chair.*) Listen . . . Thank you all very kindly for your hospitality. When Emmet gets here . . . whoever Emmet is . . . you just tell him I was here, but I just couldn't wait for him. (*Exits, screaming.*) Aaaaaaah!

(*Cats 1, 2, and 3 laugh wickedly; their parts dance around the stage.**)

Chair
Preacher Man
Fireplace
(*make to scale*)
Man in chair
(*backstage view*)

Production Notes

The preacher man progresses from being calm, to worried, to frightened, to scared half to death. Even a flat paper puppet can appear to quiver with fright: tense your forearm until it begins to shake. The preacher man must regain his original composure in order to say goodnight to the cats with utmost politeness. The cats should be played with slow and diabolical delight. Think of the wicked witch in the film, *The Wizard of Oz.*

The strangeness of the cats' come-apart bodies is most effective if they remain still and composed when not specifically directed by the script to do their tricks.

Shadow Puppets

All puppets and scenery should be made of black paper. Cut out the flames of the fireplace and cover the area with orange tissue paper. The preacher man is attached to a vertical rod, the cats to horizontal ones.

Rod Puppets

Since the cats are supernatural creatures, color them strange and unusual colors. It is even possible to use black light for the performance and to paint the puppets with fluorescent colors. Cat 3's head must be on a long, thin black rod so that it can fly up and over the other cat puppets.

*Sound Effects

Play ascending and descending notes on a xylophone or electronic keyboard in time with the eerie movements of Cats 1 and 2. A slide whistle up and down or a finger run up and down the electronic keyboard can accompany the flight of Cat 3's head. Recorded "haunted house" sound effects can be used as opening and closing music for this show.

Follow-up Activities

Who Is Emmet, Anyway?

Is Emmet a cat . . . or is he *something else?* Is he huge and frightening or small and silly? Use your imagination, and make a puppet of Emmet.

Ghostly Storytelling

Nearly everyone likes to hear ghost stories. This type of tale is the easiest for children to learn and tell. Schedule a candle-light storytelling session in

Cat 1
Cat 2

Cat 3

which children share their favorite scary stories—ones that they know already or ones learned from books, such as the following:

Southern Fried Rat and Other Gruesome Tales, by Daniel Cohen. New York: Evans, 1983.

The Thing at the Foot of the Bed and Other Scary Tales, by Maria Leach. Cleveland: World, 1959.

When the Lights Go Out: Twenty Scary Tales to Tell, by Margaret Read MacDonald. Bronx: H. W. Wilson, 1988.

In a Dark, Dark Room, and Other Scary Stories, by Alvin Schwartz. New York: Harper, 1984. (Beginning reader)

As an accompaniment to the storytelling, use a shadow screen to show tableaux of the scary creatures in the tales.

Why Mosquitos Buzz in Our Ears

This play, adapted from a Filipino folktale, tells how the mosquito was accused and convicted of a crime simply because King Crab was tired of hearing the other animals' alibis. And, it answers the perplexing question, just why *do* mosquitos buzz in our ears.

Puppeteers: Five to seven, plus narrator.

Puppets:	Crab	Firefly
	Frog	Mosquito
	Snail	Two or more other Mosquitoes

Scenery piece: Entrance to Crab's cave

Setting: The forest floor. The entrance to Crab's underground dwelling is at center stage. There are no scene changes.

Narrator: Once upon a time, the crab was king of all the animals. He had a terrible temper.

Crab: (*Enters right.*) General Frog! General Frog!

Frog: (*Enters left.*) Yes, Your Majesty.

Crab: I am going to take my royal nap now.

Frog: Very good, Your Majesty.

Crab: And I have made up a new law.

Frog: What is the new law, Your Majesty?

Crab: Everyone is to be completely quiet during my royal nap. Anyone who makes a noise and WAKES ME UP . . .

Frog: (*Frightened.*) Yes, Your Majesty.

Crab: . . . WILL BE EXECUTED!

Frog: Very good, Your Majesty.

Crab: Stand guard now, General Frog, and make sure that no one makes even the tiniest noise. (*Turns and exits down into hole.*)

Frog: Have a good nap, Your M . . . oops. (*Softly.*) Have a good nap, Your Majesty. (*Marches back and forth.*)

Snail: (*Enters right and crosses stage slowly.*) Have to . . . hurry . . . have to . . . hurry . . . have to . . . hurry. (*Exits left.*)

Frog: Shhhh! Who is that? What? I can't believe my eyes. It was the snail, and she was carrying her house on her back. (*Chuckles softly.*) That's the funniest thing I've ever seen. (*Laughs loudly.*)

Crab: (*Pops out of hole, angrily.*) All right! All right! Who did it? Who woke me up?

Frog: Um . . . er . . .

Crab: Who laughed?

Frog: I did, Your Majesty. But it wasn't my fault. I couldn't help laughing when I saw the snail. You would have laughed, too. She was . . . heh, heh . . . she was carrying her house on her back.

Crab: So it is the snail's fault. Let the snail come forward.

Snail: (*Enters right.*) Have to . . . hurry . . . have to . . . hurry . . . yes . . . Your Majesty.

Crab: I sentence you to be executed. The frog laughed and woke me up because he saw ***you*** carrying your house on your back.

Snail: Oh, Your Majesty, it isn't my fault. I have to take my house with me on my back because the firefly is carrying fire. I am afraid she will burn my house down.

Crab: I see. It is the firefly's fault. General Frog, bring the firefly here to be executed.

Frog: Firefly! (*Hops around, calling.*) Firefly! Firefly! Firefly!

Firefly: (*Flies on right. Stops in midair.*) You called, Your Majesty?

Crab: Just exactly why are you carrying that fire? Are you trying to burn down the snail's house?

Firefly: (*Alights on Crab's cave.*) No, not at all. I am carrying fire to frighten the mosquito. She keeps trying to bite me.

Crab: Oh! It is the mosquito's fault. The mosquito will be executed. Summon the mosquito.

Mosquito: (*Flies on right, buzzing*) Your Majesty called me?

Crab: Yes. The frog awakened me from my royal nap. He was laughing at the snail because she had her house on her back. The snail had her house on her back because the firefly was carrying fire. Firefly was carrying fire to frighten you, because you were trying to bite her. Therefore, you are responsible for waking me up from my royal nap, and you will be EXECUTED!

Mosquito: No fair! No fair! How do you expect me to live if I don't bite someone? I would die if I didn't bite someone.

Crab: Everyone has an excuse. I am tired of excuses, and someone must be punished. Off with her head! Off with the mosquito's head!

(*As the narrator speaks, the Frog chases the Mosquito, who exits. Then other animals exit, King Crab last of all, into his hole.*)

Narrator: The mosquito escaped, and she told all the other mosquitos in the world to go to King Crab's underground palace and to bite him.

(*As Narrator speaks, the Mosquitos buzz back and forth across the stage four times, angrily attacking the entrance to King Crab's cave.*)

Narrator: But mosquitos can't see very well. They can't tell the difference between the hole of the tunnel that leads to King Crab's palace . . . and the holes in people's ears! So they keep buzzing and buzzing in our ears, seeking revenge for King Crab's unjust decision.

(*Mosquitos exit, buzzing angrily.*)

Production Notes

The stage can be decorated with lush jungle trees and vines. The snail is very slow both in movement and speech, in contrast to the firefly and mosquito, who are quick and energetic.

Shadow Puppets

Jungle plants and trees of colored tissue paper can be placed at the sides and across the top of the shadow screen. Make the set piece (the entrance to

Frog
Crab

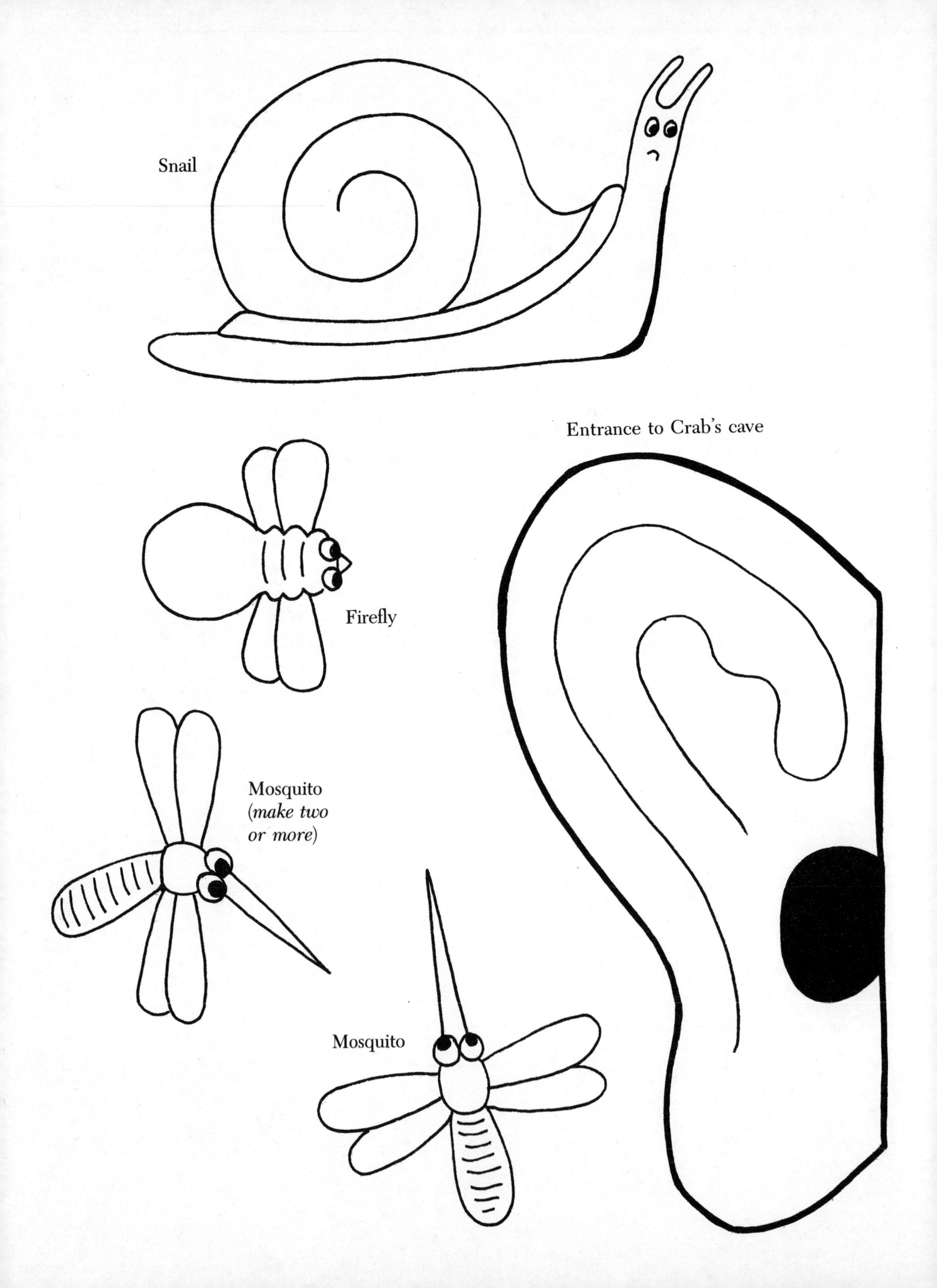
Snail
Entrance to Crab's cave
Firefly
Mosquito
(*make two
or more*)
Mosquito

crab's cave) from black paper, and use sharp scissors to cut along the interior lines, so that the audience can tell that it looks just like a human ear. If you are making the puppets from black paper, cut out the circle in firefly's tail and cover it with yellow or orange tissue paper. Attach the firefly and mosquitos to horizontal rods, the other puppets to vertical rods.

Rod Puppets

The rods on the firefly and the mosquitos will need to be long enough to allow them to fly above the other puppets.

Follow-up Activities

Buggy Poems

It's fun to learn poems and act them out with puppets. Try the following poetry collections:

> *Insects All Around Us*, by Richard Armour. Illus. by Paul Galdone. New York: McGraw-Hill, 1981.
>
> *When It Comes to Bugs*, by Aileen Fischer. Illus. by Chris Degen and Bruce Degen. New York: Harper, 1986.
>
> *Bugs*, by Mary Ann Hoberman. Illus. by Victoria Chess. New York: Viking, 1976.

Adventures in a Small World

Choose a particular species of crab, frog, snail, or insect, to portray in a scientific puppet play. Do library research, focusing on an aspect of the life cycle or behavior of that animal that has dramatic potential. Make puppets, props, and scenery, then write a narrative script to be read during the puppet performance (like the offscreen voice in a nature documentary).

The Silly Jellyfish

The daughter of the Dragon King is sick, and only the liver of a monkey can make her well again. This play is adapted from a Japanese variant of a tale which is popular throughout Asia.

Puppeteers: Three to five speak, plus narrator and musician, with the option of adding other undersea creatures in swim-on roles.

Puppets:
- Dragon King
- Dragon Princess
- Doctor Crab
- Jellyfish
- Jellyfish (for final scene)
- Monkey
- Monkey (for final scene)

Scenery pieces:
- Undersea kingdom
- Monkey Island
- Ocean waves

Scene 1

The undersea kingdom of the Dragon King. Coral, seaweed, and chests full of gold and jewels set the scene. Dragon Princess is sitting left, Dragon King right.

Dragon Princess: (*Moans.*)

Dragon King: What's the matter, child?

Dragon Princess: It hurts, Daddy.

Dragon King: What hurts, Princess?

Dragon Princess: Everything hurts. My claws hurt. My spikes hurt. My scales hurt.

Dragon King: This is serious. I'll summon the royal doctor at once. (*Yells.*) Doctor Crab! Doctor Crab! Doctor Crab!

Crag: (*Enters rights.*) Yes, yes. What's the problem?

Dragon King: Something is wrong with my daughter.

Crab: (*Hops over King.*) There certainly is something wrong. Her scales have purple splotches. (*Pinches her nose.*)

Dragon Princess: Ouch!

Crab: Her nose is hot. Say Aah!

Dragon Princess: Aaaaaaaaa. (*Continues saying it as Crab looks into her mouth.*)

Crab: Oh, it's bad.

Dragon King: How bad?

Crab: Very bad.

Dragon King: What is it?

Crab: Her fire is nearly extinguished.

Dragon King: Not that! Is there a cure, doctor?

Crab: Yes, but only one cure.

Dragon Princess: What is it?

Crab: You must . . . as soon as possible, yes . . . you must eat the liver of a monkey.

Dragon King: But monkeys live on land. How will we capture one?

Crab: You'll have to send a creature with the ability to travel on land to fetch one. I'd go myself, of course, but I'm much too important.

Dragon Princess: (*Weakly.*) Why not send the jelly fish. He's always bragging about how he can walk on land with his long stiff legs.

Dragon King: Doctor Crab, please send the jellyfish here at once.

(*Crab hops over King and exits right; Jellyfish enters right.**)

Dragon King: Jelly, in your travels on the land, have you ever encountered the creature known as the monkey?

Jellyfish: Oh, yes. Very fast they are, monkeys. Very clever.

Dragon King: I command you to go right away, capture one, and bring it back. My darling daughter is deathly ill, and only the liver of a monkey can cure her.

Jellyfish: Oh, dear. Oh, yes. I'll go right away.* (*Starts to exit.*) They are very fast, monkeys. Very clever. And strong. I will have to trick one into coming back here with me.

Dragon King: And hurry! If you're not back here tomorrow with a monkey, I'll break all your bones!

(*Jellyfish exits right.**)

Scene 2

Monkey Island. Waves across entire stage; island set piece at right of stage.

(*Monkey walks back and forth on island, making little monkey noises. When the Monkey's back is to the water, the Jellyfish pops up and looks at him, then disappears when the Monkey turns back to face the water. Repeat three times. Then the Jellyfish walks up onto the island.**)

Jellyfish: What a beautiful island you have here. In all my travels, I have never seen such a lovely island.

Monkey: Why, thank you. But to tell you the truth, it does get a bit tiresome here. I wish I could travel over the water as you do.

Jellyfish: If you did, you would be able to see the most splendid sight—the palace of the Dragon King, which lies on the bottom of the sea.

Monkey: Oh, please! Tell me what it's like.

Jellyfish: Fish of every color of the rainbow swim among trees of coral. From those trees hang pearls and precious jewels. Each day, there are new sights to see and new and different creatures to talk to.

Monkey: How I wish I could go there. But I can't swim.

Jellyfish: It would be a pleasure and an honor for me to carry you there. I will introduce you to the Dragon King . . . *and* his daughter.

Monkey: Would you?

Jellyfish: Jump on my back, and hold on tight!

(*Monkey hops on the Jellyfish's back. They exit left.**)

Scene 3

The high seas. Waves across entire stage.

(*Jellyfish, with the Monkey on his back, floats on from right.*)

Monkey: Tell me, is everyone in the Dragon's kingdom happy?

Jellyfish: Yes, usually. But the Dragon Princess has been sick. They say she might even die.

Monkey: Can't anyone help her.

Jellyfish: The royal doctor—Doctor Crab—has said that she can only be cured by eating the liver of a monkey.

Monkey: (*Frightened.*) What! The liver of a monkey?

Jellyfish: Oops.

Monkey: (*Regaining his composure.*) Why didn't you tell me about this before we left the island? If I had known that the Dragon King's daughter needed my liver, I would have brought it with me.

Jellyfish: What? You don't have your liver with you?

Monkey: No, I left it hanging in a tree on the island.

Jellyfish: We must return there at once. (*Exits right.*)

Scene 4

Monkey Island, as in scene 2.

(*Jellyfish enters left, with the Monkey on his back.* Monkey jumps off the Jellyfish's back and exits stage right, then reappears, high in the tree.*)

Monkey: My liver is up here, you silly jellyfish. Come and get it if you can! Come and get it!

Jellyfish: (*Wails.*) Waaaaah! (*Exits left.**)

Scene 5

The high seas, as in scene 3. Stage is empty. Loud, clattering noises offstage.*

Dragon Princess
Dragon King

Narrator: When the jellyfish returned to the palace of the Dragon King without the monkey, the king commanded his guards to beat the poor creature. They broke all his bones, and sent him to live far away, on the surface of the ocean.

(*Second Jellyfish puppet enters left and floats slowly across stage.*)

Jellyfish: . . . so silly? Why was I so silly? Why was I so silly? (*Repeats these words until he exits right.*)

Narrator: He is still floating there today. No longer can he walk on land; he only floats at the mercy of the tides. As for the Dragon King's daughter, she confounded the doctor by getting well—*without* eating a monkey's liver.

(*Dragon Princess rises briefly above the ocean waves, then disappears.*)

Production Notes

Design an undersea kingdom of coral trees, seaweed, and treasure chests full of gold and jewels. An opening scene may be added to the play in which puppeteers manipulate a variety of undersea creatures which they have designed and made. Use some appropriate recorded music to accompany this scene.

For scenes 2 through 5, attach a thin strip of paper, cut in a wave pattern, across the stage. The island-scenery piece can be put up behind these waves during scenes 2 and 4.

Shadow Puppets

The Dragon King, Dragon Princess, and the monkey puppet should be attached to vertical rods. The crab and the jellyfish are attached to horizontal rods. A duplicate monkey puppet, attached to a horizontal rod, is needed in scene 4, when he appears in the tree. Make the second jellyfish puppet's tentacles from a clear plastic bag.

Rod Puppets

The monkey puppet must have a thin black rod, long enough to allow him to climb to the top of the tree. Make the second jellyfish's tentacles from translucent (but not transparent) plastic film such as a plastic shopping bag.

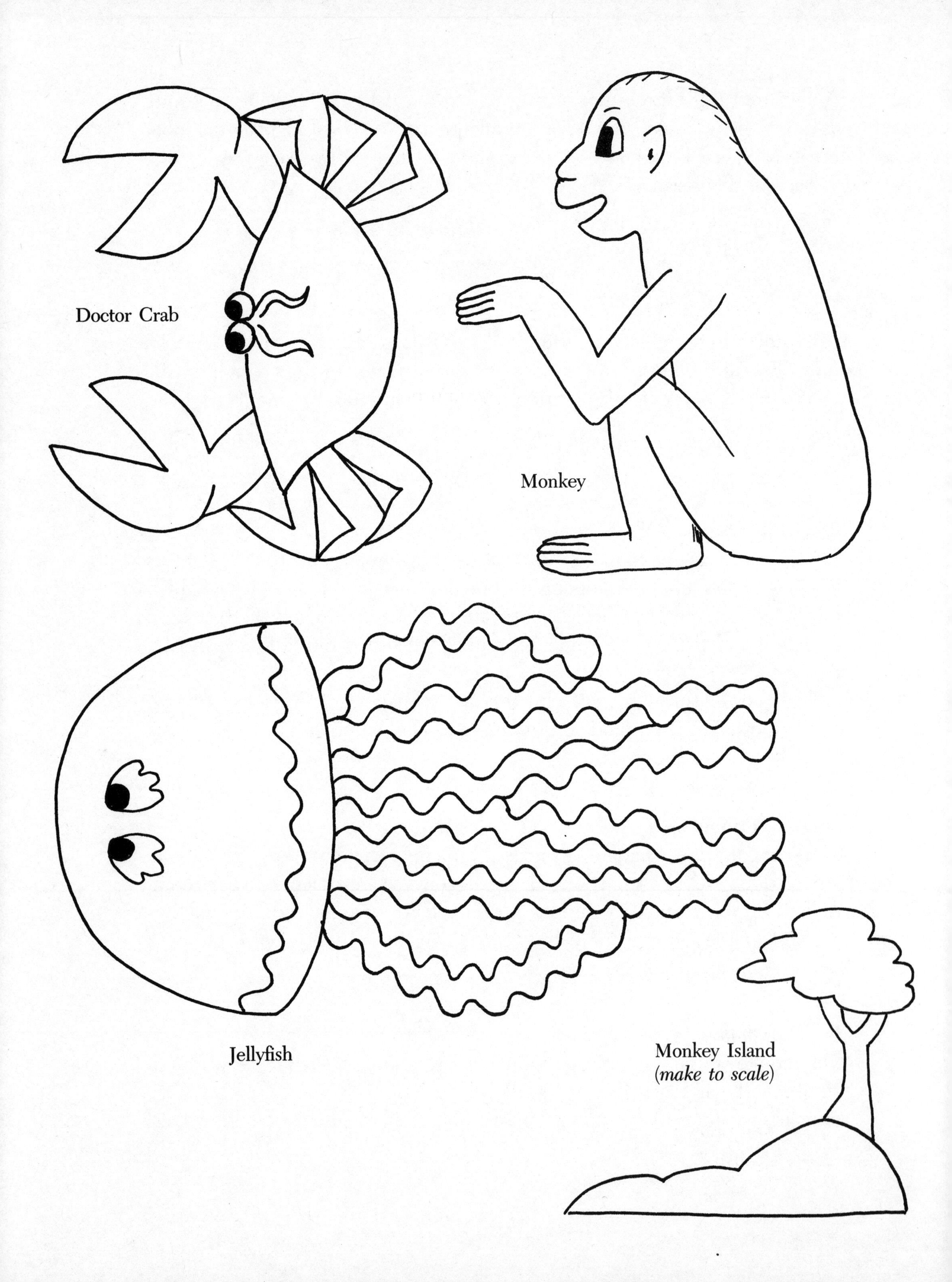
Doctor Crab
Monkey
Jellyfish
Monkey Island
(*make to scale*)

***Sound Effects**

Use a sound effect to emphasize that the jellyfish used to have stiff legs. Whenever he walks on land or on the bottom of the sea, accompany his walk with high, staccato notes on a keyboard or xylophone.

Follow-up Activities

Underwater Pantomimes

Undersea creatures make fascinating puppets, particularly in colored shadows or brightly-colored rod puppets operated on thin black rods against a black background.

Design your own undersea puppets, and perform a pantomime to symphonic music, to the Beatles' "Octopus's Garden" (on Raffi's *One Light, One Sun*), or Raffi's "Baby Beluga" (on the record and tape of the same title). Work to create small dramas within the pantomimes.

Sea Tales

Act out these deep sea stories and poems with puppets:

> "The Fish with the Deep Sea Smile," by Margaret Wise Brown. In *The Flannel Board Storytelling Book,* by Judy Sierra. Bronx: H. W. Wilson, 1987. Pages 146–151.
>
> Includes patterns suitable for a rod or colored-shadow puppet play, pantomimed to a reading of the poem.
>
> "The Little Mermaid," by Hans Christian Andersen (included in most Andersen collections).
>
> The story is a bit long, so divide it into scenes, assigning them to groups of three to five puppeteers. Watching the Disney movie of this story, then making puppets and improvising short scenes, is a good oral language exercise. Simplify scenery as much as possible, and focus on interaction and dialogue between major characters.
>
> *Swimmy,* by Leo Lionni. New York: Pantheon, 1963.
>
> Perform *Swimmy* in the round with rod puppets. Have the puppeteers make fish puppets and attach them to short rods (handles), then practice merging the school of little fish into the shape of a single big fish.

The Frog Prince

The tale of the *Frog Prince* is alive and well in modern folklore. "Kissing a frog" is a frequent subject of jokes, cartoons, and bumper stickers. In many versions of this old tale, however, the princess transforms the frog into a prince by throwing him roughly against the wall! A kiss suffices in this play.

Puppeteers: Three, plus musician.

Puppets:	Princess	King
	Frog	Prince

Props: Golden ball

Scenery pieces:	Tree	Table
	Well	Bed

Scene 1

The forest; tree and well at left.

Princess: (*Enters right, tossing her golden ball into the air and catching it, as she sings.*) La-la-la, la-la-la. La-la-la, la-la-la. La-la-la, la-la . . . oops! (*She drops the ball, which falls to the ground and bounces into the well*; she mimes bending over and trying to reach the ball. Finally, she stands beside the well and cries until the frog speaks.*)

Frog: (*Appears from well and watches Princess cry for a while before speaking*) Princess! Lovely princess! What is the matter? You are crying so much, even a stone would have pity on you.

Princess: Oh, it's you, you slimy water-splasher. I happen to be crying because my beautiful golden ball has fallen into the well.

Frog: I can bring your ball back to you. But what will you give me if I do?

Princess: Oh, I would give you anything you want—my dresses, my jewels! Just bring my golden ball back to me!

Frog: Dresses? Jewels? Feh! Those mean nothing to me. Only promise to let me be your playmate (*he moves closer and closer to Princess, as she backs away*), to let me sit by you at the table, and eat from your golden plate, and drink from your golden cup, and sleep in your bed, and then I will bring your golden ball to you.

Princess: Yes, yes, anything you want. Just hurry and get my golden ball.

Frog: (*Leaps into well. Comes up to the surface twice, sputtering and gasping for air. The third time, he has the golden ball.*) Here it is, princess.

(*Princess takes ball, turns, and exits right.*)

Frog: Stop! (*Hops.*) Wait! (*Hops.*) Princess! (*Hops.*) Wait for me! (*Exits right.*)

Scene 2

The Palace. The table is at center stage.

(*King and Princess enter from left and sit in chairs at either end of table, Princess at right, King at left.*)

Frog: (*Offstage. Knocks.**)

Sweet princess,
Open the door to me.
Don't forget the promise you made
Under the linden tree.

King: It sounds like someone is at the door.

Princess: I don't hear anything.

Frog: (*Offstage. Knocks.**)

Lovely princess,
Open the door to me.
Don't forget the promise you made
Under the linden tree.

King: Why don't you see who is at the door.

Princess: Eeeew. Please! No!

King: Is it a fierce giant come to carry you away?

Princess: No, father, it is only a slimy little frog. Today I dropped my golden ball into the well, and the frog got it out for me and . . . and . . .

King: Tell me the whole story.

Princess: . . .and I promised to be his playmate and to let him sit at the table with me and eat from my golden plate and drink from my golden cup and . . . eeeew . . .

King: What else?

Princess: . . . and then I promised to let him sleep in my little bed.

Frog: (*Offstage. Knocks.**)

Princess! Princess!
Open the door to me.
Don't forget the promise you made
Under the linden tree.

King: A princess must always keep her promise. Now, let the frog in.

(*Princess turns and goes to left, returns followed by the Frog. She sits in chair; Frog hops onto table, facing her.*)

Frog: Let me eat from your golden plate. (*Mimes eating.*) Now, let me drink from your golden cup. (*Mimes drinking.*) I'm tired now. Please take me to bed.

Princess: Father!

King: A promise is a promise.

Princess: Eeew. Very well. Eeew. (*Exits right, followed by the Frog.*)

Scene 3

The Princess's bedroom. Bed is left.

Princess: (*Enters right.*) Sleep there on the floor, frog.

Frog: No. I want to sleep on the bed, like you promised.

Princess: Eeew.

Frog: You promised.

Princess: (*Angrily.*) Oh, very well.

(*Frog hops onto pillow.*)

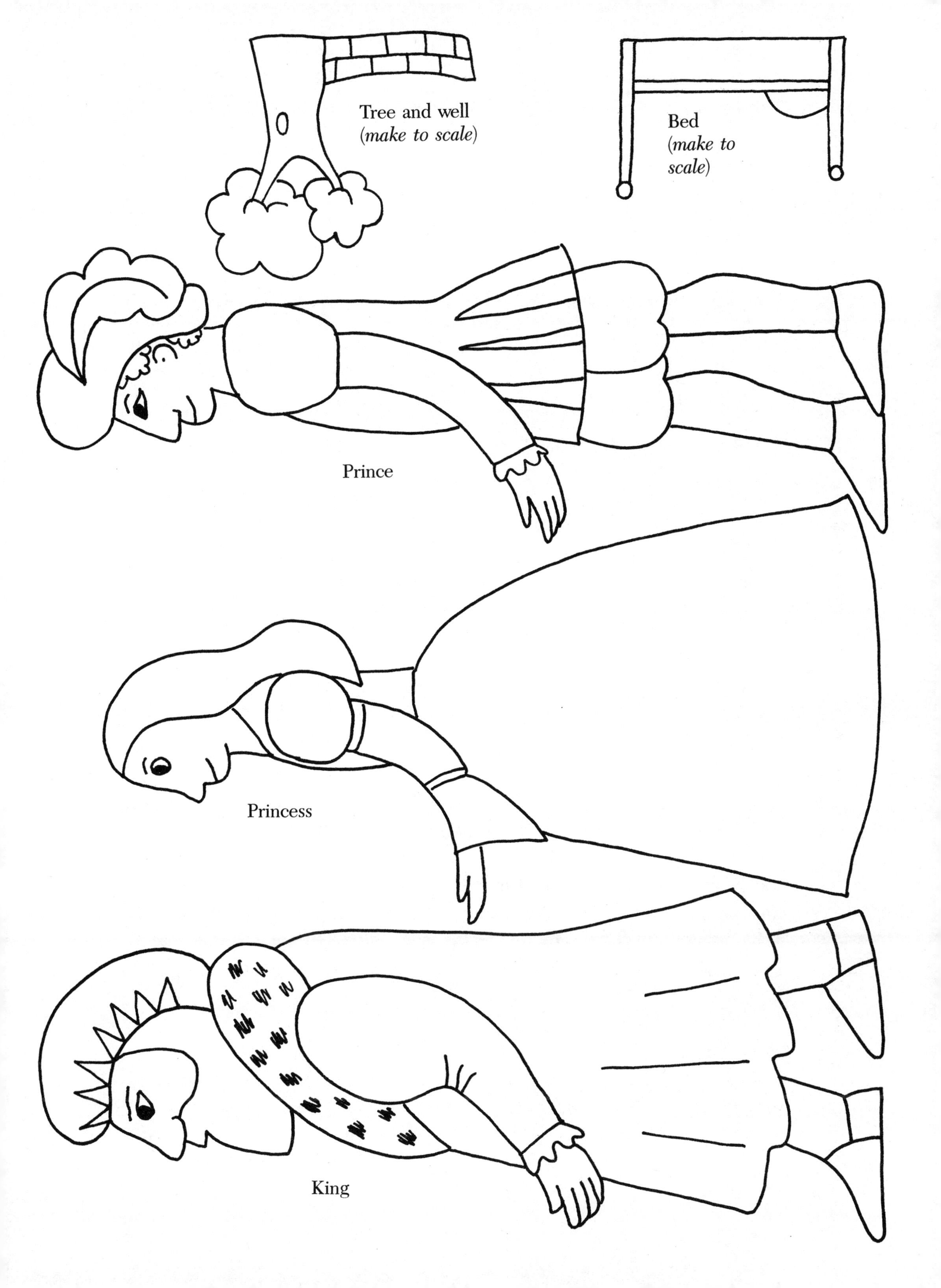
Tree and well
(make to scale)
Bed
(make to
scale)
Prince
Princess
King

Princess: No! Not on my nice pillow!

Frog: Yes. Now, kiss me goodnight.

Princess: Never.

Frog: I'll tell your father.

Princess: (*Makes noises to show how disgusted she is, but finally kisses the Frog, who transforms into Prince.**) What happened? Who are you?

Prince: I'm a prince, of course. Long ago, a wicked witch turned me into a frog, and only the kiss of a true princess could change me back into a prince again. Thank you, dear princess.

Princess: You're very welcome.

(*They kiss, then exit.*)

Production Notes

Make the bed by altering the table pattern slightly, as illustrated. The tree and the well may be combined into one scenery piece.

Shadow Puppets

The ball and the frog are attached to horizontal rods. Make two frog puppets, one facing left and one facing right; substitute one for the other when the frog needs to turn around. As a special effect—to be used when the frog jumps into the well, and when he comes up spewing water and gasping for breath—make a water-splash prop from thin strips of green and blue tissue paper taped to the end of a puppet rod.

Rod Puppets

The frog's rod should be long enough to allow him to hop and to sit on the table. A handful of confetti tossed up from below the stage, along with a sound effect, can accompany the quick replacement of the frog puppet by the prince.

*Sound Effects

Use a slide whistle to represent the ball falling into the well, a clavé for the frog knocking on the palace door. The ringing of a triangle or chimes signifies the frog's magical transformation into a prince.

Ball
Frog
Table and chairs

Follow-up Activities

Frog Wives and Frog Husbands

The following are other folktales about humans and enchanted frogs. Compare them to the Brothers Grimm's "The Frog Prince," the story upon which this puppet play is based.

"A Fortune from a Frog," in *Tales of a Korean Grandmother*, by Frances Carpenter. New York: Doubleday, 1947. Pages 97–105.

The Frog Princess, by Elizabeth Isele. New York: Crowell, 1984. (Russia)

"Noble Frog," in *Chinese Fairy Tales*, by Isabelle Chang. New York: Schocken, 1965. Pages 6–8.

Frog Videos

Two very entertaining and very different video productions have been made from the story of *The Frog Prince*. Both are available from libraries and rental outlets. Interestingly, the adapters of both versions have chosen to show—each in their own way—how and why the prince was turned into a frog in the first place. Student film critics can compare and rate the two videos. Perhaps they will want to write, design, and produce their own video version.

The Frog Prince. The Muppets. Directed by Jim Henson, 1971. 50 minutes. Distributor: Walt Disney Home Video.

The Tale of the Frog Prince. Faerie Tale Theater. Directed by Eric Idle, 1982. 55 minutes. Distributor: Playhouse Video.

The Brahman, the Tiger, and the Jackal

In this adaptation of a fable from India, a brahman lets his compassion for a caged tiger overwhelm his reason, and nearly winds up as the tiger's dinner. To escape this fate, he must find a single creature who believes that human beings are deserving of gratitude.

Puppeteers: Three to five.

Puppets: Tiger
Brahman
Jackal
(a talking) Tree
Water Buffalo

Scenery piece: Cage

Setting: A clearing in the forest. The cage is at far left, the tree at far right. There are no scene changes.

(*The Tiger is in the cage, facing right, growling fiercely as the play begins. The Brahman enters right, and the Tiger abruptly stops growling.*)

Tiger: Oh, kind and holy man! Please let me out of this cage.

Brahman: No, no, dear friend. You would surely eat me if I did.

Tiger: Me? Oh, never. Never. I would be grateful to you until the end of my days. Just open the door, please.

Brahman: No, I do not dare to let you out, for tigers are the enemies of humans.

Tiger: No! Not I! I promise to be your humble servant forever. (*Begins to blubber and cry.*) Please, dear sir. Please, dear kind sir. Save me from a terrible fate. (*Cries harder.*)

Brahman: Your words and your tears have touched my heart. (*Mimes opening door.*)

Tiger: (*Roars. Springs out of cage and pins the Brahman to the ground.*) Ha! How foolish and soft-hearted you humans are. And how ***hungry*** I am. Prepare to be my dinner!

Brahman: You should be ashamed of yourself, you ungrateful beast. I have just released you from prison; I have saved you from an early death. Is this how you show your gratitude?

Tiger: I have no reason to be grateful to a human. I must follow my nature as a beast . . . and eat you.

Brahman: Wait. Wait a moment. Why don't we make a bargain. We will ask the first three creatures who pass by here whether you should be grateful and set me free, or whether I deserve to be eaten.

Tiger: Of course they will all agree with me. I accept this bargain. In fact, if even ***one*** of the three creatures you ask agrees with you, I will set you free. (*Moves back.*)

(*Brahman stands up.*)

Tree: (*Moves its branch and comes alive.*) I'll tell you my opinion . . . All my life I have given shade and shelter to humans. In gratitude, they cut and tear off my branches. Humans are not grateful. Tigers have no reason to be grateful, either. (*Returns to original position.*)

Tiger: You see? Humans have few friends.

(*Water Buffalo enters right.*)

Brahman: Excuse me. I would like to ask your opinion in a very important matter.

Water Buffalo: Yes?

Brahman: This tiger was imprisoned in that cage. He begged me to set him free. He even promised to be my servant forever. Now, after I have let him out, he wants to eat me. Don't you think he should be grateful?

Water Buffalo: Grateful? To a human being? Ha! All my life, I have served humans, pulling a plow and turning a mill wheel. And what have I gotten in return? My master feeds me scarcely enough food for a bird, and what's more, he beats me with a stick. Humans are not grateful. Eat him, tiger. (*Exits right.*)

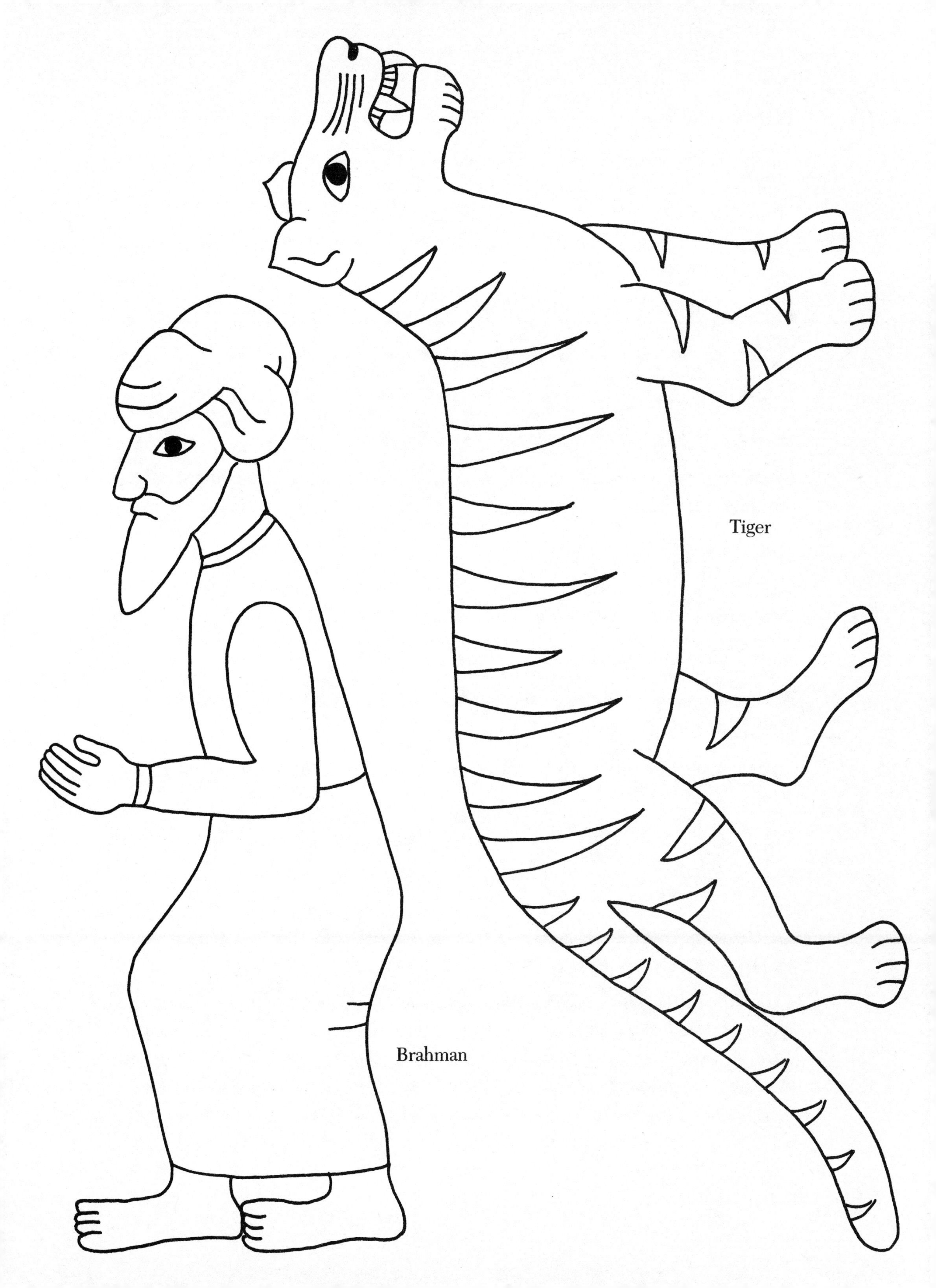
Tiger
Brahman

Brahman: Oh dear.

Tiger: You have only one more chance.

Jackal: (*Enters right.*) Excuse me, but what is all this commotion about?

Brahman: I released this tiger from his cage. Now, instead of being grateful, he wants to eat me. Do you think that is fair?

Jackal: Certainly it would not be fair for you to eat the tiger.

Brahman: No, no. The tiger wants to eat ***me.***

Jackal: Oh, I see. You were in the cage, and the tiger let you out . . .

Tiger: No, you brainless jackal! ***I*** was in the cage.

Jackal: Oh, my poor head. Let me see if I can make sense of this. The brahman was locked in the cage . . .

Tiger: ***I*** was in the cage!

Jackal: I still don't understand. Perhaps you could show me exactly how things were at the beginning.

Tiger: (*Goes into cage.*) I was in the cage, like this.

Brahman: (*Mimes closing the door.*) And the door was locked, like this. And things were much better that way.

Jackal: Just remember now, human, to show your gratitude to all living things. (*Exits right.*)

Brahman: (*Bows toward Jackal.*) Thank you. I will. (*Exits left.*)

Tiger: (*Roars.*)

Production Notes

There must be room between the tiger's cage and the tree for the tiger, the brahman, and the jackal to stand side by side, so plan the size of your puppets and sets accordingly. The tree is attached firmly to the stage and made with a moving branch. A rod is attached to the branch at the point marked on the pattern; this rod is taped into place on the back of the tree trunk. When lowered, the branch reveals a face on the tree. When the tree

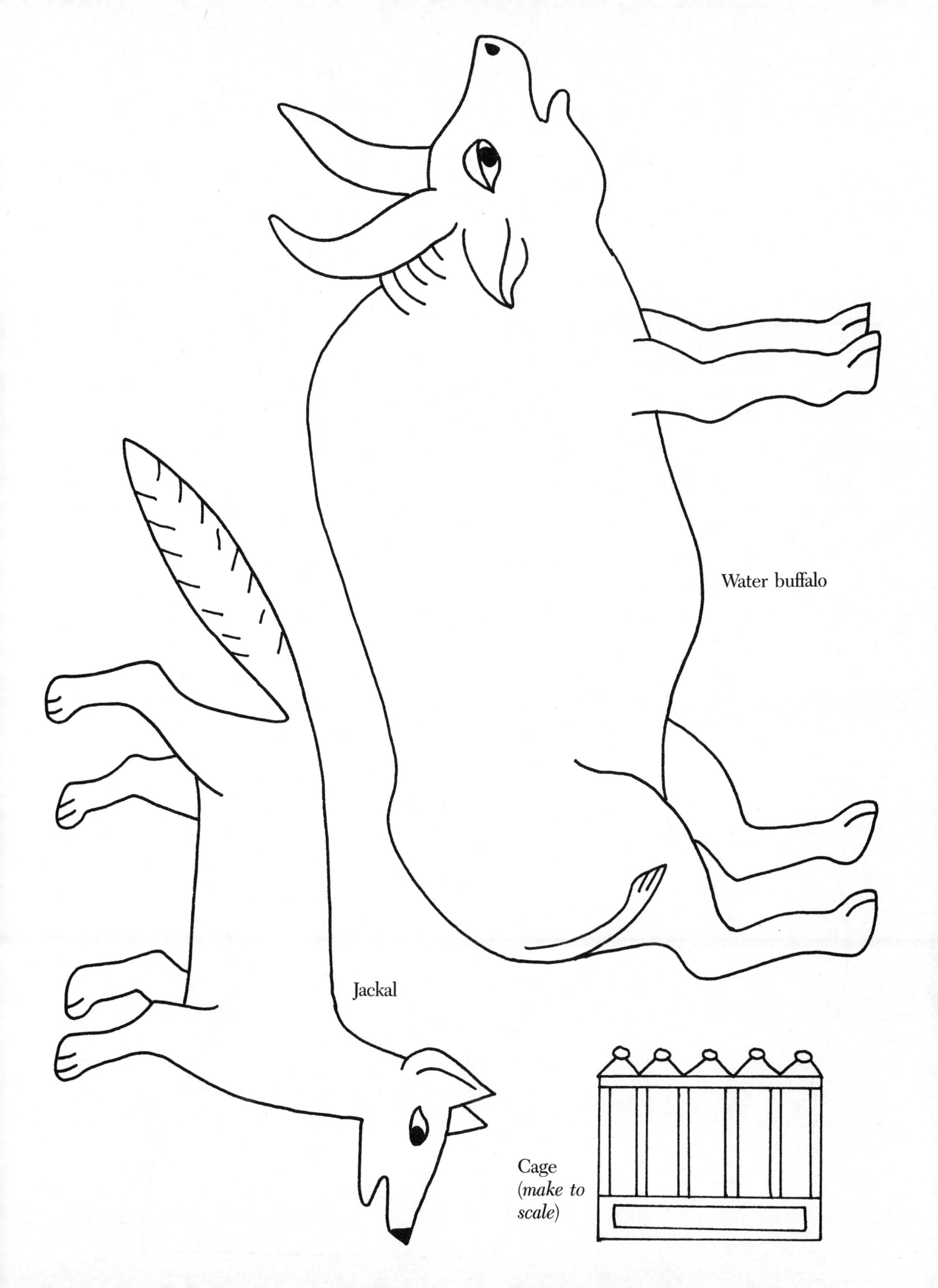
Water buffalo
Jackal
Cage
(*make to
scale*)

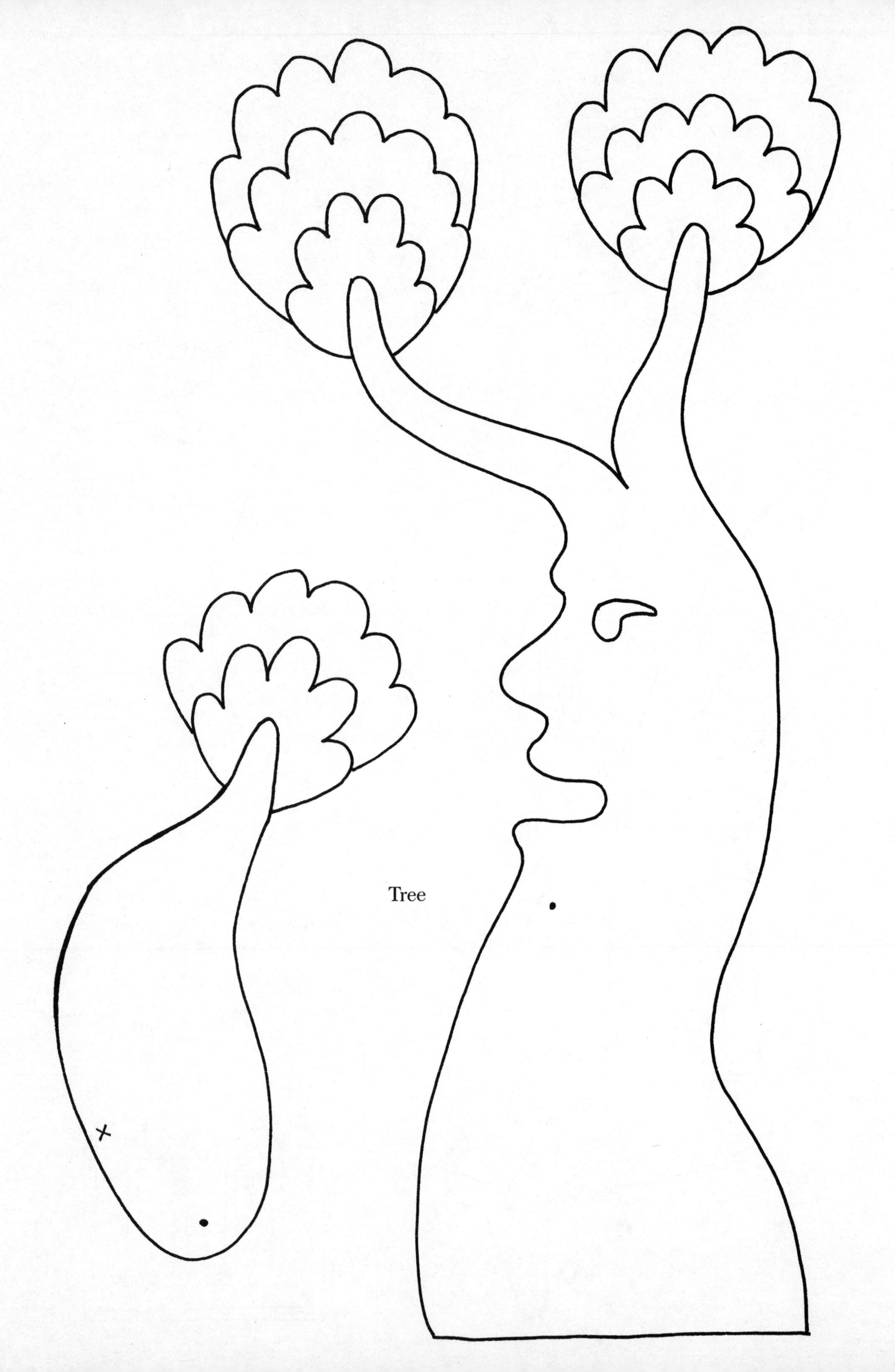
Tree

has completed its speaking role in the play, move the branch back into its original position, covering the face, and secure it again with tape.

Shadow Puppets

The cage may be made of clear acetate, and the bars colored with black marker. This will eliminate having to cut between the bars, and will also prevent the tiger puppet catching on them. All puppets are attached to vertical rods.

Follow-up Activities

Captives Recaptured

The theme of tricking a powerful creature back into captivity is found in the folktales of many cultures. Compare the following tales to *The Brahman, the Tiger, and the Jackal.*

"Bagged Wolf," in *Sweet and Sour,* by Carol Kendall and Yao-Wen Li. New York: Seabury, 1978. Pages 49–59. (China)

"The Fisherman and the Brass Bottle," in *Tales from the Arabian Nights,* by James Riordan. Skokie, Ill.: Rand McNally, 1985. Pages 26–37.

"The Snail and the Leopard," in *Fourteen Hundred Cowries,* by Aboyomi Fuja. New York: Lothrop, Lee & Shepard, 1971. Pages 69–72.

Fables from India

Act out other fables from India. The *Jataka Tales,* in the collection edited by Nancy deRoin (Houghton Mifflin, 1975), are short animal tales in verse form which conclude with morals and provide perfect short plays to be dramatized in the narration-improvisation method.

Brer Rabbit and the Wonderful Tar-Baby

The tar-baby story is the best known of the tales in Joel Chandler Harris's *Uncle Remus* collections, which are based on the animal trickster lore of African-Americans. Brer Rabbit can always upset the best plans of his enemy, Brer Fox. In the tar-baby story, Brer Rabbit uses his quick wits, and some mighty convincing acting, to escape from a sticky situation.

Puppeteers: Three, plus musician.

Puppets: Brer Fox
Brer Rabbit

Props: Bucket
Tar-baby

Scenery pieces: Briar patch
Bush

Setting: A road. Briar patch at far left, bush at right with enough space to its right for Brer Fox to stand. No scene changes.

Brer Fox: (*Enters left, carrying bucket. Walks to center and sets it down. Mimes mixing and molding something in the bucket as he talks.*) Gonna catch me a bunny rabbit. Mix up some tar and turpentine. Gonna make a fine contraption to catch a bunny named Brer Rabbit. Gonna make me a tar-baby. (*Takes tar-baby from the bucket and sets it center stage.*) Now, tar-baby, you just set by the road here and catch a rabbit for old Brer Fox!

(*Brer Fox takes bucket and hides behind the bush at right of stage. During Brer Rabbit's encounter with the tar-baby, Brer Fox peeks over the bush and reacts to what he sees.*)

Brer Rabbit: (*Offstage.*) Lippety-clippety, oh lippety-clippety. (*Enters left with a hop over the briar patch, and stops beside the tar-baby.*) Well! Good mornin'! (*Pause.*) Nice weather this mornin'. (*Pause.*) How are you feelin' this mornin'? (*Goes to right of tar-baby.*) Can't you hear me? 'Cause if you can't, I CAN HOLLER LOUDER. (*Pause.*) You know what, you are stuck-up—that's what you are. (*Pause.*) And I'm gonna cure you of your stuck-upness with a slap in the face. Take that! (*Slaps tar-baby.**) Hey! Let go of my hand, or else I'll slap you with my other hand. (*Slaps tar-baby with the other hand.**)

(*At this point, one puppeteer holds both Brer Rabbit and the tar-baby as if they are glued together, face to face, and moves them back and forth with quick, jerky motions.*)

Brer Rabbit: Let go! Watch out! (*Lifts tar-baby to mouth.*) I'm gonna bite you! Unh! (*Puppeteer says next sentence with lips closed.*) Let go of me you stuck-up somebody!

(*Brer Rabbit falls down on top of tar-baby and whines helplessly from time to time as Brer Fox gloats.*)

Brer Fox: (*Comes from behind bush, chuckling. Moves around as he talks.*) Well, what do we have here? It seems to be Brer Rabbit himself! I expect I got you for real this time. You're always running around sassin' after me, thinkin' you're the boss of the whole gang. Always messin' where you got no business. Now, who asked you to strike up an acquaintance with this little tar-baby? You just went and jammed yourself up against this tar-baby with no invitation. (*Lifts Brer Rabbit off tar-baby, which then disappears. Brer Fox keeps hold on Brer Rabbit.*) Now, Brer Rabbit, I'm gonna fire up a brush-pile, and I'm gonna ***barbecue*** you.

Brer Rabbit: I don't care.

Brer Fox: What did you say?

Brer Rabbit: I don't care what you do with me, Brer Fox, only don't fling me into that briar patch.

Brer Fox: It's a lot of trouble to kindle a fire. I expect I ought to just ***hang*** you, Brer Rabbit.

Brer Rabbit: Hang me as high as you please, Brer Fox, just don't fling me into that briar patch.

Brer Fox: I don't have any rope, so I expect I'll have to ***drown*** you, Brer Rabbit.

Brer Rabbit: Drown me deep as you please, Brer Fox, only don't fling me in that briar patch!

Brer Fox: There isn't any water nearby, so I expect I'll just have to ***fling*** you in that there ***briar patch,*** Brer Rabbit.

Brer Rabbit: Noooooo!

(*Brer Fox picks up Brer Rabbit and throws him into the briar patch.* Long pause. Brer Fox walks closer to briar patch.*)

Brer Rabbit: (*His head pops up and down, appearing from behind briar patch.*) A lippety-clippety! I was born and raised in the briar patch, and isn't it a lovely place to be! Yessir, the old briar patch is the place for me.

Brer Fox: (*Jumps up and down.*) Grrrrrrr! I'll get that rabbit yet. (*Exiting left.*) I will, I will, I will, I will . . .

Production Notes

The tar-baby is manipulated and held by a puppeteer until the point in the script where the Brer Rabbit puppeteer takes control of it.

Shadow Puppets

Attach Brer Rabbit and Brer Fox to vertical rods. The rods will show a bit when the puppets hop and jump. Attach the tar-baby to a vertical rod; cut out its facial features if you make it from black paper.

Rod Puppets

Make the tar-baby look sticky by covering the puppet with dark plastic from a garbage bag.

*Sound Effects

Use a long slide whistle when Brer Rabbit enters, and again when Brer Fox tosses him into the briar patch; give a handclap or drumbeat when Brer Rabbit slaps the tar-baby.

Follow-up Activities

Sticky Traps

Using a figure covered with a sticky substance to trap someone is a widely-used plot device, especially in African and African-American folktales. Com-

Bush
(*make to scale*)
Briar patch
(*make to scale*)
Brer Fox
Brer Rabbit
Tar-baby
Bucket

pare the following to *Brer Rabbit and the Wonderful Tar-Baby.*

Beeswax Catches a Thief, by Ann Kirn. New York: W. W. Norton, 1968. (Zaire)

A Story, A Story, by Gail E. Haley. New York: Atheneum, 1970. (Ghana).

"The Straw Ox," in *Favorite Fairy Tales from Russia,* by Virginia Haviland. Boston: Little, Brown, 1961. Pages 53–65. (Russia)

Truly Sticky Traps

Nature has devised some highly effective sticky traps of her own. Use the information and illustrations in these books to help you create science puppet plays.

Sticky plants that trap animals:

Carnivorous Plants, by Cynthia Overbeck. Minneapolis: Lerner, 1982.

Plants That Eat Insects, by Anabel Dean. Minneapolis: Lerner, 1977.

The La Brea Tar Pits:

The La Brea Story, by Gretchen Sibley. Los Angeles: Ward Ritchie, 1968.

Trapped in Tar: Fossils from the Ice Age, by Caroline Arnold.
New York: Clarion, 1987.

Who Is Strongest?

This folktale from Liberia tells how a contest of strength was held to choose a new king of the animals, and how one of the weaker animals won the competition through cunning.

Puppeteers: Five, plus narrator and musician.

Puppets:	Leopard	Elephant
	Antelope	Bat
	Monkey	Bat (rolled into a ball)

Prop: Stone

Setting: A clearing in the forest; trees at sides of stage. There are no scene changes.

(*Leopard enters left and walks very slowly to center stage as Narrator speaks.*)

Narrator: The leopard, king of the forest, was growing old and weak.

(*Leopard moans feebly.*)

Narrator: He decided that the animals needed a new king: a younger, stronger king.

Leopard: I just don't know which animal I should choose to be the new king. Maybe I should have a contest of some kind and let the winner be my successor.

(*Antelope enters left; Monkey enters right, followed by the Elephant.*)

Leopard: My loyal subjects, I have grown too old to be a good king to you any longer.

Antelope, Monkey, and Elephant: (*Sadly.*) Oh!

Leopard: The time has come for me to pass the crown and the kingdom along to one of you.

Antelope, Monkey, and Elephant: (*Happily.*) Aaaaah!

Leopard: The new king must be young and strong. I have decided to hold a competition. The winner will be our new king.

Antelope: What sort of competition will it be?

Leopard: A contest of skill and strength. We will meet here tomorrow. Whoever can throw a stone the farthest shall be king.

Elephant: You will probably win, monkey. You're the only animal who has hands for throwing.

Monkey: (*Turns.*) Use your trunk to throw the stone. You might win. (*Monkey and Elephant exit right.*)

Leopard: The contest will begin tomorrow at sunrise. (*Exits right.*)

Antelope: I would make a good king, but I don't have a chance to win the contest . . .

(*Bat flies overhead.*)

Antelope: . . . unless, somehow, brains are more important than muscles.

(*Bat flies overhead again.*)

Antelope: (*Yells.*) Bat! Baaaaaaaaat!

(*Bat flutters above Antelope.*)

Antelope: Tell me, do you think I would make a good king?

Bat: I think you would be a better king than any of the other animals. You are wise and kind and generous.

Antelope: Then will you agree to be my stone tomorrow morning?

Bat: Your stone? (*Pauses.*) Oh, I understand. Yes. I will come before sunrise, and roll up in a ball on the ground. You'll be able to recognize me easily. I will be the only stone wearing a fur coat! (*Flies off.*)

Antelope: See you there! (*Exits left.*)

Leopard: (*Enters left and walks very slowly to center.*) Who will be first to compete in the stone-throwing contest?

Monkey: (*Enters right, hopping and talking very excitedly.*) I'll be first! Let me be first! I'll be first! I have hands! I'm sure to win! I'll be first! Let me be first! (*Picks up stone, leans far back, and throws. The stone goes straight up and falls straight down, onto the Monkey's head.**) Ouch! (*Turns.*) Ow! Ow! Ow! Ow! Ow! (*Exits right, still crying.*)

Leopard: (*Disgusted.*) Next!

Elephant: (*Enters right.*) I am going to throw the stone with my trunk—high, high, high! (*Picks up stone with trunk and tosses it. Stone rises and falls on the Leopard's head.**)

Leopard: Ouch! Ow! Oh, go away, go away. Such a clumsy animal will never be king.

(*Elephant turns and exits right.*)

Leopard: Who will be next to throw?

Antelope: (*Enters right. Mimes looking on ground for the Bat.*) I will kick the stone up from the ground with my hoof.

Leopard: Very well. (*Ducks.*)

(*Antelope turns his back on Leopard and kicks with his hind legs. Use the second Bat puppet—it flies up from ground and exits left, still flying high.**)

Leopard: (*Turns left.*) That stone flies as if it has wings!

Elephant: (*Enters right, behind Antelope.*) It's still going!

Leopard: I can't see it anymore. (*Turns right.*) Congratulations, Antelope . . . I mean, Your ***Majesty.*** You are now king of the animals.

Elephant: I never knew you were that strong.

Antelope: Sometimes brains are more important than muscles.

(*Monkey enters left.*)

Monkey: Long live the new king!

Monkey, Elephant, and Leopard: Long live the new king!

Bat: (*Flies overhead.*) Long live the new king!

Production Notes

Leopard should walk and talk very slowly. When he enters or exits, have him move a few inches, pause and sigh, move a few more inches, pause and sigh, etc. This will contrast with the liveliness of the other animals.

Shadow Puppets

The bat puppets and the stone are attached to horizontal rods; all other puppets are on vertical rods.

Rod Puppets

Attach both bat puppets and the stone to rods that are long enough to make their flight convincingly high.

***Sound Effects**

Use a slide whistle for the flight of the stone. Give very deliberate up and down slides for the first two throws. Use a clavé to indicate the stone hitting the monkey, then the leopard, on the head. The flight of the bat can be represented as a slide up, then a fast trill, on the slide whistle.

Follow-up Activities

Contests Won by Trickery

Many folktales tell of small, weak animals who outsmart larger, stronger opponents. Try writing puppet plays based on the following stories of physical contests won by mental power. To represent races, see the description of *traveling* in the Glossary.

The Extraordinary Tug-of-War, by Letta Schatz. Illus. by John Burningham. Chicago: Follett, 1968. (Nigeria)

The Great Race of the Birds and the Animals, by Paul Goble. New York: Bradbury, 1985. (Native American: Plains tribes)

The Hare and the Tortoise, a fable by Aesop. Illus. by Paul Galdone. New York: Whittlesey House, 1962. (Greece)

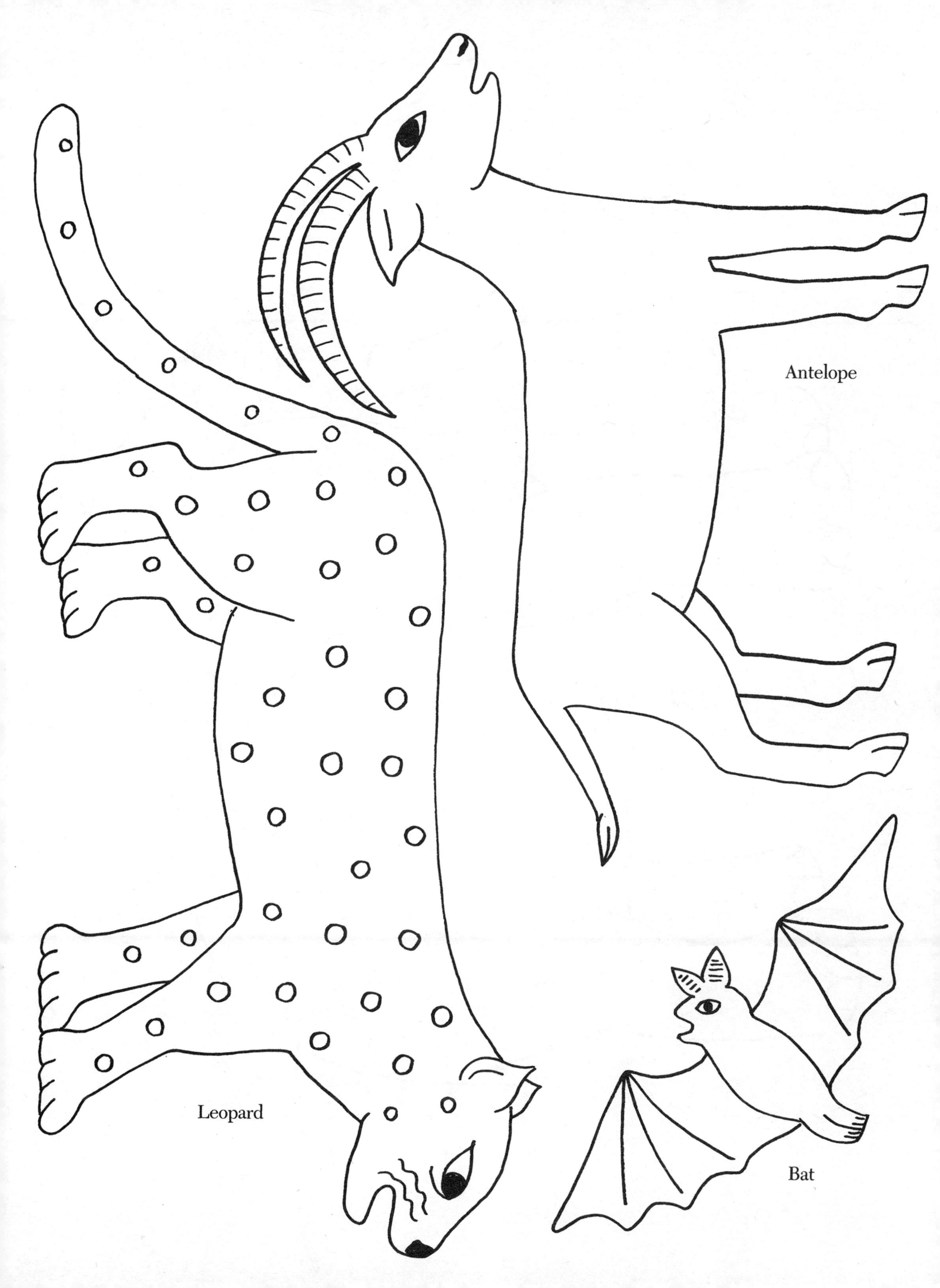
Antelope
Leopard
Bat

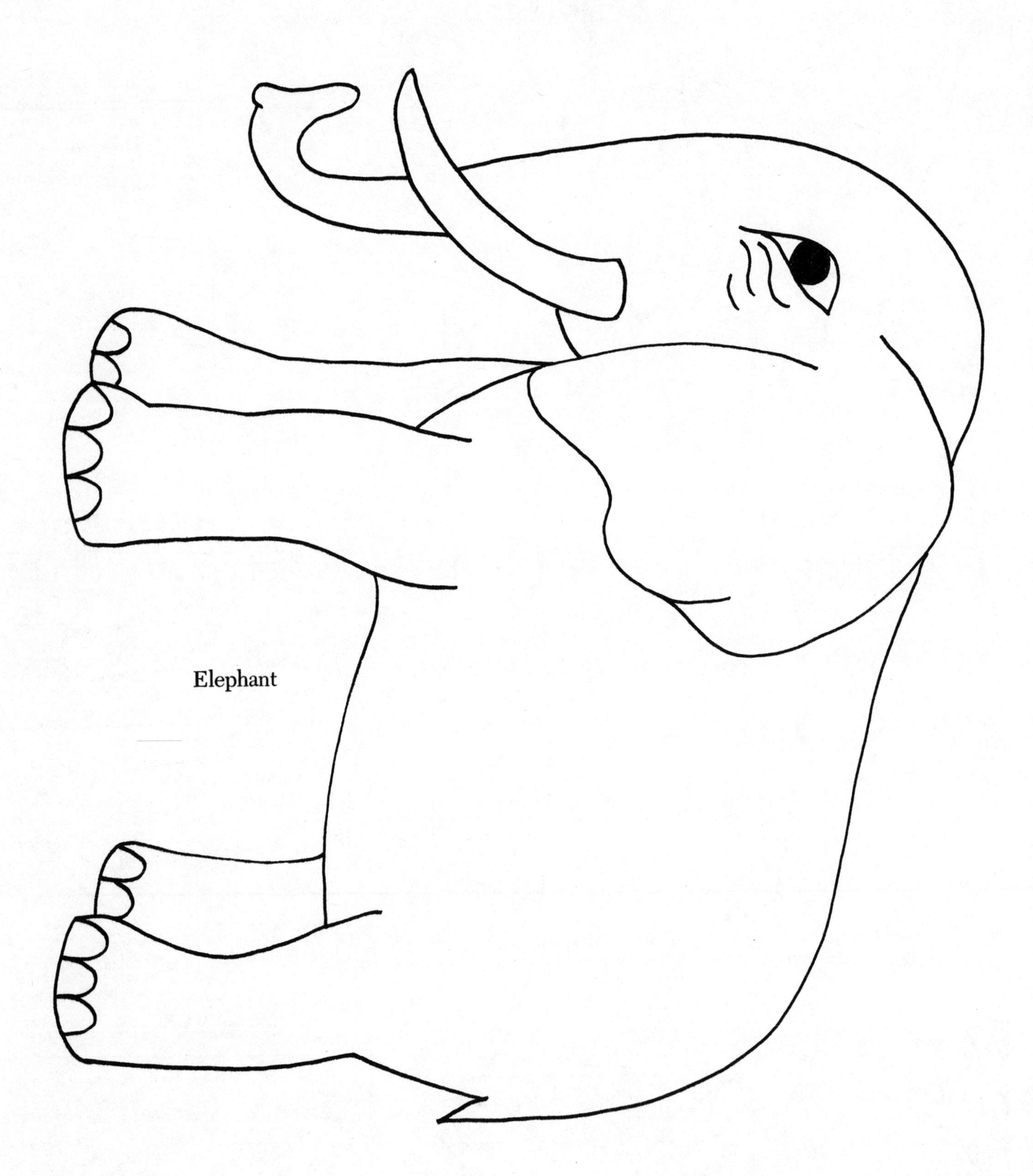

Elephant

Brains over Brawn

Announce your own contest: who can throw a piece of paper the farthest. Don't tell anyone, but one such contest was won, not by a sleek paper airplane, but by a tightly-wadded paper ball! Airplanes are more fun, and the contest takes on added excitement if you can launch them from a balcony or other high place.

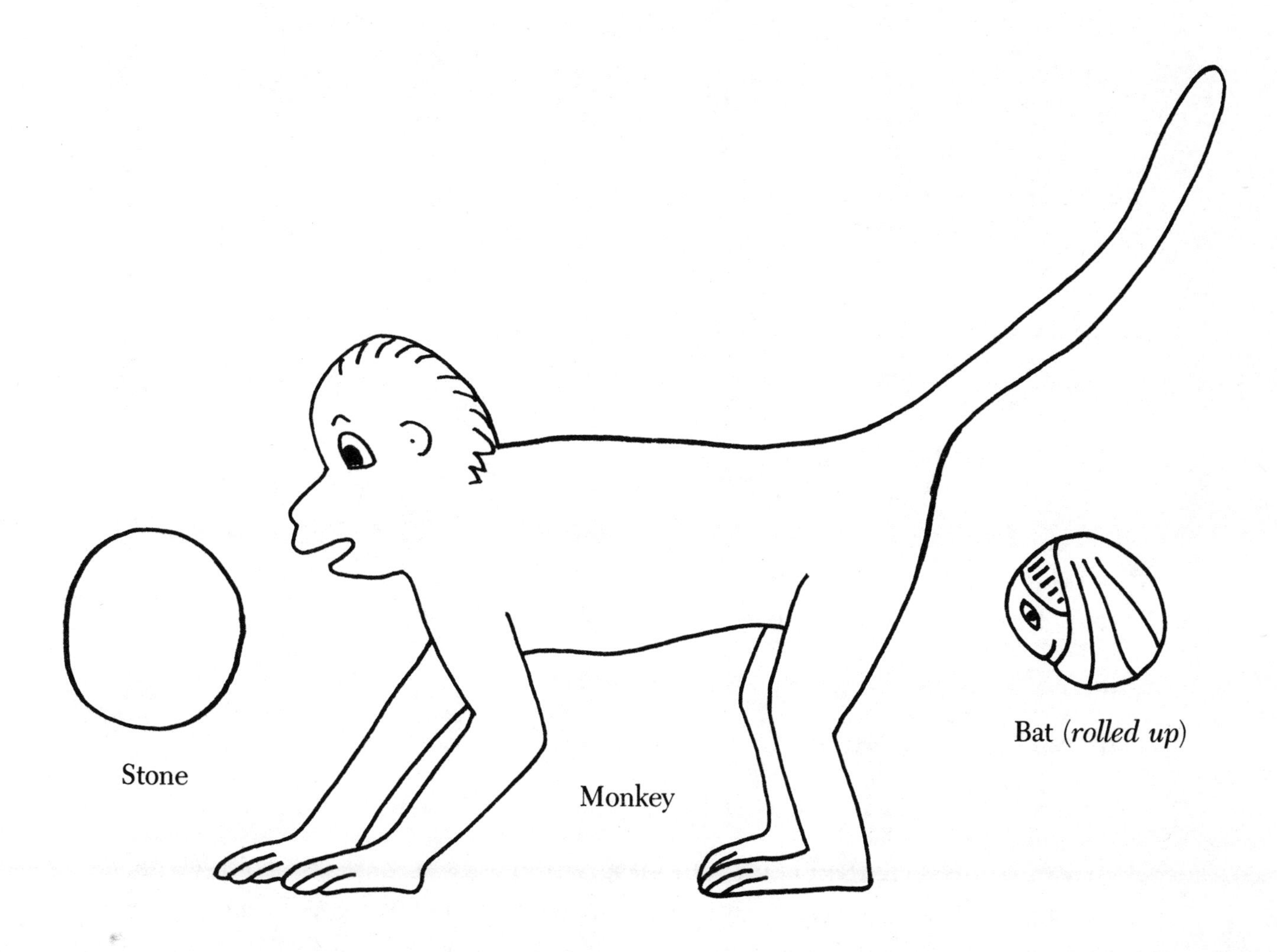

How the Sun and Moon Came to Live in the Sky

People from many cultures tell stories in which the sun and moon behave like human beings. In this play, adapted from a myth of the Maidu Indians of California, the sun and moon are sister and brother and would rather stay inside their house of stone than travel the heavens. The house is built in native Northern-California style—its door is the smoke-hole in the roof.

Puppeteers: Four to seven, plus narrator and musicians.

Puppets: Sun, Moon, Coyote, Jackrabbit, Grizzly Bear, Gopher, Earthworm

Scenery piece: Sun and moon's house

Setting: The early world. House at left, with the Sun and Moon visible inside. No scene changes.

Narrator: Long ago, in the days when animals lived on the Earth as people do today, the sun and moon went inside their house. They refused to travel across the sky. The animals were cold. The world was in darkness.

Sun: I don't want to go outside, do you?

Moon: No, I don't want to go outside.

Sun and Moon: Let's just stay right here in our house.

Coyote: (*Enters right.*) I can't stand it anymore. It's so dark. So cold. (*Walks to house.*) I'll try politely asking them to come out. (*In a loud voice.*) Sun! Moon! Would you mind coming out and giving us some light? (*Waits for an answer. Silence.*) Will you ***please*** come out!

Sun and Moon: (*Loudly.*) No.

Coyote: (*Bangs on house* and yells.*) Come out here right now, or else!

Sun and Moon: (*Softly.*) No.

Coyote: (*Turns, speaking as he exits.*) Jackrabbit, see if you can make them come out.

Jackrabbit: (*Enters left.*) I'll just jump up the side of their house and go down the smoke-hole. (*Jumps up side of house, loses balance.*) Uh oh! (*Slides down to ground.**) Yeeeee-owwwwww! (*Exits left.*)

Grizzly Bear: (*Enters left.*) Come out! Come out! Come out, sun! Come out, moon! (*Bangs loudly on house.**) I know you're in there. I'm going to push your house down.

Sun: I don't think so.

Moon: It's made of stone.

Grizzly Bear: (*Pushes against house and groans; repeat three times.*) Oh, I give up! (*Exits right, growling angrily.*)

(*Earthworm enters right, followed by Gopher.*)

Gopher: We'll start our tunnel right here, earthworm. I'll dig down, then across, and up into the sun and moon's house.

Earthworm: (*Turns to face Gopher.*) Sure thing, gopher. Do you have your secret weapon?

Gopher: Here it is. (*Holds up bag.*) My bag of fleas. (*Giggles.*) When we get inside, I'll let my fleas loose on them.

Earthworm: I don't think you need a ***bag*** of fleas, gopher. There are hundreds hopping around on your back already!

Gopher: Shut up and dig, earthworm.

(*They mime digging and disappear into the ground.**)

Earthworm: (*Offstage, softly.*) Gopher! Let the fleas out. Now.

Gopher: (*Offstage, softly.*) Here they come.

(*Long pause,* then the Sun and Moon begin to jiggle.*)

Sun: Ouch!

Moon: Ye-ouch!

Sun: Something is biting me!

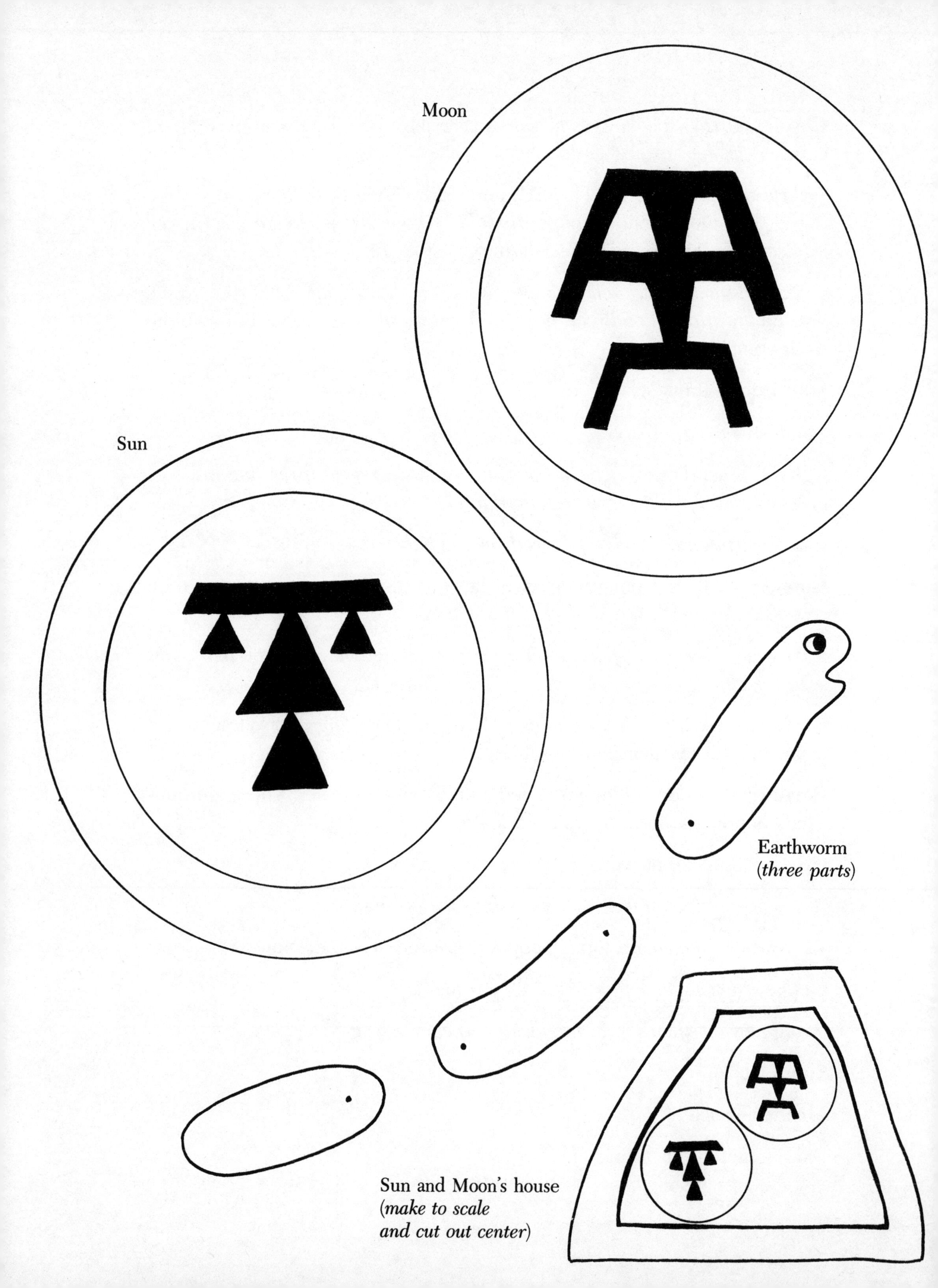
Moon
Sun
Earthworm
(*three parts*)
Sun and Moon's house
(*make to scale
and cut out center*)

Moon: Something is biting me, too!

Sun and Moon: Oh, no! Fleas!

Sun: Let's get out of here right now!

(*The Sun and Moon exit their house through smoke-hole, and come to a stop in the sky, above center stage. Gopher and Earthworm appear inside the Sun and Moon's house and giggle.*)

Sun: What are we going to do, brother moon. Our house is full of fleas now.

Moon: We may as well travel across the sky and light the world.

Sun: You travel by night, brother moon, and I will travel by day.

(*The Sun and the Moon exit right slowly, in an arc, as if they were setting.*)

Narrator: So it has been ever since. The sun travels by day.

(*Sun makes a slow arc across the sky, left to right.**)

Narrator: And the moon travels by night.

(*Moon makes a slow arc across the sky, left to right.**)

Production Notes

The house of the sun and moon is cut away to show them inside. The sun and moon are haughty and arrogant; give them snooty voices. When sun or moon speaks, the puppet moves slightly, so that the audience will know which one is speaking. Gopher and earthworm have high-pitched voices and laughs.

Shadow Puppets

Cover the cut-out section of the sun and moon's house with light blue tissue paper. Both sun and moon should be attached to long horizontal rods. The other puppets should be attached to vertical rods, except the earthworm, who is made in three parts with horizontal rods attached to its front and back sections.

If your shadow screen light is on a dimmer, try playing the show at slightly less than full illumination; turn the light up to full when the sun and moon come out of their house. Adjust it up and down as each travels across the sky.

Rod Puppets

The sun and moon's house should be made of strong cardboard. If you are using a large rod-puppet stage, cut the house from a corrugated cardboard box. The sun and moon, and the jackrabbit, will need long rods. Animal puppets have moving arms, and the earthworm is made in three parts, with a rod attached to each of the two end segments.

***Sound Effects and Music**

A clavé provides the sound of the animals knocking on the sun and moon's house. Light drumbeats simulate the noise of the jackrabbit hopping up the side of the house; a hard drumbeat marks his fall to the ground. A guiro makes the noise of gopher and earthworm tunneling through the ground. The sound of the fleas jumping around inside the sun and moon's house can be represented by some high "pings" on an electronic keyboard, or high notes on a xylophone. A slow, steady drumming accompanies the sun and moon's journeys across the sky at the end of the performance.

These are the minimum musical sound effects required; others will greatly enliven the show—for instance, drum and flute music as an overture and to mark transitions after one character exits and another is about to enter.

Follow-up Activities

Native American Tales of Sun and Moon

Use the narration-improvisation technique to act out scenes from these Native American sky tales:

> *Arrow to the Sun,* by Gerald McDermott.
> New York: Viking, 1974. (Pueblo)
>
> *The Angry Moon,* by William Sleator. Illus. by Blair Lent.
> Boston: Little Brown, 1970. (Northwest Coast)
>
> The illustrations in both of these picture books make beautiful rod or colored shadow puppets.

Puppet Storyboard

Transform this puppet play into a giant cartoon storyboard. Use white paper to cover a bulletin board or large wall area. Remove the rods from the puppets. Attach the house to the bulletin board, then arrange the puppets

Coyote
Jackrabbit

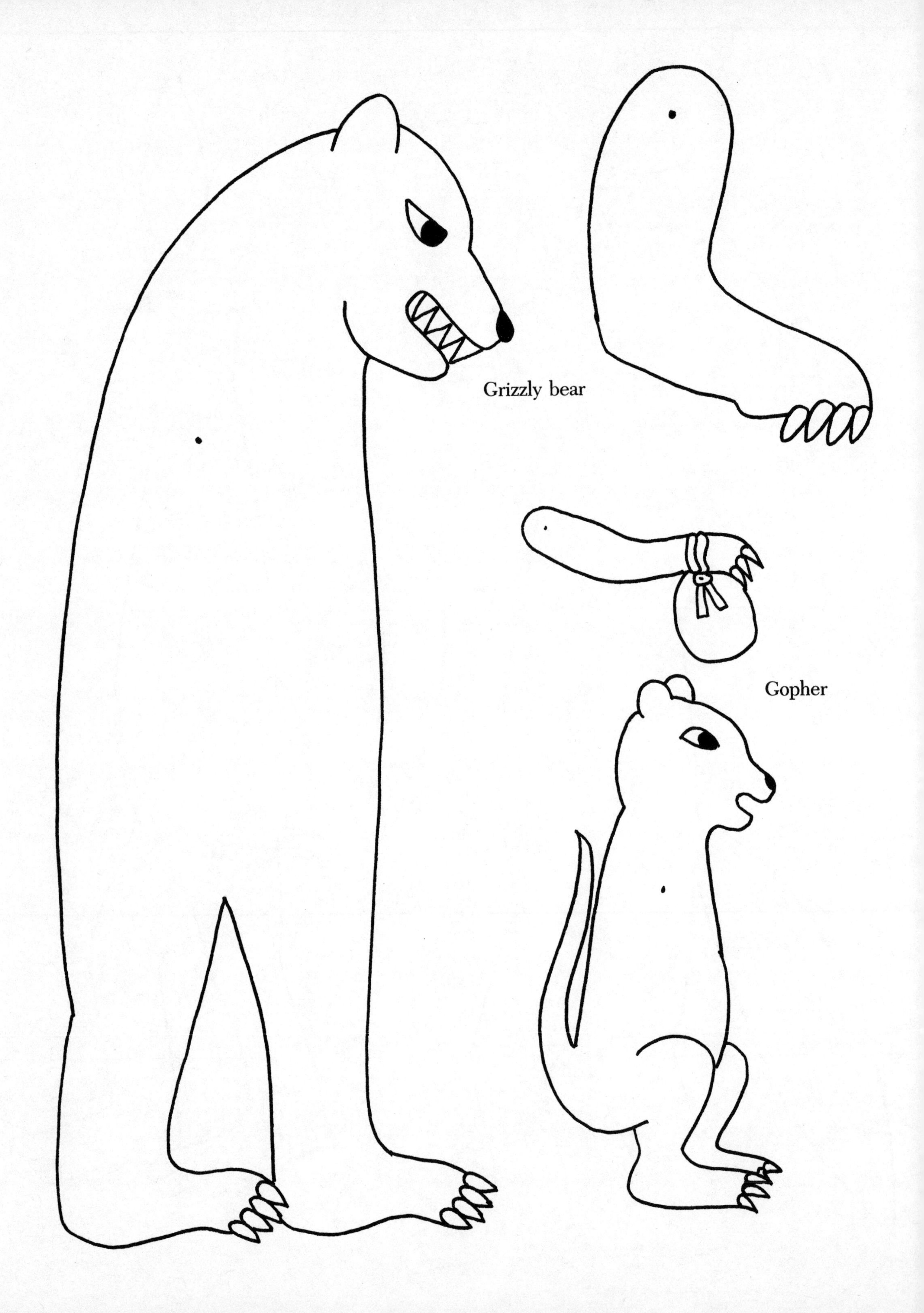
Grizzly bear
Gopher

in groups: sun and moon in the sky; gopher and earthworm inside the house; coyote, bear, and rabbit outside the house. Imagine what each puppet might be saying or thinking at this point in the story; make balloons above their heads, as in a comic strip, and write their words or thoughts inside.

All Stories Belong to Anansi

Stories about tricky Anansi, the spider, are part of the oral tradition of West Africa, the Caribbean islands, and the United States. Among the Ashanti people of West Africa, *anansesem* is the name for a certain type of story that was traditionally told to children as part of their education. This play is adapted from a tale which explains how these stories came to be called *anansesem*—Anansi stories.

Puppeteers: Four to seven, plus narrator and musicians.

Puppets:
- Anansi
- Anansi with one eye closed
- Three Spider children
- Nyame, the sky god
- Snake
- Leopard

Props:
- Bamboo pole
- Gourd

Scenery piece: Baobab tree with hornets' nest

Scenery is optional in all scenes except scene 4.

Scene 1

Anansi's house.

Narrator: Once upon a time, when animals could talk, Nyame, the sky god, owned all the stories. That was because he was so mighty, so powerful. All the other creatures were afraid of him. But then Anansi the spider, although he was small and weak, got all the stories for himself. He made Nyame give them to him. This is how it happened.

Anansi: (*Enters left, followed by his children, Spiders 1, 2 and 3*) Time for your nap, spider babies.

Spider 1: No.

Spider 2: It's too early.

Spider 3: Tell us a story first.

Spider 1: Yes, Papa, tell us a story.

Spider 2: Tell us one of Nyame's stories.

Spider 3: Yes, one of Nyame's wonderful stories.

Anansi: (*Paces back and forth angrily.*) Why do all the stories belong to Nyame? It just isn't fair. Everyone knows that I, Anansi the spider, am the very best storyteller in this whole, entire country. The stories should belong to *me*.

Spider 1: Tell us a story, please, Papa.

Anansi: Not now. I am going to see Nyame. And when I get back, I'll have a brand new story to tell you. Now go to bed.

(*Little Spiders kiss Anansi and exit left. Anansi exits right.*)

Narrator: So, Anansi traveled to the place where Nyame lived.

Scene 2

The sky country. Nyame sits right. Scenery optional.

Anansi: (*Enters left, timidly.*) Good afternoon, Nyame.

Nyame: Good afternoon, Anansi.

Anansi: It certainly is . . . um . . . a nice day, isn't it, Nyame.

Nyame: Do you want something from me, Anansi? Speak up! I can tell that you want something.

Anansi: Well, as a matter of fact, I do. You know the stories we all tell . . . the stories about Mr. Rabbit and Miss Bush Hen and Mr. Turtle and all the rest of us?

Nyame: Do you mean ***my*** stories?

Anansi: I think . . . I mean . . . I would like them to be called. . .

Nyame: What, Anansi?

Anansi: Anansi stories.

Nyame: Oh? Really? (*Chuckles.*) Let me think. Hmmmm. Hmmmm. Hmmmm. Yes, yes, I think I could sell you the stories, Anansi.

Anansi: (*Jumps up and down.*) Oh, thank you, thank you, thank you . . .

Nyame: ***If*** you do three things for me, Anansi. Three small, simple things.

Anansi: Anything. Whatever you ask, I'll do it.

Nyame: I would like you to bring me three things, Anansi. Bring me Mr. Snake, who lives by the river. Bring me the hornets from the baobab tree. And bring me Mr. Leopard, who stalks the plain. And bring them to me alive!

Anansi: Is that all?

Nyame: No. Bring them to me TODAY!

Anansi: Thank you. Oh, thank you, Nyame. You'll be seeing me again real soon. (*Exits left.*)

Scene 3

Snake's neighborhood. Scenery optional.

Narrator: Anansi went along until he reached the place where Mr. Snake lived.

(*Snake enters left. Anansi enters right, carrying pole. He puts the pole on the ground, beside Mr. Snake, then paces back and forth behind the Snake and the pole.*)

Anansi: Yes, he is. No, he isn't. Yes, he is. No, he isn't. Yes, he is. No, he isn't. Yes, he is. No, he isn't.

Snake: What? What? What are you talking about, Anansi?

Anansi: Oh, I was just wondering if you are longer than this bamboo pole, or whether this bamboo pole is longer than you.

Snake: Of course I am longer than that bamboo pole! (*Moves behind, and even with, the pole. Raise the Snake slightly so that he remains in view of the audience.*)

Anansi: (*Talking and acting quickly.*) Why, yes. I think you are longer than this bamboo pole. Let me tie your tail to one end, just to make sure. (*Mimes tying tail.*) Let me tie your belly to the middle, just to make sure. (*Mimes tying belly.*) Let me tie your head to the other end, just to make sure. (*Mimes tying head.*) Now, I'll take you to see Nyame. (*Picks up Snake and pole. Exits right.*)

Narrator: Then, Anansi went to the baobab tree, where the hornets had their nest.

Scene 4

Hornets' neighborhood. Baobab tree center stage.

Anansi: (*Enters carrying gourd, and paces back and forth behind tree.*) Yes, they can. No, they can't. Yes, they can. No, they can't. Yes, they can. No, they can't. Yes, they can. No, they can't.

Hornets: (*Voices only, no puppets.*) Bzzzzz! What are you talking about, Anansi?

Anansi: Oh, I was just wondering if there are enough of you to fill this big gourd jar.

Hornets: Of course there are enough of us. There are hundreds of us. Put that jar next to our nest.

Anansi: (*Puts jar next to hornets' nest*) Here it is.

Hornets: Bzzzzzzzzzzzzzzzzzzzzzzzzzzzzzzzzzzzzzzzzzz. (*Voices muffled.*) We're all in the jar and the jar is full.

Anansi: Good. Now I'll put the lid on the jar and take you to see Nyame. (*Exits.*)

Narrator: Anansi closed his right eye and went to see Mr. Leopard.

Scene 5

Leopard's neighborhood. Use Anansi puppet with one eye closed for this scene only.

Anansi: (*Enters right, dancing and jumping.*) Oh, I am going to see paradise. Oh, I am going to see paradise. Sew up my eyelids and see paradise. Sew up my eyelids and see paradise.

Leopard: (*Enters left.*) What are you talking about, Anansi?

Anansi: Oh, Mr. Leopard, haven't you heard. It's a miracle. If you sew up your eyelids and go to the magic place, you can see paradise. Look, I've sewn up my right eyelid already.

Leopard: I would like to see paradise too, Anansi. But I can't sew with these clumsy big paws of mine. (*Pauses.*) Say, would you sew up my eyelids for me?

Anansi: Certainly. (*Mimes sewing. Place the Anansi puppet over the Leopard's head, so that the audience can't see the Leopard's eye.*) Now, follow me to the magic place.

Leopard: Where is the magic place?

Anansi: (*As they exit together, right.*) It's up above in the sky. Very near Nyame's house, yes, very near.

Scene 6

Anansi's house. Transition to this scene should be long, to suggest that quite a bit of time has elapsed. Anansi enters left, followed by his three children.

Spider 1: What happened then, Papa?

Anansi: I took Mr. Snake and the hornets and Mr. Leopard, and I delivered them all to Nyame. I did just exactly what he had asked me to do.

Spider 2: Then did he sell you the stories?

Anansi: He had no choice. He gave them all to me, every last one.

Spider 3: They aren't called Nyame's stories anymore.

Anansi: No, now all the stories are called *anansesem*—Anansi stories!

Spiders 1, 2, and 3: *Anansesem! Anansesem!* Hooray!

(*All exit.*)

Production Notes

Introduce this play by singing "Anansi," from *The Raffi Singable Songbook* (Crown, 1980), or playing the recording (on Raffi's *The Corner Grocery Store*).

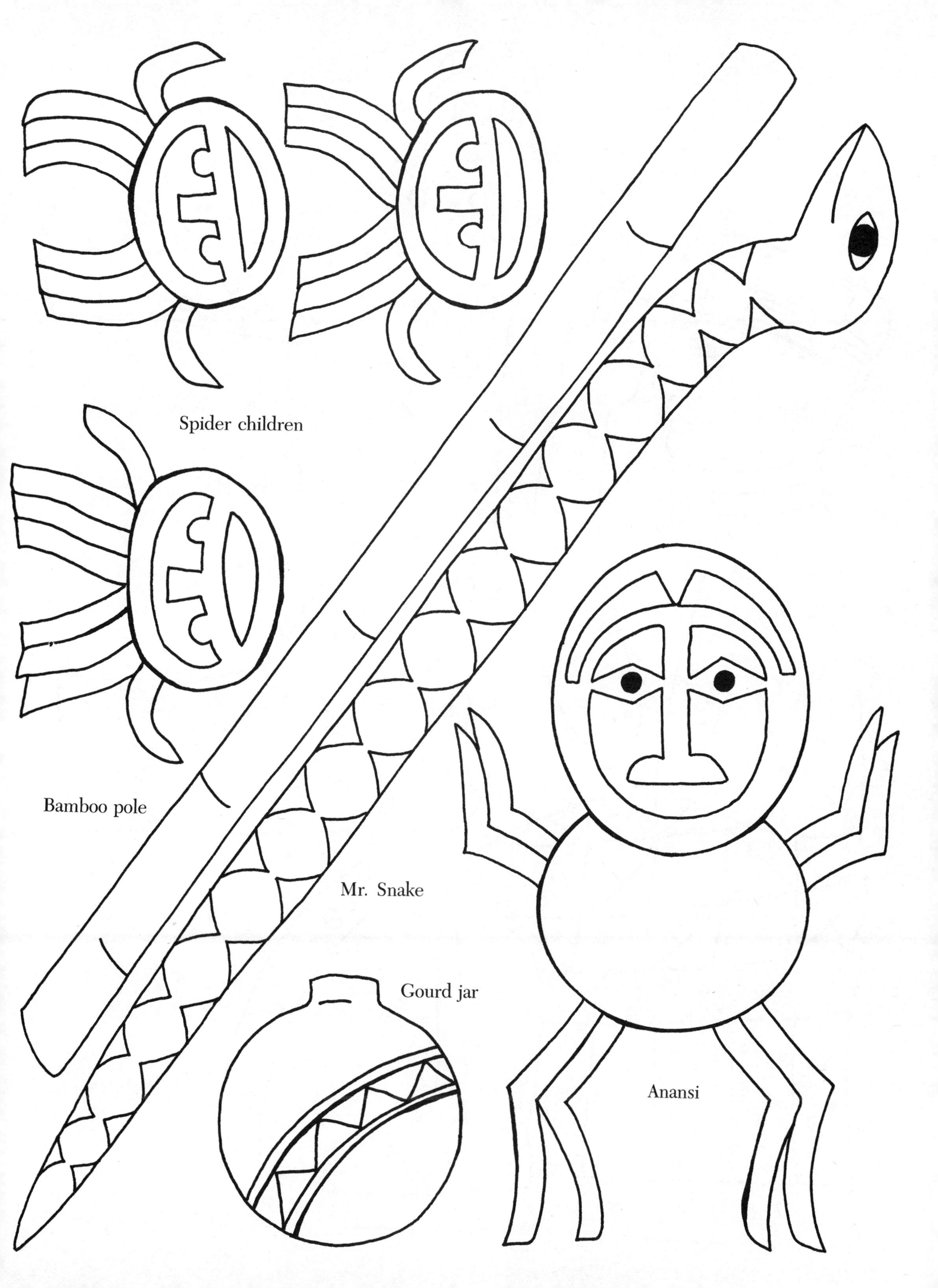
Spider children
Bamboo pole
Mr. Snake
Gourd jar
Anansi

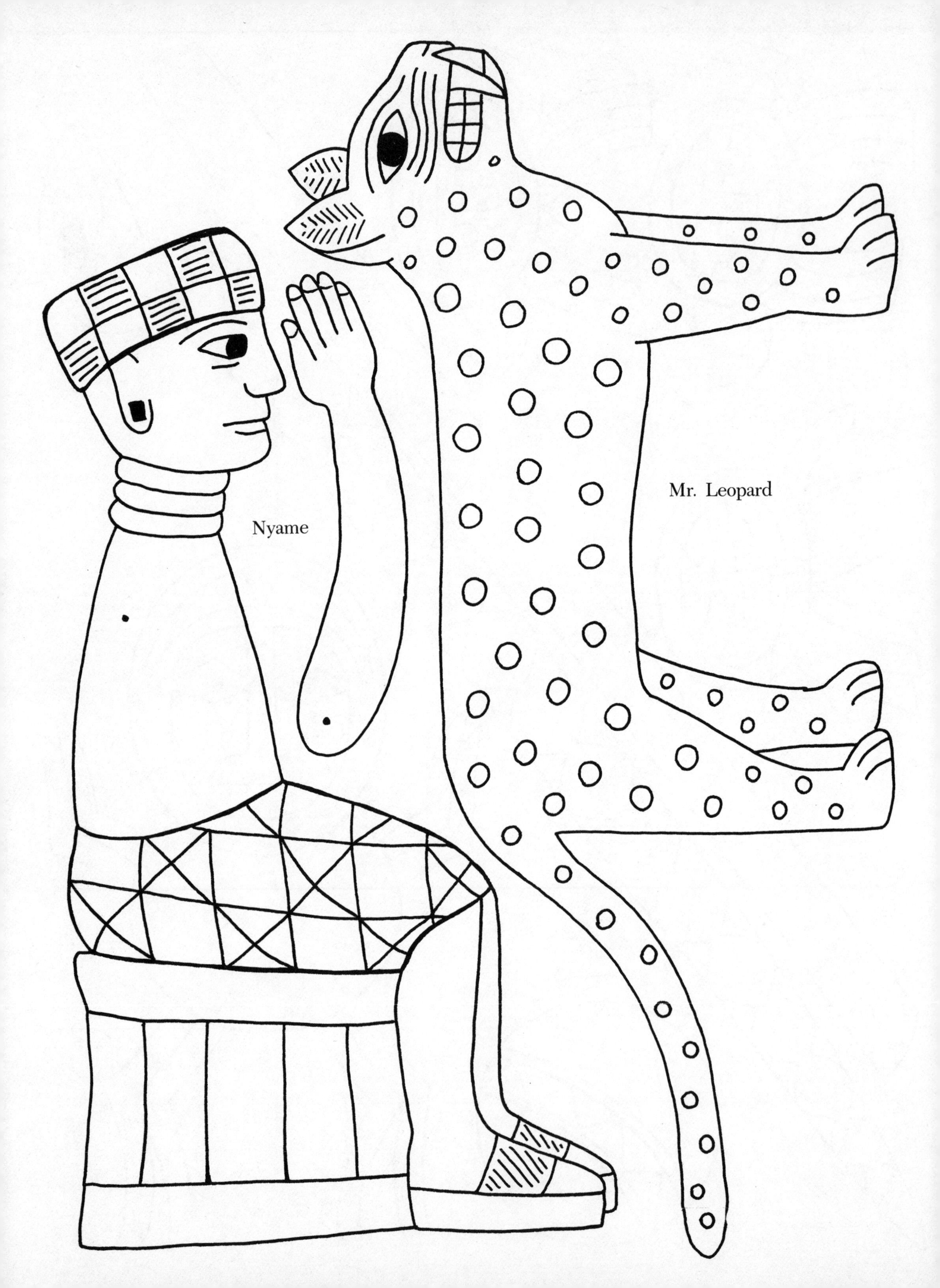
Nyame
Mr. Leopard

The hornets are represented by voices only. Have three or more of the backstage personnel speak their lines together in small, nasal voices, using very clear articulation. After the hornets are inside the gourd jar, the speakers can give their voices a muffled quality by cupping one or both hands around mouth.

Attach the rods to Mr. Snake and to the bamboo pole at their exact centers, so that one puppeteer can hold the two rods together in one hand as Anansi pretends to measure Mr. Snake against the pole and as he carries him off.

There are six scenes in this play, but only one really requires scenery. Otherwise, the scene can be set by the narration. Transition in time and space can be conveyed through music played between scenes.

Shadow Puppets

If you are making the puppets from black paper, cut out the areas around the spiders' facial features with small, sharp scissors. Vertical rods can be used on all puppets. Cut out the leopard's spots and the markings on the baobab tree with a hole punch.

Rod Puppets

In rod puppetry, the two Anansi puppets can be made as the two sides of one puppet, since the puppet is designed to face forward.

***Sound Effects and Music**

A lively way of marking the transition from scene to scene is to play a bit of improvised music for ten to fifteen seconds while the scenery is being changed (or, if you opt for little or no scenery, while the stage is empty). Use thumb piano, gourd rattle, flute, and/or drum.

Follow-up Activities

Anansi Wins Again

Choose a dangerous or hard-to-catch African animal—a rhinoceros, a gazelle, a rabbit, or a mosquito, for instance—and write a short scene in which Anansi captures this animal by trickery. Make puppets of these animals and act out the scenes on the puppet stage.

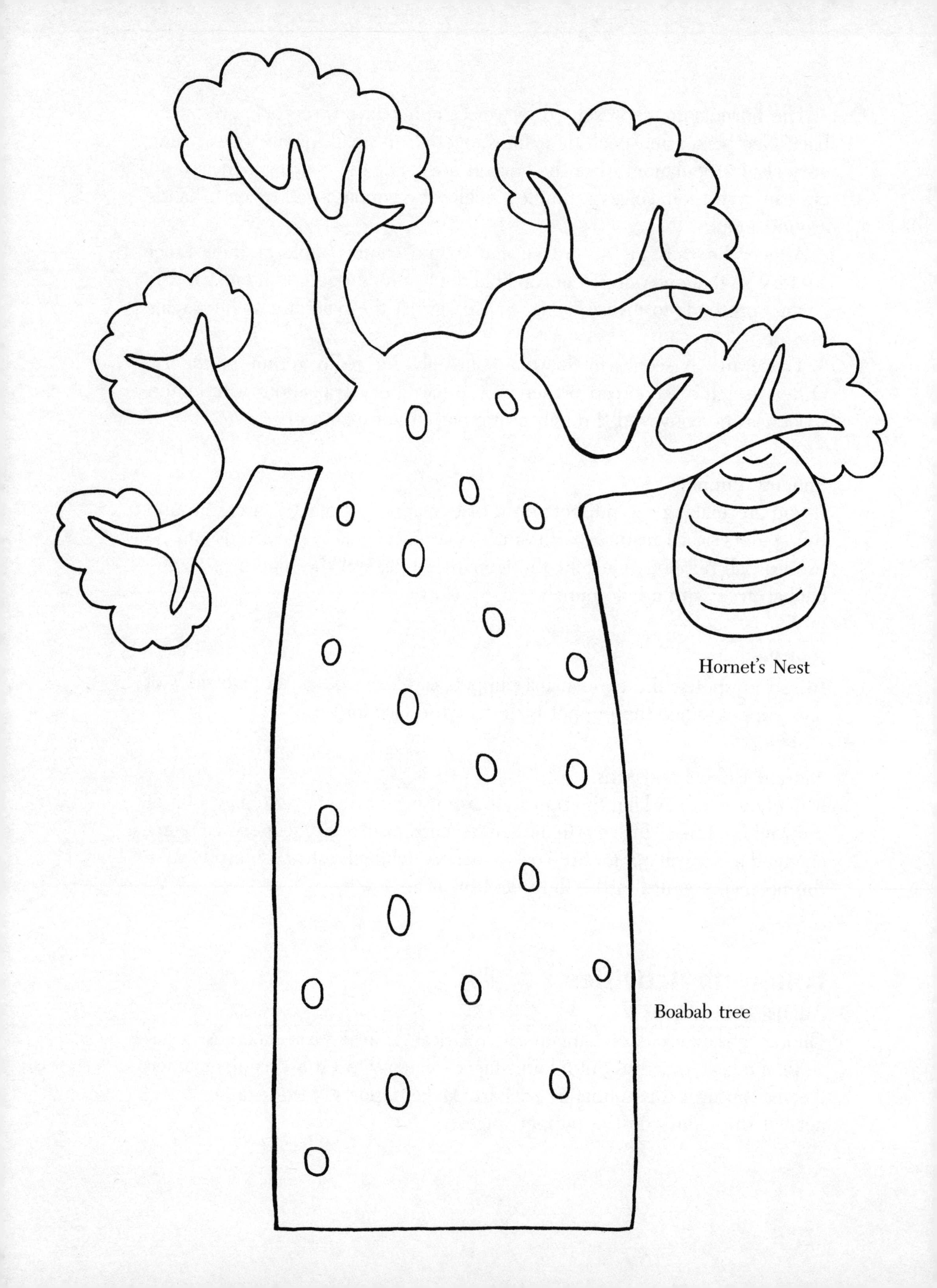
Hornet's Nest
Boabab tree

More Anansesem

The following Anansi stories are also recommended for dramatization, using the narration-improvisation technique:

> *Anansi and the Moss Covered Rock,* by Eric Kimmel. Illus. by Janet Stevens. New York: Holiday, 1988.
>
> *Anansi the Spider,* by Gerald McDermott. New York: Holt, 1972.
>
> "Ticky-Picky Boom-Boom," in *Twice Upon a Time,* by Judy Sierra and Robert Kaminski. Bronx: H. W. Wilson, 1989. Pages 35–39.

Toad Visits the Emperor

This adaptation of a Vietnamese folktale tells how a toad, a tiger, a bee, and a rooster travel to the sky in order to persuade the Jade Emperor to send rain down to the parched earth. The tale also explains why a toad's croaking precedes a storm.

Puppeteers: Six, plus musician.

Puppets:	Toad	Tiger
	Rooster	Emperor on cloud throne
	Bee	Guard

Scenery pieces: Cloud with rain.

Scene 1

A dried-up lake bed. There is no scenery. Toad is hopping back and forth; Rooster is pecking at the ground.

Toad: Croak! Croak!

Rooster: I can't find a single bug in this hard dried-up mud.

Toad: My skin is shriveling. I'm not long for the world.

Rooster: If only it would rain!

Toad: All the animals are suffering from this endless drought.

Rooster: The Jade Emperor has always sent us rain from his palace in the clouds. Why isn't he doing his job? What could be the matter?

Toad: Croak! Croak!

Rooster: Don't just sit there and say "croak, croak." We have to ***do*** something.

Toad: (*Hops back and forth.*) I have an idea. I am going to visit the Jade Emperor and ask him to let the rain fall. (*Exits left.*)

Rooster: Wait for me! I'm coming, too. (*Exits left.*)

(*Toad and Rooster re-enter right; Bee buzzes in left.*)

Toad: Good morning, friend bee.

Bee: Good morning, friend toad, friend rooster. Where are you going?

Rooster: We are off to ask the emperor to send down the rain.

Bee: I can't live without the flowers, and the flowers can't bloom without the rain. May I come with you to visit the emperor?

Toad: Yes. Please come with us, friend bee.

(*Tiger enters left.*)

Toad: Good morning, friend tiger.

Tiger: Good morning, friend toad, friend rooster, friend bee. You haven't seen any water around here, have you? I am so very thirsty.

Toad: No, the rivers and the lakes are all dry. That's why we're off to ask the emperor to send down rain from his palace in the clouds.

Tiger: May I come with you?

Rooster: Please do, friend tiger. (*All exit right.*)

(*The four animals walk in procession across the stage, three times left to right. The third time, they are tired and walk slowly, improvising groans and complaints.*)

Scene 2

The Emperor's palace in the clouds. Emperor's throne right. The Emperor is seated on his throne, and his Guard stands in front of him.*

Toad: (*Enters left.*) Croak! Croak! Croak!

Emperor: What's that noise?

Toad: Croak . . . er . . . um . . . Excuse me . . . um . . . Your Majesty.

Emperor: Guard, do you hear a small, annoying sound?

Guard: Yes, Your Majesty.

Toad: (*Jumps onto Guard's head, then into Emperor's lap.*) Croak! Your Majesty! Send us rain!

Emperor: Guard! Seize this horrid toad.

Toad: Help me, friend rooster!

Rooster: (*Enters left.*) Co! Co! Co! (*Crosses behind Guard and chases him offstage left.*)

Emperor: Guard! Come back here!

Guard: (*Enters left.*) Your Majesty, that creature pecked me!

Toad: Croak!

Emperor: I asked you to remove this annoying toad from my royal lap!

Guard: Yes, Your Majesty.

Toad: Help me, friend bee!

Bee: Bzzzzzzz. (*Flies in from left, over Guard's head. Chases Guard offstage left.*)

Emperor: Guard! Come back here!

Guard: (*Enters left.*) Your Majesty, that impudent insect stung me!

Toad: Croak! Croak!

Emperor: This toad is laughing at me. Lock him up in the dungeon.

Guard: Yes, Your Majesty.

Toad: Help me, friend tiger!

Tiger: Grrrrrrr. (*Enters left.*)

Guard: Yipes! (*Turns and exits right, behind Emperor's throne.*)

(*Tiger remains stage left.*)

Emperor: Guard? Guard?

Guard: (*Offstage.*) I resign my position.

Emperor: (*Angrily.*) Toad, what do you want?

Emperor
(*made in one piece
with his throne*)

Toad: Your Majesty, I have come to ask you to send rain down to the earth. Otherwise, the animals will die.

Emperor: Oh, is that all? How forgetful I am. Return home, and I will send you one of my most magnificent storms.

Toad: (*Hops off Emperor's lap.*) Thank you, Your Majesty.

Emperor: And, Uncle Toad . . .

Tiger: Did you hear that? The emperor called you ***uncle!***

Emperor: Uncle Toad, whenever you want the rain to fall, just croak, and I will hear you. (*Leans forward.*) And don't ever bring your friends back here.

(*Toad and Tiger exit left.**)

Scene 3

The earth. No scenery. Toad, Rooster, Bee, and Tiger enter right.

Tiger: Well, Uncle Toad, try your new power.

Bee: Yes, toad, see if you can make the Emperor send rain.

Rooster: Go ahead and croak!

Toad: (*Jumping.*) Croak! Croak! Croak! Croak!

(*Thunder rolls.* Cloud with rain passes overhead.*)

Tiger, Bee, and Rooster: (*Dancing.*) Hooray! Hooray for Uncle Toad!

Production Notes

The emperor puppet is made in one piece with his cloud throne, which is attached to the stage like a set piece. He has a moving arm. The guard, the rooster, and the tiger also have moving parts.

Shadow Puppets

Attach the emperor and his throne to the shadow screen like a set piece, manipulating his arm with a horizontal rod. Make duplicate puppets of the toad, one facing right and one facing left, attached to horizontal rods, and substitute one puppet for the other when he needs to turn around. The rooster, the tiger, and the guard are on vertical rods. Design and make a

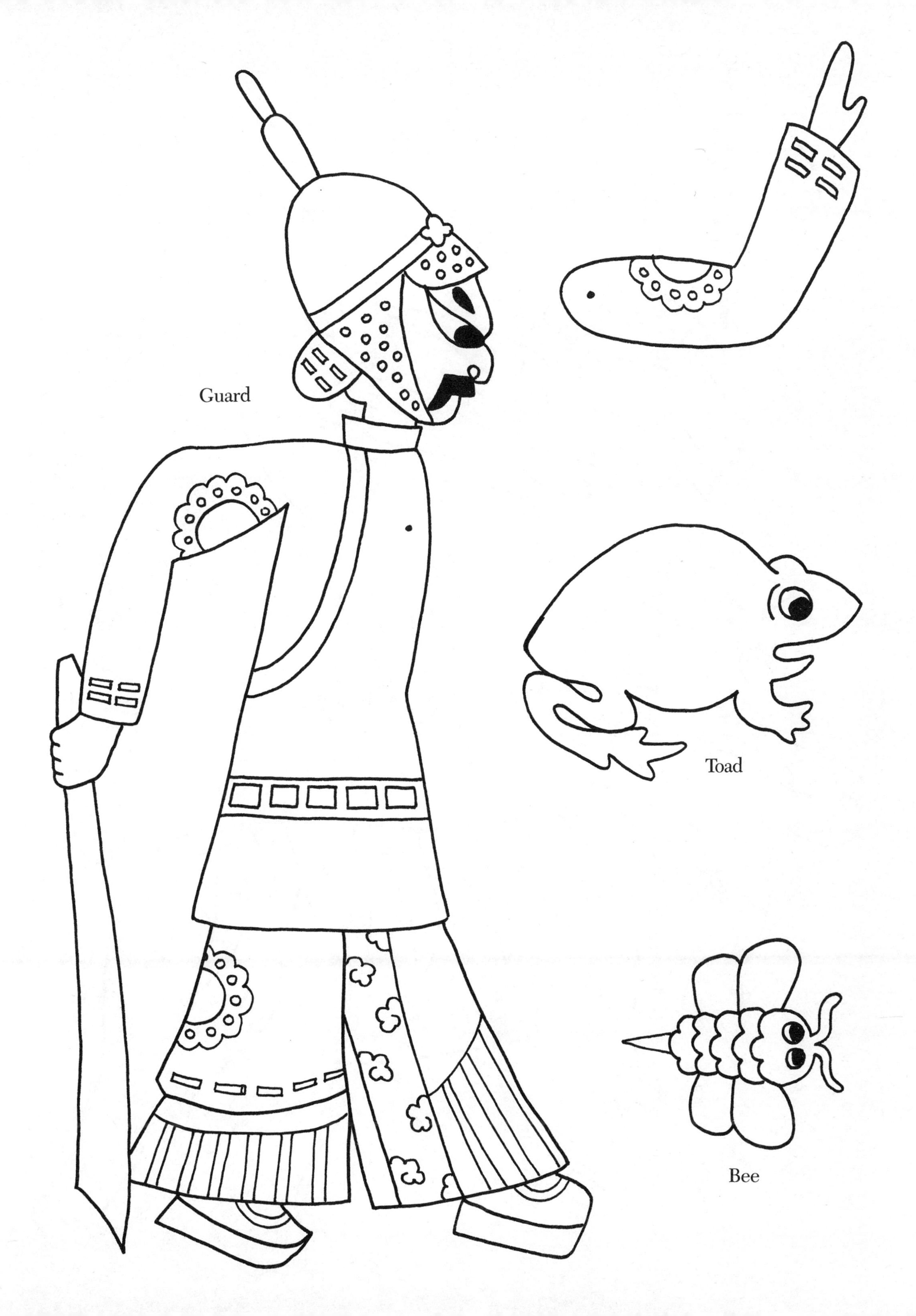
Guard
Toad
Bee

Rooster
Tiger

large rain cloud, and attach a long fringe of clear, thin plastic film—a polyethylene bag, for example—to represent the rain coming from it. The cloud, as well as the bee, should be on horizontal rods.

Rod Puppets

Secure the emperor on his cloud throne to the stage like a scenery piece. Design and make a rain cloud, and attach it to a long black rod. The rain is made by attaching a fine fringe of clear plastic to the bottom of the cloud.

***Sound Effects and Music**

Add some rhythms, played on a keyboard or xylophone, when the animals are traveling to see the Emperor. Begin and end the scene at the Emperor's palace with a crash of cymbals. Make the sounds of the rainstorm with loud drumming and a crash of cymbals for thunder; whirl a rattle for the sound of raindrops.

Follow-up Activities

Adventuresome Puppets

The following tales of friends joining together, one by one, to go on a journey also make very good puppet plays:

> "The Bremen Town Musicians." Pages 122–127.
> "Henny Penny." Pages 56–60.
> In *The Flannel Board Storytelling Book*, by Judy Sierra.
> Bronx: H. W. Wilson, 1987.
>
> Includes patterns suitable for rod or shadow puppets.
>
> "Peach Boy," in *Japanese Children's Favorite Stories*, ed. by Florence Sakade. Rutland, Vt.: Tuttle, 1958. Pages 9–16.

The Water Cycle

A scientific shadow play of the water cycle can be presented with puppets playing the parts of sun, clouds, and raindrops. Script and puppet patterns can be found in Judy Sims' *Puppets for Dreaming and Scheming* (Early Stages, 1976); or make your own puppets and write your own script based on Jeanne Bendick's *How to Make a Cloud* (Parents, 1971) or Franklyn Branley's *Rain and Hail* (Crowell, 1983).

The Blue Jackal

The tale of the Blue Jackal comes from the *Panchatantra,* an ancient collection of wisdom stories from India. In Hindu symbolism, the color blue signifies divinity, a color which could never rightly belong to a lowly, carrion-eating scavenger like the jackal.

Puppeteers: Four to eight, plus narrator and musician.

Puppets: Fierce Howl, the jackal
Fierce Howl (blue)
Three other Jackals
Pack of Dogs (a single puppet)
Elephant
Monkey
Tiger

Scenery pieces: Two houses.

Scene 1

A remote mountainside in India. Scenery optional.

Narrator: In the mountains near a village in India, there lived a family of jackals.

(*Fierce Howl and three other Jackals enter and begin to howl.*)

Jackal 1: I am soooooooo hungry.

Jackal 2: I haven't eaten in a weeeeek.

Jackal 3: My belly huuuuuuuurts. I'm staaaaaaaarving.

Fierce Howl: I'm going into the village to see if I can find anything to eat.

Jackal 1: Be careful.

Jackal 2: Keep a sharp eye out for dogs.

Jackal 3: Bring something back for us.

(*Fierce Howl exits right; other Jackals exit left.*)

Scene 2

The village. Houses at far left and right of stage.

Narrator: That brave—or foolish—jackal, whose name was Fierce Howl, crept into the silent village.

(*Fierce Howl enters right, walks slowly to center stage. Dogs bark offstage, softly, then louder.*)

Fierce Howl: Oh no! Dogs! (*Runs. Dogs chase him across the stage four times, left to right, barking loudly. Then, Fierce Howl crosses left to right alone.*)

Narrator: At last, Fierce Howl ran into an empty shop, the shop of a dyer. Desperate to escape the dogs, the frightened jackal leaped into a tub of indigo blue dye.

(*The blue Fierce Howl enters right, very slowly at first, then trots across stage and exits.*)

Scene 3

The mountains again. Scenery optional.

(*Three Jackals enter left, walk to center stage, and howl. Fierce Howl enters right.*)

Jackal 1: Who are you?

Fierce Howl: Don't you recognize me?

Jackal 2: No, we have never before seen a creature like you.

Jackal 3: You are so . . . so *blue.*

Fierce Howl: (*Coughs.*) I am called Sataga. I have been sent by the god, Sakra, to be king of all the animals.

Jackal 1: What may we do to serve you, King Sataga?

Fierce Howl: Go away immediately! Get out of my sight! Send the more important beasts to see me at once.

(*The other Jackals exit left.*)

Elephant: (*Enters left.*) Your Majesty, King Sataga, how may I serve you?

Fierce Howl: I hereby appoint you to be my royal horse. You may carry me on your back.

Elephant: Yes, Your Highness. It will be an honor.

(*Fierce Howl climbs up the Elephant's trunk and turns around. In shadow puppetry, quickly substitute the other blue Fierce Howl puppet, so that it looks as if he has turned around.*)

Tiger: (*Enters right.*) Yes, Your Majesty. How may I serve you?

Fierce Howl: You will be my steward. Go at once and fetch me some fresh meat.

Tiger: Yes, Your Majesty. (*Turns and exits right.*)

Monkey: (*Enters right.*) King Sataga, how may I serve you?

Fierce Howl: You will be my prime minister. Please go and find all the lowly, disgusting jackals in my kingdom. Tell them to get out of the country, to go away and stay away. I don't want to see them again, ever.

Monkey: Yes, your majesty. (*Turns and exits right.*)

(*Tiger enters right; mimes putting meat on ground. Fierce Howl walks down the Elephant's trunk and mimes eating meat.*)

Fierce Howl: This is good. You must fetch me meat every day.

(*Monkey enters right.*)

Monkey: The jackals have all fled in terror, Your Majesty.

Fierce Howl: Good. Very good.

Narrator: That evening, Fierce Howl found himself well fed, and surrounded by animals who were his willing servants. He felt very satisfied with himself and his newly found royal position. Then, a noise echoed through the valley from distant mountaintops. For Fierce Howl, it was a familiar sound. An irresistible sound.

Jackals 1, 2, and 3: (*Offstage. Howl.*) Arooooooorooooooroooo.

Fierce Howl: (*Jumps up and down.*) Mmmmmmmph! Mmmmmmmph! (*Says this with lips closed.*)

Narrator: When he heard his fellow jackals howling at the moon, Fierce Howl couldn't contain himself. He threw back his head and howled along with them.

Fierce Howl
Tiger
Monkey

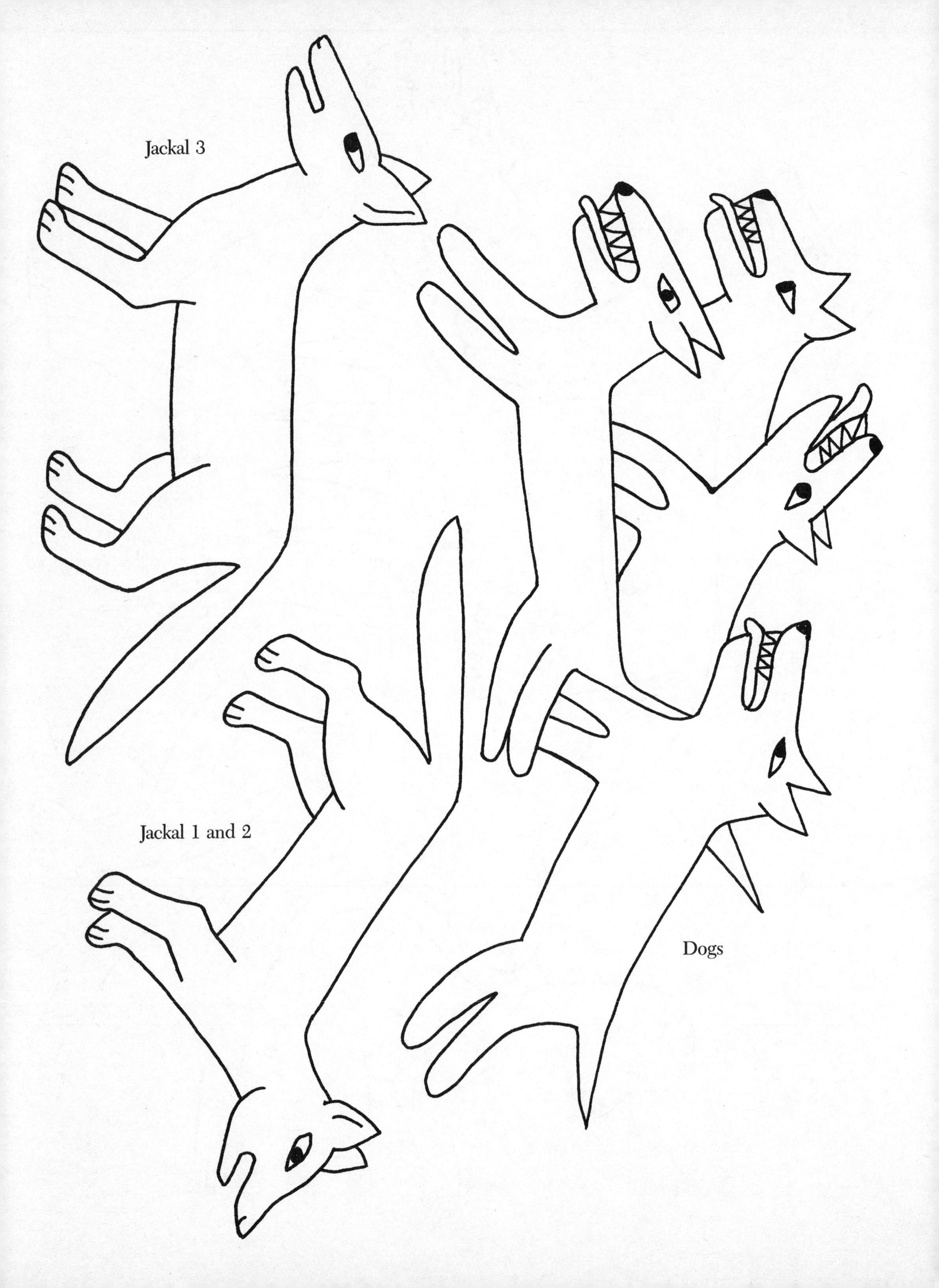
Jackal 3
Jackal 1 and 2
Dogs

Fierce Howl: (*Howls.*) Oh, excuse me. (*Howls twice.*) Oh no! Here it comes again. (*Howls three times.*)

Tiger: What's this? What is our king doing?

Monkey: He's howling with the jackals.

Elephant: He ***is*** a jackal. We've been tricked.

(*The Tiger, the Monkey, and the Elephant roar in anger. Fierce Howl exits left. They pursue him.*)

Narrator: Fierce Howl was never seen again in that country. For although he was raised high by accident, he forgot his friends and family, and he was brought down.

Production Notes

The pack of dogs will only require one puppeteer, but several others will need to join in the barking. Jackal puppets can be made with a moving head, which can be tilted back when they howl.

Shadow Puppets

Because the color of the puppets is of such importance, shadow puppets for this play should be made of colored acetate. All puppets are attached to vertical rods, except the blue Fierce Howl, who needs to sit atop the elephant. Make two identical puppets of this character, attaching the horizontal rods so that they face in opposite directions.

Rod Puppets

The blue Fierce Howl will need a rod long enough to allow him to sit on the elephant's back.

Follow-up Activities

A Bluer Jackal

The script of this play does not describe exactly what happened to Fierce Howl after the more powerful animals drove him away (in most versions, they kill him). Write another scene for the script, showing what happened to Fierce Howl. Did he lose his blue color? How? Did he try to rejoin his fellow jackals? What happened?

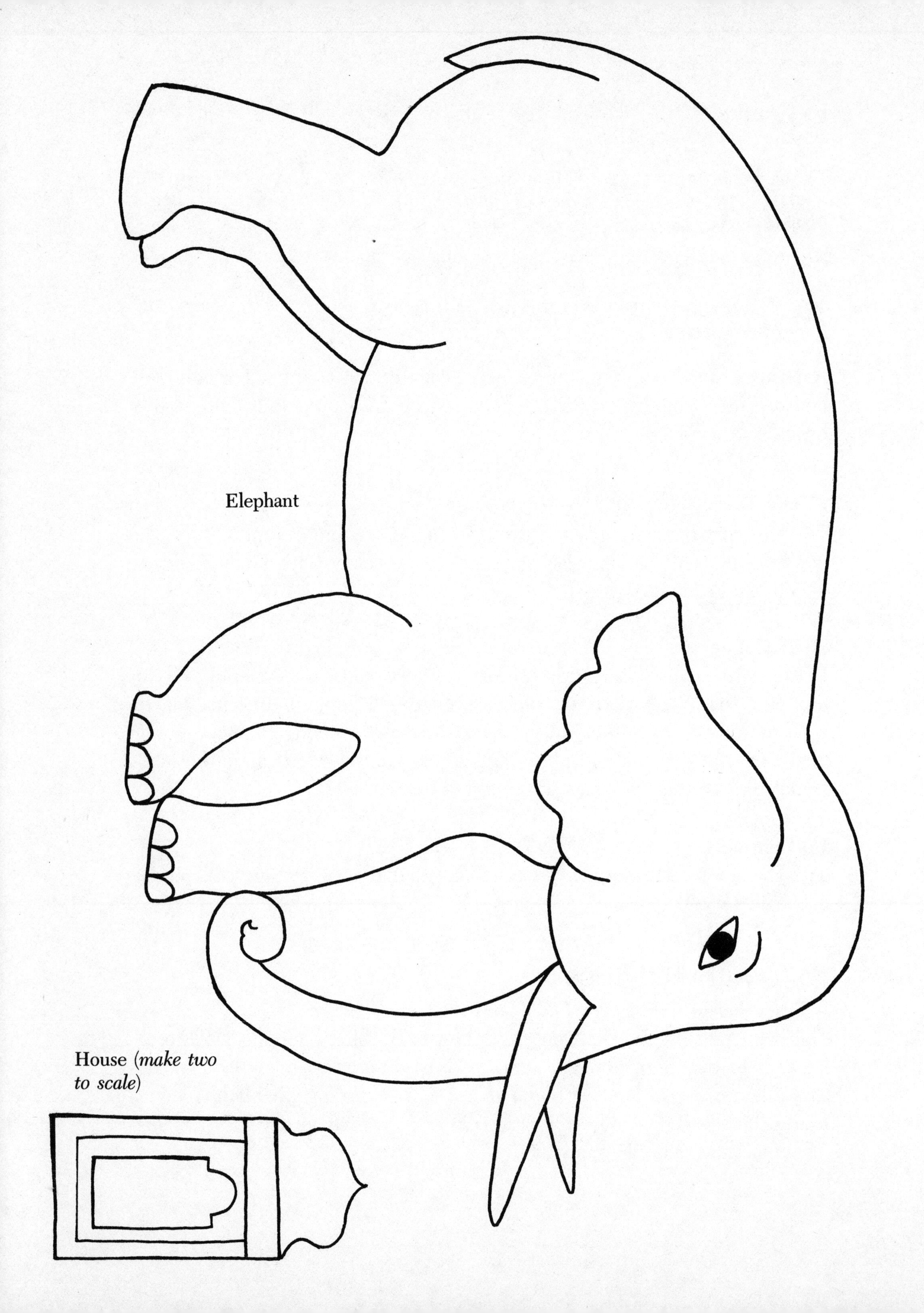
Elephant
House (*make two to scale*)

A Little Blue . . .

. . . and a little yellow. Create a shadow puppet play of Leo Lionni's classic picture book, *Little Blue and Little Yellow* (Ivan Obolensky, 1959), using colored pens on acetate. Be sure that the yellow and the blue you are using will make a bright green when superimposed on the shadow screen. With acetate, you can make a group of little pieces as one puppet. Use horizontal rods, being sure to attach the rods near the top edge of each puppet, so that they can easily be placed on top of each other.

The Turkey Maiden

This tale is from the Zuñi people of New Mexico. It tells of a poor girl who dreams of having fine clothes and attending a dance. Her dream comes true through magic performed by the turkeys she tends, but she disobeys their warnings not to forget them after she gets to the dance.

Puppeteers: Four to nine, plus narrator and musicians.

Puppets: Maiden (in rags)
Maiden (in dancing clothes)
Tom Turkey
Two other Turkeys
Priest
Four Dancers

Props: Girl's clothing

Scenery pieces: Ladder
Building
Rock with turkey tracks

Scene 1

A plain outside a village in New Mexico. The stage is empty as the play begins.

Narrator: In Matsaki, long ago, there lived a young maiden. She was very poor. She had no family. It was her job to watch the turkeys. Day after day, dressed in old, ragged clothes, she fed and cared for the turkeys as if they were her children.

Turkeys: (*Enter left, making little noises.*) Tot-tot tot-tot tot-tot. (*Continue making noises as they exit right.*)

Maiden: Turkeys! My turkeys! I have water and corn for you. (*Mimes putting these on the ground.*)

Turkeys: (*Enter right.*) Tot-tot tot-tot tot-tot tot-tot. (*They mime eating and drinking, then turn and exit right.*) Tot-tot tot-tot tot-tot.

Priest: (*Enters right.*) In four days, we will perform the Yaa-ya dance on the plaza.

Maiden: I would like to dance the Yaa-ya dance.

Priest: All the young men and all the young women will be there. They will wear their finest clothes. (*Exits right.*)

Maiden: I have no fine clothes. (*Paces back and forth sadly.*)

Tom Turkey: (*Enters right.*) What is the matter? Why are you so unhappy?

Maiden: In four days, they will celebrate the Yaa-ya dance on the plaza. All the young men and all the young women will be there. They will be dressed in their finest clothes. I want to go to the dance, too—but I have no fine clothes.

Tom Turkey: If you went to the dance, you would forget us. Who would feed us? Who would take care of us?

Maiden: I would not forget you. I would return after the dance to take care of you. (*Exits left.*)

(*Other Turkeys enter. They huddle together and "tot-tot."*)

Tom Turkey: If she is still sad on the day of the dance, we will help her. But she must promise not to forget us.

(*Turkeys exit. Drumming begins, softly.*)

Maiden: (*Enters left.*) I can hear the musicians. That means the Yaa-ya dance will soon be starting.

Turkeys: (*Enter right.*) Tot-tot tot-tot tot-tot.

Tom Turkey: Are you still sad? Do you still want to go to the dance?

Maiden: Yes.

Tom Turkey: Then we will help you.

(*Turkeys huddle and dance. Drumbeats become louder as the Turkeys sing.*)

Turkeys:
Kyaa-naa to! to!
Kyaa-naa to! to!
Ye e!
Kyaa-naa to! to!
Kyaa-naa to! to!
Yee huli huli!

(*A pile of clothes appear on ground where Turkeys have danced.*)

Maiden: Such beautiful dancing clothes! (*Picks them up.*) Thank you, my turkeys. (*Exits left; returns dressed in new clothes.*)

Tom Turkey: Go to the dance, but do not forget us. Stay only for four dances. Be sure you return to us before the sun sets.

Maiden: (*Exits right.*) I will! I promise!

Turkeys: (*Exit left.*) Tot-tot tot-tot tot-tot.

Scene 2

The plaza. Buildings at both sides of stage; ladder leans against building at left. The Dancers enter, two from each side, and dance for awhile as the drums beat loudly. Drums become soft again as the Maiden enters from right.

Dancer 1: Who is that maiden?

Dancer 2: I've never seen her before.

Dancer 3: She's beautiful. I wonder where she comes from.

Dancer 4: She looks a little bit like the Turkey Maiden.

Dancer 1: No, that isn't possible.

(*Drumming becomes louder. They all dance for a while. The drumming becomes soft again as Tom Turkey enters left, perching on the ladder.*)

Tom Turkey: One, two, three, four dances—yet she does not return. The sun is setting, but she does not notice. (*Other Turkeys, offstage, join him in singing.*)

Kyaa-naa to! to!
Kyaa-naa to! to!
  Ye e!
Kyaa-naa to! to!
Kyaa-naa to! to!
  Yee huli, huli!

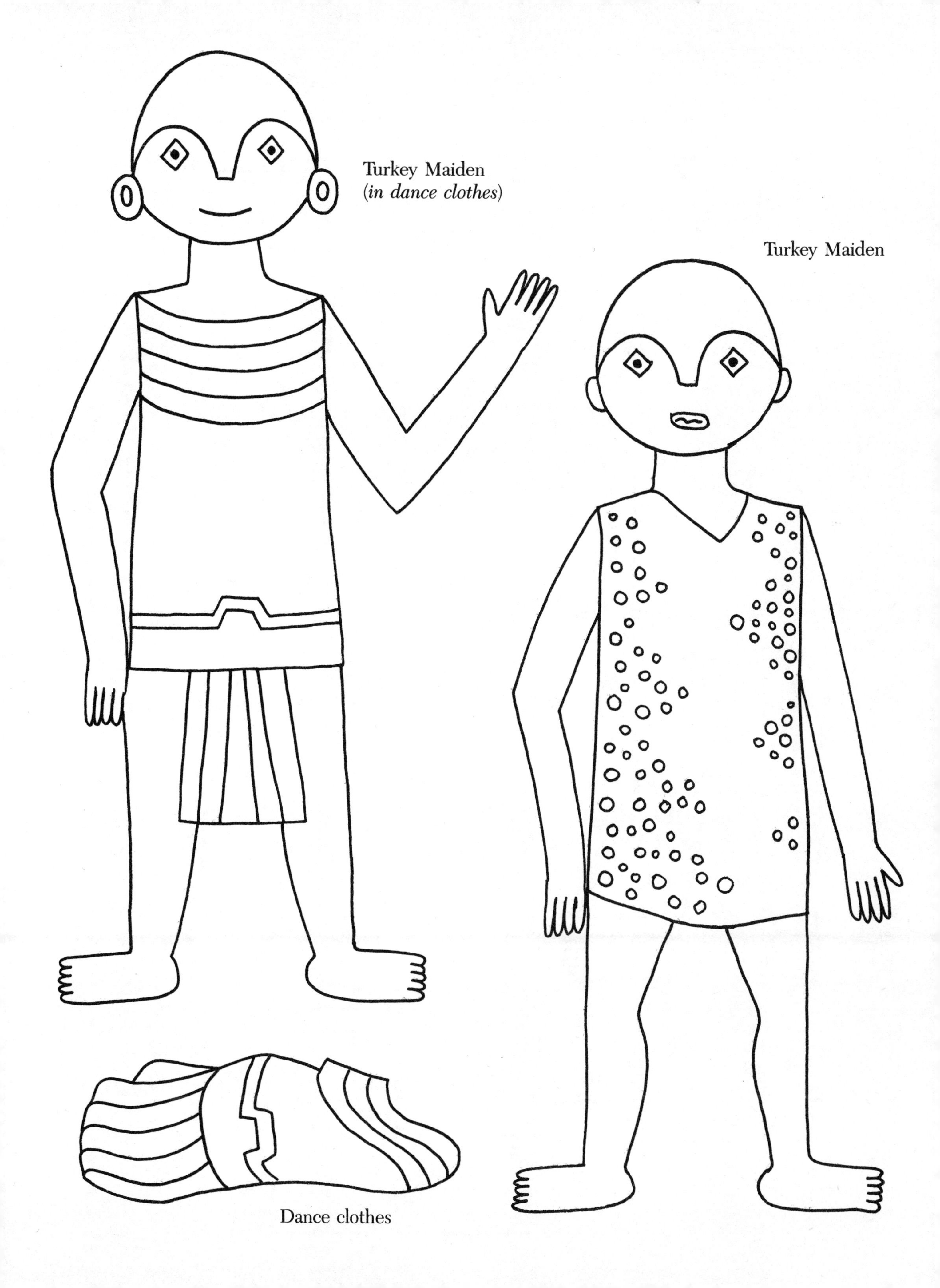
Turkey Maiden
(*in dance clothes*)
Turkey Maiden
Dance clothes

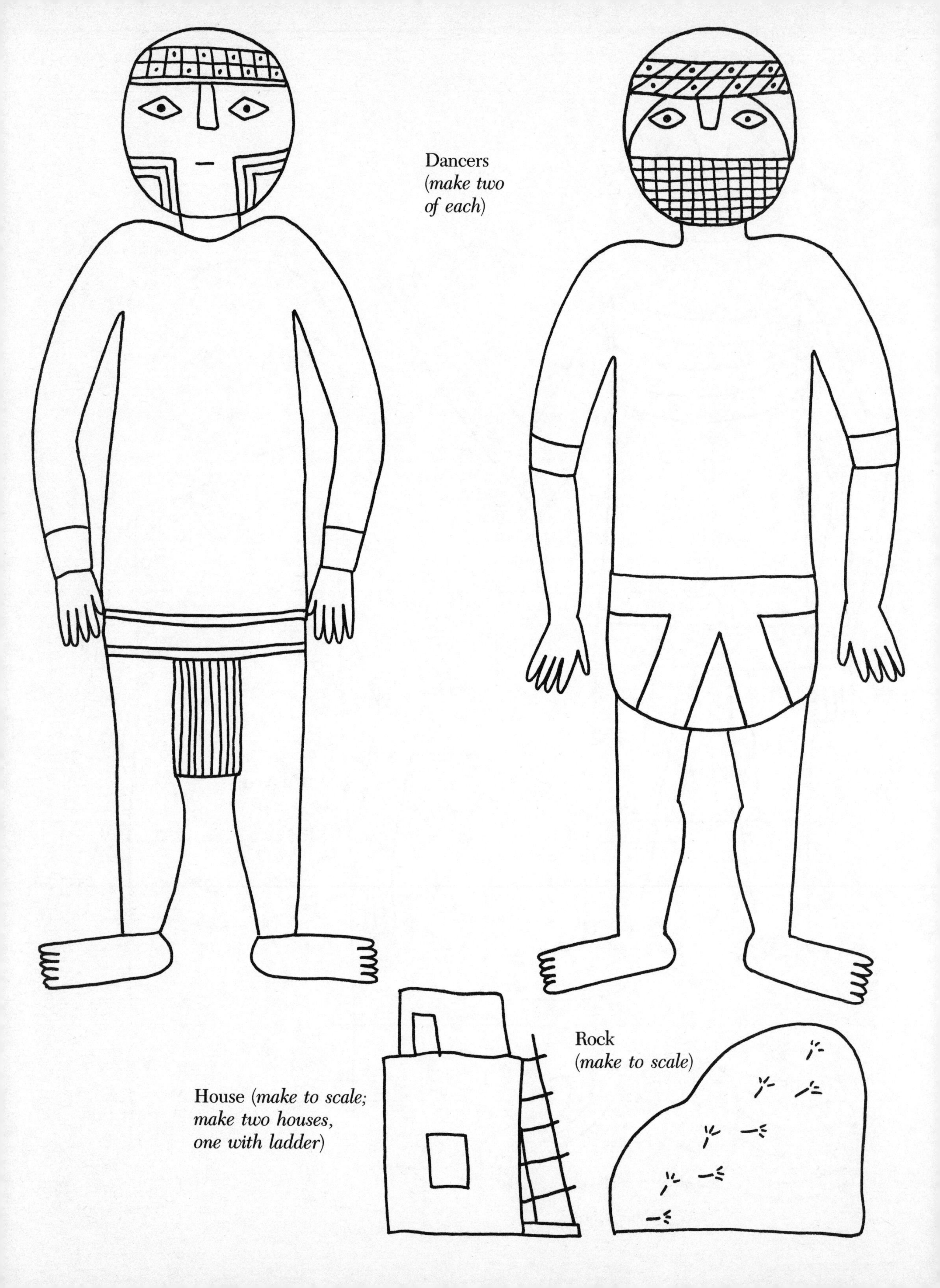
Dancers
(*make two of each*)
House (*make to scale; make two houses, one with ladder*)
Rock
(*make to scale*)

(*Tom Turkey exits left.*)

Maiden: My turkeys! My turkeys! I forgot my turkeys! (*Exits left.*)

(*Dancers exit right.*)

Scene 3

The plain; rock with turkey tracks at left.

Narrator: The maiden ran and ran, calling to her turkeys.

Maiden: (*Substitute the puppet of the Maiden dressed in rags. She crosses left to right.*) Turkeys, my turkeys!

Turkeys: (*Cross right to left.*) Tot-tot tot-tot tot-tot.

Maiden: (*Crosses right to left.*) Come back, my turkeys!

Turkeys: (*Cross left to right.*) Tot-tot tot-tot tot-tot.

(*Repeat this chase sequence.*)

Narrator: The maiden heard her turkeys, and she saw their tracks, but she never found them again. You can still see the tracks of those turkeys on the walls of Zuñi canyon. The tracks of those turkeys remain on the rock to this day. They remind us to tell the story of the Turkey Maiden.

Turkeys: (*Offstage, faraway.*) Tot-tot tot-tot tot-tot tot-tot.

Production Notes

The four dancers can be made separately or as one or two "group puppets," so that one puppeteer can manipulate all of them.

Shadow Puppets

The puppet designs are based on the black-on-white Mimbres pottery paintings. Because some of them are front-facing, the puppets should be made from clear acetate, colored with markers. The front-facing puppets can be made with horizontal rods; the others should have vertical ones. Tom Turkey's vertical rod needs to be long enough to allow him to perch on the ladder. The scenery pieces should be cut from black paper. The turkey tracks should be cut out of the rock using a knife or sharp scissors.

Turkey
(*make two*)
Tom Turkey
Priest

Rod Puppets
Tom Turkey will need a rod long enough to allow him to perch on the ladder in the final scene.

***Sound Effects and Music**
One or more drums accompany the dancing. The songs of the turkeys can be chanted on two tones. The songs are magical and serious. The turkeys make small steps in unison while chanting.

Follow-up Activities

A Cinderella Story?
Some folklorists have called this story a version of "Cinderella." Read Charles Perrault's classic "Cinderella," and compare it to the story of the Turkey Maiden. In what ways are they similar? How do they differ? Compare these two stories to two other American tales, the Appalachian Cinderella story, "Ashpet," and the Native American Micmac tale.

"Cinderella," in *The Classic Fairy Tales,* by Iona and Peter Opie. New York: Oxford, 1974. Pages 117–127. (Perrault version)

"Ashpet," in *Grandfather Tales*, by Richard Chase. New York: Houghton Mifflin, 1948. Pages 115–123. (Appalachian)

"The Indian Cinderella," in *North American Indian Legends,* by Virginia Haviland. New York: Collins, 1979. Pages 94–96. (Micmac)

Native American Rock Art
The tale of the Turkey Maiden ends with a reference to rock art that depicts turkey tracks. The rock drawings of the native peoples of the American Southwest can be brought to life in a shadow puppet production of Byrd Baylor's *Before You Came This Way* (Dutton, 1969). Make black puppets of all the drawings in the book, and have the puppets pantomime the book's poetic text as it is read by a narrator. This performance can actively involve a group of up to thirty performers. With the use of moving parts and props, hunters can shoot with bows and arrows, warriors can fight with clubs, and the coyote can throw his head back to howl at the moon.

Perseus and Medusa

The tale of Perseus, the young Greek hero who beheads the frightful Gorgon, Medusa, is told in the literature of ancient Greece and is depicted in Greek vase paintings. it is an exciting story of heroism, of magic, and of the tables turned on a wicked king.

Puppeteers: Five to seven, plus narrator and musician.

Puppets: King Polydectes
Perseus
Perseus (with winged sandals and kibisis)
Athena
The Three Gray Sisters (one puppet)
Medusa (two separate pieces for head and body)

Props: Winged sandals
Cap of darkness
Kibisis bag
Athena's shield

Scene 1

The court of Polydectes. The play is presented without scenery; narration and imagination set the scene.

Narrator: Perseus was the son of the king of the gods, Zeus, and a mortal woman, Danae. When Perseus reached the age of manhood, an evil king named Polydectes wanted to force Perseus' mother to marry him against her will. In order to get Perseus out of his way, Polydectes sent him on a dangerous mission.

King: (*Enters left.*) Perseus, come here.

Perseus: (*Enters right.*) Yes.

King: (*Pretending to flatter him.*) You are a fine lad, Perseus. I tell you, your talents are wasted in a small place like this. You ought to go off on an adventure, perform some great deed, like the ***real*** heroes.

Perseus: What do you mean? Just tell me something worth trying, and I'll do it!

King: Very well, bring me the head of the Gorgon, Medusa.

Perseus: Who is Medusa?

King: She is the only one of the three horrible Gorgon sisters who is mortal, and can be killed. I want her head. And never mind why.

Perseus: Where will I find her?

King: Far away in the west, in the land of darkness. You must find your own way, for I do not know any more about it. (*Exits left.*)

Athena: (*Enters right.*) Perseus, do you know me?

Perseus: (*Turns.*) Indeed I do! You are the goddess Athena.

Athena: Because you are a brave young man, and the son of Zeus, the gods have decided to assist you, Perseus. First of all, look at this. (*She holds her hand up toward his face and mimes showing the portrait of Medusa.*)

Perseus: (*Looks and reacts.*) Ugh!

Athena: This is a portrait of Medusa. If you were to look at her real face, even for an instant, you would turn to stone.

Perseus: Then how can I possibly get her head?

Athena: I will follow you and hold up my shield as a mirror. When you come to Medusa, keep your back to her and watch her reflection in the shield. Strike her over your shoulder, then cut off her head.

Perseus: Perfect! And is it far to the land where Medusa lives?

Athena: Very far. And you will need three magic objects to help you—the winged sandals, so that you may fly through the air, the cap of darkness, so that you can become invisible, and the magical sack, Kibisis, in which to put her head.

Perseus: Well, give them to me.

Athena: Not so fast. These things are in the possession of the three gray sisters.

Perseus: Oh, yes . . . the wisest of the old ones. They have lived so long that they only have one eye and one tooth left amongst the three of them. But they live practically at the edge of the earth!

Athena: I will go with you. The winds will help us travel quickly.

(*Perseus and Athena exit right.*)

Narrator: Perseus and Athena soon arrived at the cave where the three gray sisters lived. As Perseus approached, they were arguing over who would use their one eye and their one tooth.

(*Three Sisters enter left, and stop at left side of stage. Sister 1 is left, 2 center, 3 right.*)

Sister 3: It's my turn to use the eye. Let me have it, sister.

Sister 2: First, give me the tooth.

Sister 1: Isn't it my turn to use the tooth?

(*Perseus and Athena enter right, slowly, as the Sisters speak.*)

Sister 2: Here is the eye, sister.

Sister 1: She has to give me the tooth first.

(*Perseus reaches toward Sister 3 and mimes taking the eye from her.*)

Sister 3: Give me the eye. You promised.

Sister 2: I did give it to you.

Sister 3: I can't find it. (*Upset.*) Where is the eye? I can't find it.

Perseus: I have it.

Sister 1: Who is that? Give back our eye!

Perseus: You have something that I want in exchange.

Sister 3: You're a thief! Give back our eye.

Perseus: First, I must have the winged sandals.

Sister 2: (*Gives sandals to Perseus.*) Here, take them.

Perseus: And the cap of darkness.

Sister 1: (*Gives cap to Perseus.*) Take it, and give us back our eye.

Perseus: Oh, and one more thing.

Sisters 1, 2, and 3: Our eye! First give us the eye!

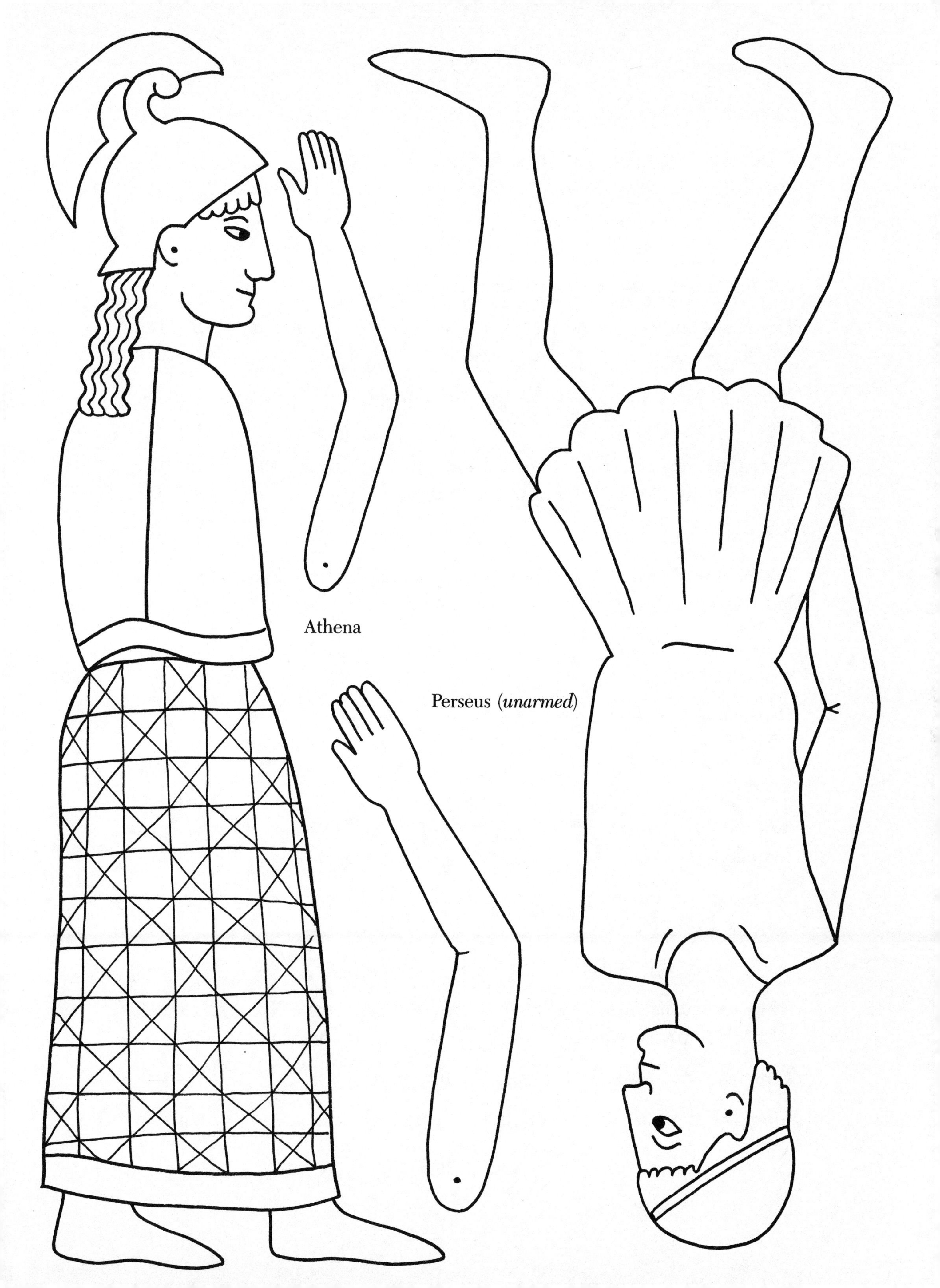
Athena
Perseus (*unarmed*)

Perseus: After you give me the bag, Kibisis.

Sister 3: Young man, you must be going to slay the Gorgon Medusa. The bag, Kibisis, is the only thing on earth which can contain her head. Take the bag. And remember to use all these gifts wisely. (*Gives bag to Perseus.*)

(*Perseus exits right—quickly substitute second Perseus puppet with winged sandals and Kibisis—and re-enters right.*)

Perseus: Here is your eye, good women. (*Mimes giving it to them.*) Thank you for the loan of these magic objects.

(*Perseus and Athena exit right, quickly. Three Gray Sisters exit left, slowly. Place Medusa right.*)

Narrator: Perseus and Athena traveled swiftly through the air, until they arrived at the dwelling place of the hideous Gorgons.

Medusa: (*Snores loudly.*)

Perseus: (*Offstage.*) She's asleep. I can take off the cap of darkness. (*Enters left, backwards.*)

Athena: (*Enters left, carrying shield in front of her.*) Can you see her reflection?

Perseus: Yes. Keep following me.

Medusa: (*Snores.*)

(*Perseus reaches behind his back and cuts off Medusa's head,* then puts it into the bag, Kibisis. Athena turns, and both exit left. Medusa's body sinks offstage.*)

Narrator: Perseus returned to the court of King Polydectes, who was very surprised to see him.

(*King enters left. Perseus enters right.*)

King: (*Sarcastically.*) Why, Perseus. You're back so soon. I thought you had left on a heroic adventure. Was your quest too frightening for you?

Perseus: No. In fact, I have completed my quest.

King: (*Frightened.*) But you didn't. . . . You couldn't have. . . . No!

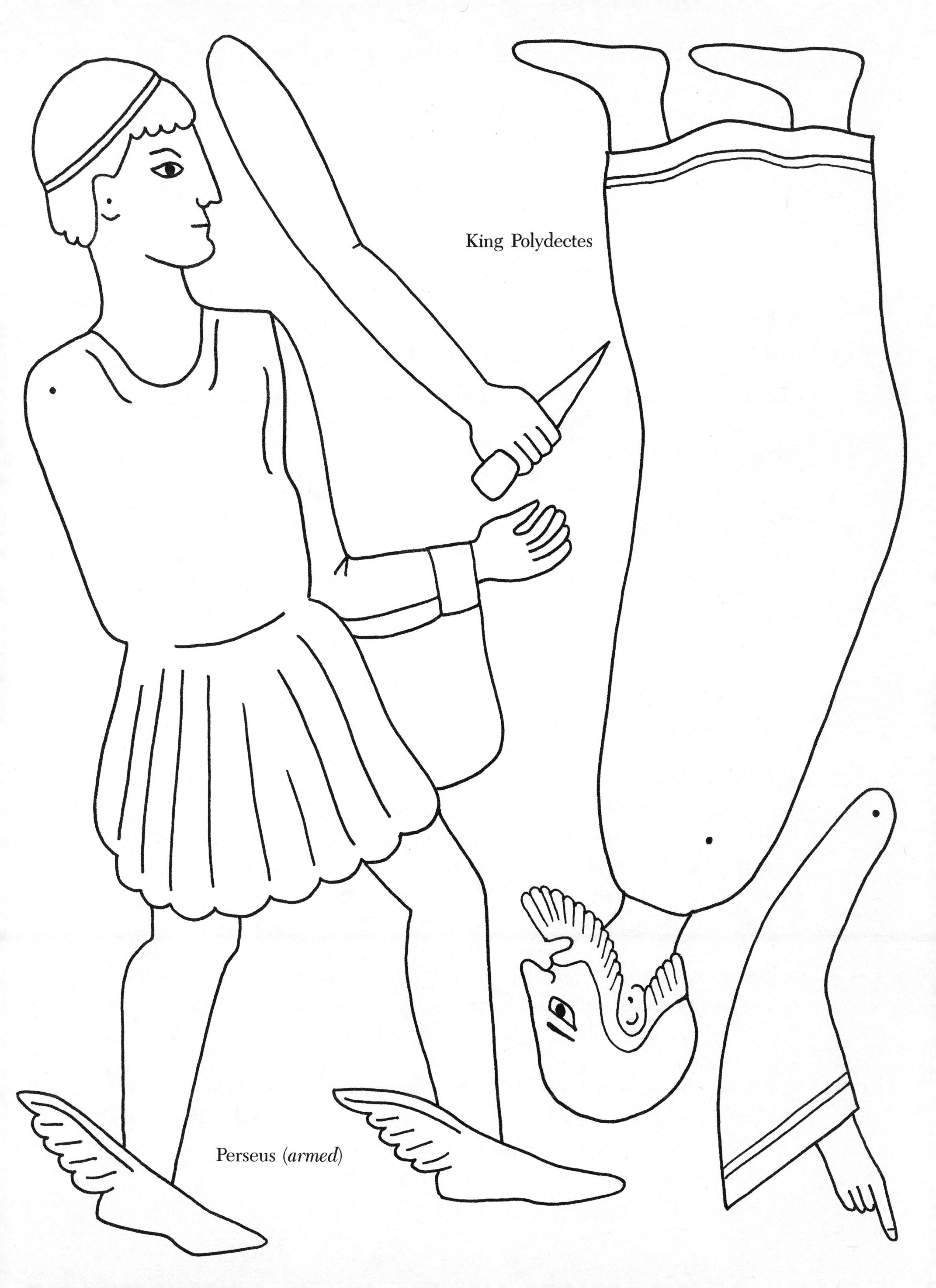
King Polydectes
Perseus (*armed*)

Perseus: (*Lifts Gorgon head from bag.*) Here, King, is the head of the Gorgon Medusa.

(*King freezes, falls slowly backward, hits ground,* and disappears.*)

Athena: (*Enters left and takes head. It appears on her shield.*) I shall take the head now, and it will forever be a blazon on my shield to strike fear into the enemies of the Greek people. Go now, Perseus. More adventures await you. (*Exits left.*)

Perseus: Thank you, goddess. (*Exits right.*)

Narrator: Perseus became a great hero. He found and tamed the winged horse, Pegasus, and rescued Andromeda from an evil sea serpent. But that's another story. . . .

Production Notes

The three sisters are made as one "group puppet" with a moving arm at either end. The puppet requires two puppeteers; these two can supply all three voices, or get an assist from another puppeteer. The portrait of Medusa, which Athena shows to Perseus, as well as the three sisters' eye, are nonexistent props which are simply mimed.

Shadow Puppets

The puppet designs have been adapted from ancient Greek vase paintings of mythological scenes. These paintings are very dark in color, emphasizing the characters' silhouettes, so black shadow puppets are quite effective. Because of the actions required, all puppets except Medusa are made with a moving arm. Human puppets are operated on vertical rods, props on horizontal ones. The body and the head of Medusa are separate, both on horizontal rods. A puppeteer holds them in place together until Perseus beheads Medusa, then that puppeteer makes the head follow Perseus' hand, as if he were carrying it, and lifts it off the shadow screen as it reaches the sack. This puppeteer will again be needed to operate Medusa's head when Perseus takes it out of the bag to show Polydectes and when Athena takes it to put on her shield.

Athena's shield is a hoop of black paper covered with yellow tissue. Medusa's head is placed behind it at the end of the play, so that the head appears to have become a design on the shield.

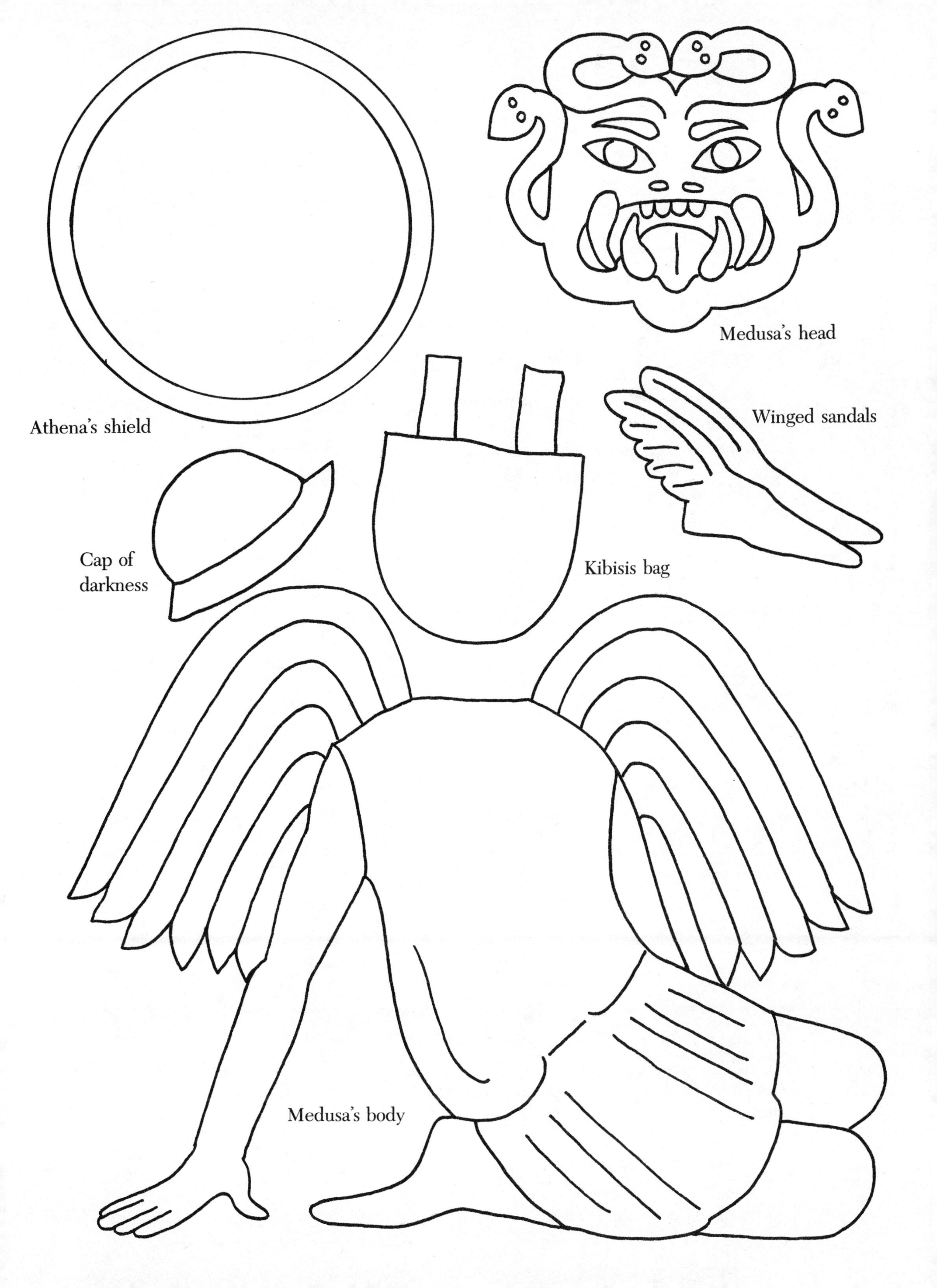
Medusa's head
Athena's shield
Winged sandals
Cap of
darkness
Kibisis bag
Medusa's body

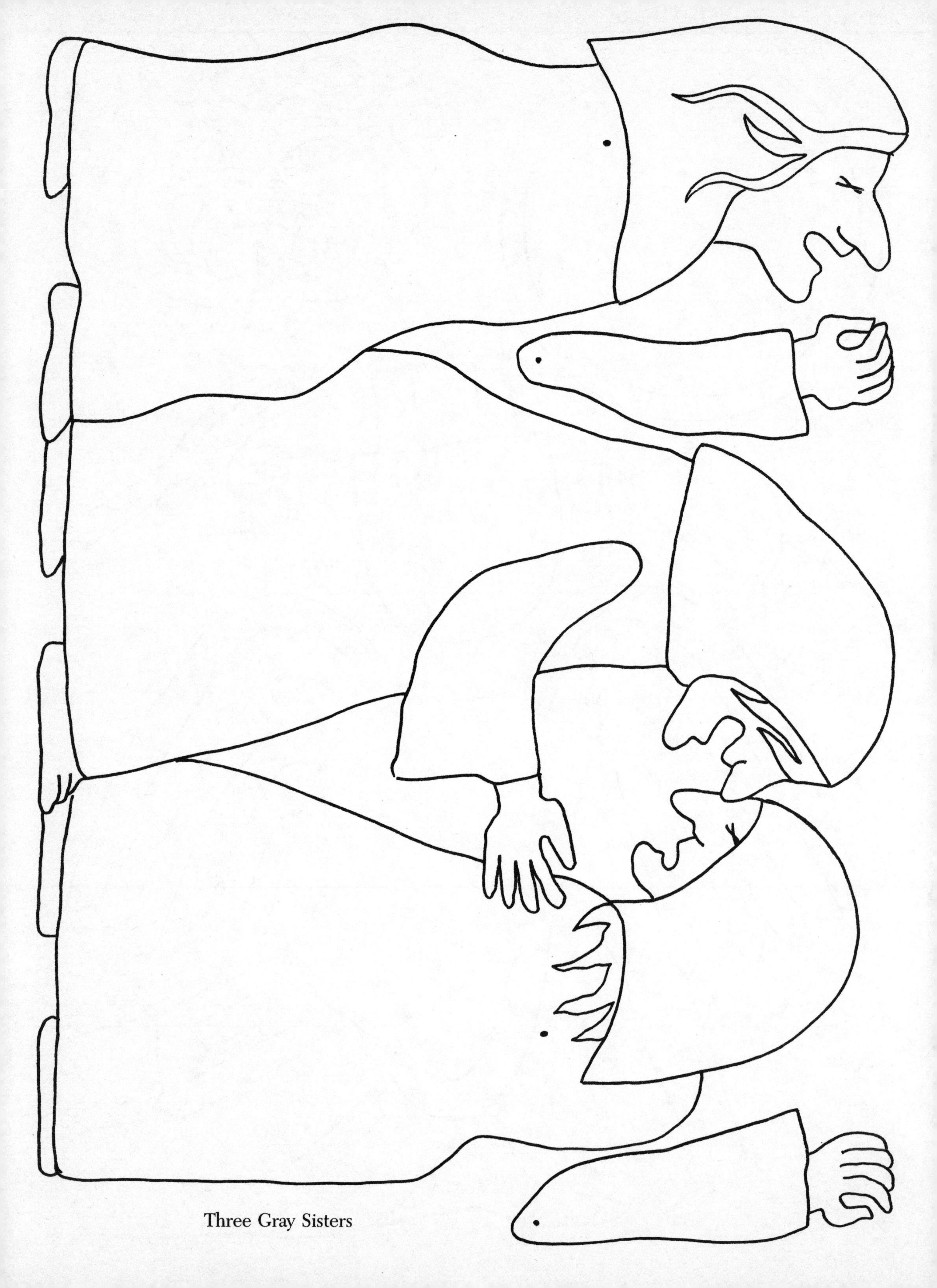

Three Gray Sisters

Rod Puppets

When Perseus puts Medusa's head into the bag, tilt the puppet forward so that the bag touches the stage, and quickly bring the head down and offstage. Reverse this procedure later when Perseus removes the head from the bag.

Athena's shield should be plain on one side and have a drawing of Medusa's head on the other. Keep the plain side toward the audience until Athena takes the head from Perseus, then simply flip the shield so that the second side is visible.

***Sound Effects**

Use a guiro for the sound of Perseus cutting Medusa's head off; a long, slow slide whistle when King Polydectes falls stiffly to the ground; and a clavé or drum as he lands.

Follow-up Activities

Greek Myths

The following myths, which are widely available in children's anthologies, make good puppet performances. Because of the episodic nature of the Greek myth texts, narration is always a necessity to set the stage and facilitate transitions from scene to scene. In fact, the myths may be entirely pantomimed by the puppets to narration. The following myths adapt particularly well to puppetry:

Arachne
Demeter and Persephone
Daedalus and Icarus
King Midas and the Golden Touch
Orpheus and Eurydice
The Labors of Hercules

Mythical Monsters

Research monsters from Greek myths, or from other world mythologies, and design puppets of them with moving parts. Puppeteers use a documentary style, moving the puppet on the screen while telling a bit about its special powers and its mythical adventures. The following books can serve as resources:

Creature Catalog, by Michael Berenstain. New York: Random, 1982.

Fabulous Beasts, by Alison Lurie. New York: Farrar, Straus, 1981.

Hunahpu and Xbalanque

The story of Hunahpu and Xbalanque comes from the *Popol Vuh*, sacred book of the Quiché Maya. The twin boys of the title are the heroes of a long mythological cycle, and this play is based on an episode of their youthful adventures. Young Hunahpu and Xbalanque wish to live with their grandmother but are opposed by their two older brothers, who are already living with her. The young heroes find a comical way to drive the older brothers away, and take their places in their grandmother's house.

Puppeteers: Five to seven, plus narrator and musicians.

Puppets:
- Hunahpu
- Xbalanque
- Grandmother
- First Brother
- Second Brother
- First Monkey
- Second Monkey

Props:
- Bird
- Drum
- Flute

Scenery pieces:
- House
- Tree
- Anthill
- Bramble bush

Setting: A clearing in the jungle: tree at far left, house at far right. There are no scene changes.

Narrator: Hunahpu and Xbalanque were born in the woods. When they were old enough, they came to their grandmother's house.

(*Hunahpu and Xbalanque enter left and walk to house; Grandmother and two Brothers appear inside house.*)

Narrator: Their two older brothers were living there already.

Hunahpu: (*Calls out.*) Hello, Grandmother. I am your grandson, Hunahpu.

Xbalanque: And I am your grandson, Xbalanque.

Hunahpu: We left our mother, and we want to live with you.

Brother 1: Get those brats out of here!

Brother 2: We don't want them living with us.

Grandmother: You two, Hunahpu and Xbalanque! Go sleep over there on that anthill.

(*Put up anthill next to tree. It is held by a puppeteer and removed as soon as the twins are finished lying on it.*)

Brother 1: Those stinging ants should take care of our brothers once and for all.

(*Hunahpu and Xbalanque lie down on anthill for a while. Then they walk to the house again.*)

Xbalanque: We had a good nap. Can we come in now?

Brother 1: No! Go take another nap on those bramble bushes, and leave us alone.

(*Hunahpu and Xbalanque lie down on bramble bush for a while. Then they walk to the house again.*)

Hunahpu: This bed is very comfortable, but I still want to live in Grandmother's house.

Xbalanque: Let's ask her again.

(*Hunahpu and Xbalanque walk to house.*)

Xbalanque: May we come inside now?

Grandmother: No. Your brothers do not want you to live here. Go live in the woods.

(*Hunahpu and Xbalanque exit behind tree.*)

Narrator: So Hunahpu and Xbalanque returned to the woods. But every day they caught birds and brought them to their grandmother's house.

(*Hunahpu and Xbalanque walk from woods to house, carrying a bird.*)

Hunahpu: Here is a bird for your supper.

Grandmother: Thank you, boys. (*She takes bird.*)

(*Grandmother and older Brothers mime cooking and eating the bird.*)

Xbalanque: May we have some too?

Brother 1: No! Get lost!

Brother 2: Don't let us see you around here unless you have one of these good-tasting birds for us.

(*Hunahpu and Xbalanque exit.*)

Narrator: But still, Hunahpu and Xbalanque brought the birds each day, until one day they came to the door of their grandmother's house empty-handed.

(*Hunahpu and Xbalanque enter left and walk to house.*)

Grandmother: Haven't you brought us any birds?

Hunahpu: We have shot birds for you, but they just won't fall down from the tree.

Xbalanque: We think our older brothers must come, and climb the tree, and bring the birds down.

Grandmother: Go along, then, you two. Go with your younger brothers, and get some of those tasty birds.

(*The two older Brothers follow Hunahpu and Xbalanque to the tree, then cross behind them to exit left. Hunahpu and Xbalanque remain onstage.*)

Hunahpu: There are the birds! Up there! Do you see them?

Brother 1: (*Offstage.*) No!

Xbalanque: Climb higher.

Brother 2: (*Offstage.*) There are lots of birds up here, but we are afraid. We might fall.

Hunahpu: Unwrap your loincloths. Let them hang down. That way you will be able to climb down.

Grandmother
Anthill
Grandmother's house
(*make to scale*)
Tree (*make to scale*)

Narrator: The two older brothers let their loincloths hang down. Then the loincloths turned into tails, and the two brothers turned into monkeys!

(Monkeys 1 and 2 appear in the branches of the tree, make monkey noises, and jump around. Hunahpu and Xbalanque exit behind tree and return carrying the drum and the flute. They walk to Grandmother's house.)

Grandmother: Where are those boys? What have you done to my favorite grandsons? I want to see them.

Hunahpu: Grandmother, our older brothers have become like animals, and they are ashamed to come back here to your house.

Xbalanque: But we can try to call them with a song.

(Hunahpu and Xbalanque begin to play on the flute and drum. The Monkeys enter right, dance, and make monkey noises.)*

Grandmother: Are these my grandsons? They look more like monkeys! *(Laughs.)*

(Monkeys exit left.)

Xbalanque: Grandmother, if you laugh, they will run away. We can only use this special song to call them back four times.

(Hunahpu and Xbalanque play flute and drum. Monkeys come and dance, as before.)*

Grandmother: They look so funny! *(Laughs.)*

(Monkeys exit left, crying. Hunahpu and Xbalanque play flute and drum again. Monkeys dance on, as before.)*

Grandmother: I can't help it . . . *(Laughs.)*

(Monkeys exit left, crying.)

Xbalanque: Now, Grandmother, this is your last chance. If you laugh at our brothers this time, they will never come back to live with you.

(Hunahpu and Xbalanque play flute and drum. Monkeys come and dance, as before.)*

Grandmother: *(Laughs.)*

(Monkeys exit left.)

Brother 2
Brother 1
Bramble bush

Narrator: So the older brothers remained monkeys, and they and their descendants lived in the forest.

(*Monkeys appear in treetop and make angry noises.*)

Narrator: They had been cruel to Hunahpu and Xbalanque, so they were punished. This is the story of how the great Mayan heroes, Hunahpu and Xbalanque, came to live in the house of their grandmother.

(*Hunahpu and Xbalanque follow their Grandmother into house.*)

Production Notes

The names of the heroes are pronounced hoo-nah-POO and shh-bah-lan-KAY. Puppet designs are adapted from the Mayan codices, books of picture writing.

This is a play for an experienced group of puppeteers. The production requires good backstage management, and skillful handling of puppets and props. Make the scenery for this play to fit your stage. The grandmother's house is open, consisting only of support beams and a roof at either end. It must be wide enough to allow as many as three puppets to appear inside at once. The space between the house and the tree needs to accommodate as many as four puppets at one time—Hunahpu and Xbalanque playing their instruments and the two monkeys dancing.

The bramble bush and anthill are affixed to vertical rods like puppets and held on the screen only when they are needed in the drama.

If you wish to reproduce the authentic coloring of the figures, look in books on the art of the Maya and of Ancient Mexico, listed on page 231.

Shadow Puppets

The puppet designs are based on the brightly colored Mayan codices, therefore, colored shadow puppets are highly recommended for this production. Scenery should be made of black paper; tree leaves can be made of green tissue or acetate.

All human puppets are attached to vertical rods. The monkey puppets are attached to horizontal rods, so that they can jump and turn somersaults. This will prevent them from turning around, and they will have to exit by backing offstage.

Flute
Bird
Drum
Xbalanque
Hunahpu

Monkey 1
Monkey 2

Rod Puppets
Both the house and the tree should be made from corrugated cardboard or foam core board. Rods on the monkeys need to be long enough to allow them to sit on a branch of the tree.

***Sound Effects and Music**
The ringing of a triangle should accompany the first appearance of the brothers-turned-monkeys in the treetops. Hunahpu and Xbalanque play a magic song on flute and drum, and their older brothers—now monkeys—dance and caper to the tune. This music is important to the production, so choose two talented musicians to work on creating and playing it. A plastic recorder or penny whistle can be used for the sound of the flute. Each time it is played, the music should last long enough for the monkeys to perform some choreographed tricks.

Follow-up Activities

More about the Maya
The Maya were one of the great pre-Columbian civilizations of Central America, and a Mayan culture lives on there today. Read the following books to find out more about the life and art in this fascinating culture.

The Ancient Maya, by Barbara Beck. New York: Franklin Watts, 1983.

The Art of Ancient Mexico, by Shirley Glubok. New York: Harper & Row, 1968.

Codex Nuttall, by Zelia Nuttall. New York: Dover, 1975.

Mysteries of the Ancient Maya, by Carolyn Meyer and Charles Gallenkamp. New York: Atheneum, 1985.

A Mayan Sport: *Pok-a-tok*
After replacing their brothers at their grandmother's house, Hunahpu and Xbalanque challenged the lords of the underworld to a game of *pok-a-tok.* This Mayan game was played with a small, hard rubber ball on a long, stone court with high walls at either end. Players had to put the ball through a small hoop, barely larger than the ball. This hoop was about 25 feet up the wall, and, unlike a basketball hoop, it was placed perpendicular to the ground.

Use shadow puppets to show Hunahpu and Xbalanque playing a game of *pok-a-tok*. Cut out a ball and put it on a horizontal rod. Place a circular hoop of paper at each side of the shadow screen, near the top. Three puppeteers will be needed—one for each puppet and one for the ball—along with a musician to hit a drum, making the sound effect of the ball hitting the boys' leather clothing, the ground, or the wall of the playing court. According to the rules of the game, players could not touch the ball with their hands.

What other sports can be played by shadow puppets?

Glossary of Puppetry Terms

Backlight. Light coming from behind the puppet stage.

Backstage. The area behind the puppet stage, out of sight of the audience.

Cue. The words, actions, or music which come directly before a performer's speech in a play.

Director. The person in charge of rehearsals and performance.

Formal performance. A planned performance for an audience, presented in a theater or in a theater-like environment.

Ground. A four-inch high strip of dark paper across the bottom of a shadow screen. The ground hides the hands of puppeteers who are operating puppets on vertical rods.

Group puppet. A single puppet representing several people or animals—even a crowd—that is manipulated by one or two puppeteers.

Hand puppet. A cloth puppet which the puppeteer wears on the hand, like a glove.

Improvise. To perform with little or no preparation, without a script, or using words and actions which are not in the script.

Informal performance. A theater performance presented with little advance planning, with or without an audience.

Horizontal rod. A shadow-puppet rod that is attached perpendicular to the flat surface of the puppet.

Manipulation. The act of moving puppets in an artistic and dramatic way.

Moving part. A piece of a shadow or rod puppet, joined to another piece of the puppet in a way that allows it to be moved by the puppeteer during performance.

Narrator. A person who tells or reads some parts of the story the puppets are acting out.

Offstage. A theater direction meaning that a character is heard, but not seen, by the audience.

Overture. A musical introduction to a theater performance.

Pantomime. A puppet play in which the puppeteers move the puppets but do not speak.

Playboard. A flat, fairly wide, horizontal surface, which is used as the lower edge of the playing area on some puppet stages.

Program. A printed sheet or booklet that describes a play and lists the actors and support crew.

Prompter. A person who helps performers when they forget their lines.

Prop. Any object which the puppets (appear to) pick up and handle during performance.

Lines. The words a performer speaks in a play.

Rehearsal. Practice for a performance.

Rod. A stick attached to a puppet, prop, or scenery piece, which the puppeteer holds and uses to manipulate that item.

Rod puppet. A performing figure that is operated by a puppeteer from below, by means of rods.

Scene. A short section of a play which takes place in one location.

Scenery. Everything that is used to represent the surroundings of a play.

Scenery piece. A shape cut from paper or plastic, and attached to the rod or shadow stage, which depicts part of a play's scenery.

Script. A text which describes the setting and actions of a play and gives the lines which each character is to speak.

Shadow screen. A white, translucent rectangle of paper, fabric, or plastic, upon which a shadow-puppet performance takes place. It is mounted perpendicular to the ground and lit from behind, from the side away from the audience.

Shadow puppet. A flat figure which is moved on a shadow screen by means of rods.

Sound effects. Sounds made on musical instruments to represent the sounds of the puppet play, such as footsteps, knocking at the door, or thunder.

Stage manager. A person who is in charge of the backstage area during the performance of the play.

Stop. A thread, tied between two pieces of a shadow puppet, which limits the motion of a moving part.

Traveling. A method of representing puppets walking long distances on the puppet stage. The puppet or puppets travel across the stage three or more times in the same direction, accompanied by soft, rhythmic music.

Vertical rod. A shadow puppet rod that is attached flush with the puppet and extends below the bottom of the puppet forming a handle for the puppeteer.

Appendix

Plays Listed by Size of Group

These are the minimum and maximum number of puppeteers required by each of the plays in this book. A narrator and/or musician may also be necessary (in some cases, puppeteers can play these roles), and additional support crew can always be used in puppet productions.

	Number of puppeteers								
Play	1	2	3	4	5	6	7	8	9+
Hey Diddle Diddle		×	×	×	×	×	×		
Little Miss Muffet	×	×							
Hickory Dickory Dock	×								
Old MacDonald		×	×	×	×	×	×	×	×
Over in the Meadow		×	×	×	×	×	×	×	×
There Was an Old Lady Who Swallowed a Fly		×	×	×	×	×	×	×	×
The Fox and the Grapes	×								
The Dog and His Bone	×								
The Hungry Monster			×	×	×	×	×	×	×
Mr. Bear Squash-You-All-Flat						×			
The Crocodile and the Hen		×							
The Deer, the Fox, and the Tiger		×	×						
The Rabbit of Inaba			×	×	×				
The Runaway Pancake			×	×	×	×	×		
The North Wind and the Sun			×						
Red Riding Hood				×	×				
Wait Till Emmet Comes				×					
Why Mosquitos Buzz in Our Ears					×	×	×		
The Silly Jellyfish			×	×	×				
The Frog Prince			×						
The Brahman, the Tiger, and the Jackal			×	×	×				
Brer Rabbit and the Wonderful Tar-Baby			×						
Who is Strongest?					×				
How the Sun and Moon Came to Live in the Sky				×	×	×	×		
All Stories Belong to Anansi				×	×	×	×		
Toad Visits the Emperor						×			
The Blue Jackal				×	×	×	×	×	
The Turkey Maiden				×	×	×	×	×	×
Perseus and Medusa					×	×	×		
Hunahpu and Xbalanque					×	×	×		

Plays Listed by Geographic Area

Where known, specific tribes or ethnic groups are indicated as sources for the material on which the plays are based. Folk material does not honor strict national, or even tribal boundaries; these designations are not carved in stone.

North America

Old MacDonald (*Anglo-American*)
There Was an Old Woman Who Swallowed a Fly (*Anglo-American*)
The Hungry Monster (*adapted from the Anglo-American tale, "The Greedy Old Fat Man"*)
Wait Till Emmet Comes (*African-American*)
Brer Rabbit and the Wonderful Tar-Baby (*African-American*)
How the Sun and Moon Came to Live in the Sky (*Maidu*)
The Turkey Maiden (*Zuñi*)
Hanahpu and Xbalanque (*Maya*)

Europe

Hey Diddle Diddle (*England*)
Little Miss Muffet (*England*)
Hickory Dickory Dock (*England*)
Over in the Meadow (*England*)
The Fox and the Grapes (*Greece*)
The Dog and His Bone (*Greece*)
Mr. Bear Squash-You-All-Flat (*Russia*)
The Runaway Pancake (*Sweden*)
The North Wind and the Sun (*Greece*)
Red Riding Hood (*France*)
The Frog Prince (*Germany*)
Perseus and Medusa (*Greece*)

Africa

The Crocodile and the Hen (*Congo*)
Who is Strongest (*Luba*)
All Stories Belong to Anansi (*Ashanti*)

Asia

The Deer, the Fox, and the Tiger (*China*)
The Rabbit of Inaba (*Japan*)
Why Mosquitos Buzz in Our Ears (*Philippines*)
The Silly Jellyfish (*Japan*)
The Brahman, the Tiger, and the Jackal (*India*)
Toad Visits the Emperor (*Vietnam*)
The Blue Jackal (*India*)

Pantomimes for Large Groups

Books and Stories Recommended for the Narration-Improvisation Technique

Scriptwriting Projects

Puppet Design Projects

Science-based Puppet Performances

Poetry for Puppets

Comparative Folklore Activities

About the Plays

The scripts in this book are adapted from fables, folktales, and myths. By their nature, folk narratives exist in many variants, and, although variants may be written down, folklore owes its existence chiefly to the oral tradition. In researching the material for these plays, I sought out all the versions I could find of each tale, both in children's literature, and in the scholarly literature of folklore, linguistics, and anthropology. No play is based on any one version, translation, or interpretation. In each case, I have tried to rely on older, unedited sources, rather than on adaptations for children.

Of course, these plays *are* adaptations for children, but they are my adaptations. I have taken the liberties that a playwright must, such as putting words into characters' mouths, reducing the number of characters, and favoring certain scenes and actions over others. I don't think anyone can claim to read the minds of the departed storytellers of other cultures. Yet, the stories they have left us are good, and strong, and continue to be meaningful even across so much time and space. I hope I have preserved their unique essence, without forcing any one, exclusive interpretation onto them.

If you wish to find written versions of these folktales, be aware that none will agree in all details with these playscripts. Even the Greek myths exist in conflicting variants. The following bibliographic tools will help you locate prose versions of these tales in picture books and in children's folktale collections:

Eastman, Mary Huse. *Index to Fairy Tales, Myths and Legends.* 2nd ed. Boston: F.W. Faxon, 1926.

———. *Index to Fairy Tales, Myths and Legends: First Supplement.* Boston: F.W. Faxon, 1937.

———. *Index to Fairy Tales, Myths and Legends: Second Supplement.* Boston: F.W. Faxon, 1952.

Ireland, Norma O. *Index to Fairy Tales 1949–1972: Including Folklore, Legends and Myths in Collections.* Metuchen, N.J.: Scarecrow, 1973.

———. *Index to Fairy Tales 1973–1977: Including Folklore, Legends and Myths in Collections.* Metuchen, N.J.: Scarecrow, 1985.

———, and Joseph W. Sprung. *Index to Fairy Tales 1978–1986: Including Folklore, Legends and Myths in Collections.* Metuchen, N.J.: Scarecrow, 1985.

MacDonald, Margaret Read. *The Storyteller's Sourcebook: A Subject, Title, and Motif Index to Folklore Collections for Children.* Detroit: Gale/Neal-Schuman, 1982.

Ziegler, Elsie B. *Folklore: An Annotated Bibliography and Index to Single Editions.* Boston: F.W. Faxon, 1973.

Bibliography

Puppetry for Children

Andersen, Benny E. *Let's Start a Puppet Theater.* New York: Van Nostrand Reinhold, 1973.

Batchelder, Marjorie. *Puppet Theater Handbook.* New York: Harper & Row, 1947.

Cochrane, Louise. *Shadow Puppets in Color.* Boston: Plays, 1972.

Kraska, Edie. *Toys and Tales from Grandmother's Attic.* Boston: Houghton Mifflin, 1979.

Paludan, Lis. *Playing with Puppets.* Boston: Plays, 1975.

Renfro, Nancy. *Puppetry and the Art of Story Creation.* Austin, Tex.: Nancy Renfro Studios, 1979.

———. *Puppets for Play Production.* New York: Crowell, 1969.

Sims, Judy. *Puppets for Dreaming and Scheming.* Walnut Creek, Ca.: Early Stages, 1976.

World Puppet Traditions

Baird, Bil. *The Art of the Puppet.* New York: Crown, 1973.

Böhmer, Günter. *The Wonderful World of Puppets.* Boston: Plays, 1969.

Fettig, Hansjürgen. *Hand and Rod Puppets: A Handbook of Technique.* Boston: Plays, 1973.

Keeler, Ward. *Javanese Shadow Plays, Javanese Selves.* Princeton University Press, 1984.

Malkin, Michael R. *Traditional and Folk Puppets of the World.* Cranbury, N.J.: A. S. Barnes, 1977.

Simmen, René. *The World of Puppets.* New York: Crowell, 1972.

Stalberg, Roberta Helmer. *China's Puppets.* San Francisco: China Books, 1984.

Union Internationale des Marionettes (UNIMA). *The Puppet Theatre of the Modern World.* Boston: Plays, 1967.

Wimsatt, Genevieve. *Chinese Shadow Shows.* Cambridge: Harvard University Press, 1936.

Index